Emancipating the Banking System and Developing Markets for Government Debt

This book, published in association with the Bank of England, assesses the damaging effects of inflationary finance, financial repression and excessive government borrowing from abroad on economic performance in 111 countries. It then presents a practical guide to developing voluntary domestic markets for government debt.

As ways of financing government deficits, inflationary finance, financial repression and excessive government borrowing from abroad are associated with higher inflation, lower saving ratios and lower growth rates. Borrowing from voluntary domestic lenders in the private sector is the least harmful way of financing any given government deficit. However, the typical developing country makes little use of this fourth source, in part because of the practical difficulties involved in developing voluntary domestic markets for government debt.

Developing such markets involves a major change in the approach to financing the government deficit. Typically, the change occurs from a system in which most institutional interest rates are fixed and the government is financed at favourable fixed rates by unwilling captive buyers of its debt. To obtain a better understanding of this dramatic and possibly traumatic change to voluntary market financing, the Bank of England asked the central banks in Ghana, India, Jamaica, Malaysia, Mexico, New Zealand, Sri Lanka and Zimbabwe, countries that had recently developed voluntary domestic markets for government debt, to answer some questions about the process of change. All eight central banks responded and much of the material in this book is based on these questionnaire responses.

Maxwell J. Fry holds the Tokai Bank Chair in International Finance at the University of Birmingham. He is also Director of the University's International Finance Group.

Emancipating the Banking System and Developing Markets for Government Debt

MAXWELL J. FRY
University of Birmingham

Foreword by Eddie George
Governor of the Bank of England

London and New York

First published 1997
by Routledge
11 New Fetter Lane, London EC4P 4EE

Simultaneously published in the USA and Canada
by Routledge
29 West 35th Street, New York, NY 10001

Typeset in New Times Roman by the author using Leslie Lamport's
LaTeX, a set of macros for Donald Knuth's TeX typesetting software.

Printed and bound in Great Britain by
TJ Press (Padstow) Ltd, Padstow, Cornwall

British Library Cataloguing in Publication Data
A catalogue record for this book is available from the British Library

Library of Congress Cataloging in Publication Data
A catalogue record for this book has been requested

ISBN 0–415–15640–8 (hbk)
ISBN 0–415–15641–6 (pbk)

Contents

Figures

xi

Tables

Foreword

IN JUNE 1996 THE BANK OF ENGLAND hosted its third Central Bank Governors' Symposium. The paper presented at the Symposium and the discussion which followed form the basis of this book.

Our first Symposium was held in 1994, when more than 130 governors or former governors from central banks around the world gathered to mark the Bank of England's tercentenary. The two main papers on that occasion were by Stanley Fischer on "Modern Central Banking" and by Forrest Capie, Charles Goodhart and Norbert Schnadt on "The Development of Central Banking" (Capie, Goodhart, Fischer and Schnadt 1994). In keeping with the occasion, these papers concentrated primarily on the history and circumstances of central banks in the developed countries. This study was complemented at the second Symposium, held during the 1995 meeting of governors drawn mainly from central banks from the erstwhile Sterling Area, when a paper by Maxwell Fry, Charles Goodhart and Alvaro Almeida was presented on "Central Banking in Developing Countries" (Fry, Goodhart and Almeida 1996). That paper found, among other things, that inflation was *positively* related to the proportion of government borrowing from the central bank and in total domestic credit; and that inflation was *negatively* related to growth. This gave rise to the question: how should a government best meet its borrowing requirements? This was the question I asked Professor Maxwell Fry to address at our 1996 Symposium, "Emancipating the Banking System and Developing Markets for Government Debt".

The draft paper presented by Professor Fry forms the main part of this book. At the Symposium he raised a number of questions for consideration by the assembled governors, and the final chapter of this book reflects the ensuing discussion. We are grateful to Dr Donald Brash, Governor of the Reserve Bank of New Zealand, Mr Miguel Mancera, Governor of the Banco de México, and Dr Leonard Tsumba, Governor of the Reserve Bank of Zimbabwe, for acting as discussants.

We would also like to thank the governors of the central banks of Ghana, India, Jamaica, Malaysia and Sri Lanka who, together with the three discussants, assisted Professor Fry by responding to a detailed questionnaire on their experiences in developing voluntary markets for government debt.

As Dr Tsumba noted during the Symposium, the diverse experiences of a wide range of countries—Professor Fry used statistical data from over a hundred countries in addition to the information provided by the eight case studies—cannot all be boiled down into a few simple conclusions; and indeed, Professor Fry explicitly acknowledges that there exists no single ideal model for the transition from controlled to liberalised markets, and that the example of other countries cannot simply be mimicked. There are, nonetheless, a number of common themes in the success stories. Perhaps chief among these is the need for a *commitment* to allowing the markets to determine the price for borrowing and lending. Market forces not only allow borrowers and lenders to see the true cost of money, but also allow, and indeed stimulate, a response to that, whether encouraging a reduction in the budget deficit or an increase in private sector savings. But if the government and central bank are not *committed* to liberalisation, then the transition from controlled to liberalised markets will tend to be slower and more painful.

The time available at the Symposium for discussion of the issues raised in Professor Fry's paper was, perhaps inevitably, far too short to allow us to tackle all the questions in the depth we would have liked. I know that for some the discussion continued over lunch; and I hope that the publication of this book will provoke further debate. But I also hope it will do more than that. I hope it will play its part in increasing our understanding of how markets develop and so inform the labours of those involved, in central banks and elsewhere, in encouraging and facilitating such development—not for its own sake, but for the benefits which it brings to the wider economy. My colleague Ian Plenderleith noted at the Symposium that we in the United Kingdom see our markets as still developing. The move from controlled to liberalised markets is not from one static position to another, but from rigidity to constantly evolving flexibility. No central banker can afford to rest on his or her laurels!

Eddie George
Governor of the Bank of England

Acknowledgements

F IRST AND FOREMOST, my thanks go to the central banks of the eight case study countries (Ghana, India, Jamaica, Malaysia, Mexico, New Zealand, Sri Lanka and Zimbabwe) that kindly agreed to answer the questionnaire reproduced in Appendix 1. Furthermore, I am particularly indebted to Simon Gray (Bank of England) and Robin McConnachie (Bank of England) for providing extremely salient comments on both the Symposium report and the manuscript of this book.

I am also most grateful to Nabeel Al-Mannae (Central Bank of Kuwait), Tomás Baliño (International Monetary Fund), Donald Brash (Reserve Bank of New Zealand), Gerard Caprio, Jr (World Bank), Christine Chaplin (Bank of England), Roger Clews (Bank of England), Carlo Cottarelli (International Monetary Fund), Andrew Crockett (Bank for International Settlements), Rudiger Dornbusch (Massachusetts Institute of Technology), Stanley Fischer (International Monetary Fund), John Footman (Bank of England), Bernie Fraser (Reserve Bank of Australia), Thomas Fry (Sidmouth), Manuel Guitián (International Monetary Fund), Nadeem Ul Haque (International Monetary Fund), John Hawkins (Hong Kong Monetary Authority), George Iden (International Monetary Fund), Randall Kroszner (University of Chicago), Ronald McKinnon (Stanford University), Miguel Mancera (Banco de México), David Marston (International Monetary Fund), Paul Meek (Burke, Va), Hassanali Mehran (International Monetary Fund), Charles Nolan (Bank of England), Gill O'Riley (Bank of England), Lionel Price (Bank of England), Robert Price (International Monetary Fund), Andrew Sheng (Hong Kong Monetary Authority), Peter Stebbing (Central Bank of Yemen), Venkataraman Sundararajan (International Monetary Fund), Mark Swinburne (International Monetary Fund), Leonard Tsumba (Reserve Bank of Zimbabwe), David Wilton (World Bank), Brian Wynter (Bank of Jamaica) and participants at the Bank of England's 1996 Central Bank Governors' Symposium for their help with this project and comments on the Symposium report.

The questionnaire responses are incorporated into Chapter 1 and Part III, which deal with the practical issues of developing voluntary domestic markets for government debt. Quotations attributed either implicitly or explicitly to the monetary authorities of the case study countries indicate questionnaire responses. Part III also draws on written comments by Donald Brash, Bernie Fraser, Miguel Mancera and Leonard Tsumba on the report I presented at the Symposium, as well as the Symposium Minutes themselves, which were prepared by Simon Gray.

I used David Lilien's *EViews,* version 2.0, his new version of *Micro-TSP* for *Windows,* to run the regressions and simulations reported in this book. *EViews* was also used to prepare all the data-based graphs. The *EViews* graphs were edited and all the other graphs drawn in *CorelDraw.*

At Routledge, Sally Carter, Alison Kirk, Chantal Latchford and Kate Smith provided much help and encouragement. Christine Firth (Editorial Services, Checkendon, Oxon) copy-edited the manuscript and Maria Coughlin (Editorial Services, Annapolis, Md) prepared the index.

Financial support for the report prepared for the Bank of England's 1996 Central Bank Governors' Symposium on which most of this book is based was kindly provided by the Bank of England. Additional funding from the Economic & Social Research Council under its Research Programme on Pacific Asia (grant L 324253010), the Development Centre of the Organisation for Economic Co-operation and Development and the World Bank for some of the research reported here is also gratefully acknowledged. Finally, I am grateful to Penguin Books for permitting me to quote 12 lines from Aristophanes' *The Frogs.*

The views expressed in this book do not necessarily reflect those of the Bank of England, the International Monetary Fund, the World Bank, or any individual acknowledged above. All errors remain the sole responsibility of the author.

Part I

Introduction and Debt-Deficit Dynamics

Chapter 1

Why Develop Markets for Government Debt? Overview and Summary

1.1 Introduction

FOR THE BANK OF ENGLAND'S 1995 Central Bank Governors' Symposium, Charles Goodhart, Alvaro Almeida and I (Fry, Goodhart and Almeida 1996) surveyed the objectives, activities and independence of central banks in developing countries. One striking finding was that developing countries suffered considerably higher inflation than the OECD countries. While the proximate cause was more rapid money growth, we suggested that a more fundamental cause was that developing country governments resorted to their central banks much more for deficit financing.

For the Bank of England's 1996 Central Bank Governors' Symposium, therefore, we decided to investigate in more detail the four major ways that governments can finance their deficits:[1]

- Monetising the deficit by borrowing at zero cost from the central bank.

- Borrowing at below-market interest rates by thrusting debt down the throats of captive buyers, primarily commercial banks.

---

[1] Under cash-based budgets, arrears and other deferred payment arrangements together with unfunded future liabilities such as state pensions constitute additional techniques of disguising the true magnitude of a deficit.

- Borrowing abroad in foreign currency.

- Borrowing at market interest rates from voluntary domestic private sector lenders.

The typical OECD country finances about 50 percent of its deficit from voluntary domestic sources, while the typical developing country finances only about 8 percent of its deficit from this source. Why this matters is that, for any given persistent government deficit, greater use of the first three sources is associated with higher inflation rates, lower saving ratios and lower rates of economic growth. Government recourse to the central bank inevitably leads to inflation. Indeed, such inflationary finance can be considered a source of tax revenue in that inflation imposes a tax on money holders. Throughout this book, the terms monetising the government deficit, government recourse to the central bank, inflationary finance and the inflation tax are treated as synonymous and are used interchangeably.

Financial repression, the second way of financing the government deficit, is also tax-like in that it involves forcing captive buyers to hold government debt at interest rates below market yields. By reducing its interest costs, this method reduces the government's recorded deficit. Foreign borrowing, which for all developing countries implies borrowing and repaying foreign rather than domestic currency, constitutes the third method of financing a deficit. Part II of this book demonstrates that excessive reliance on these three ways of financing government deficits impedes economic development.

All this conflicts with the views of Robert Barro (1974, 1989) and James Buchanan (1976) on Ricardian equivalence. Barro (1989, 39) states that the Ricardian equivalence theorem, proposed only to be dismissed by David Ricardo (1817, 336–338) himself, holds that

> the substitution of a budget deficit for current taxes (or any other rearrangement of the timing of taxes) has no impact on the aggregate demand for goods. In this sense, budget deficits and taxation have equivalent effects on the economy—hence the term "Ricardian equivalence theorem." To put the equivalence result another way, a decrease in the government's saving (that is, a current budget deficit) leads to an offsetting increase in desired private saving, and hence to no change in desired national saving.

It also follows that Ricardian equivalence implies that the method of financing government deficits has no impact on the macroeconomy.

While Barro (1989, 52) interprets the empirical evidence to provide general support for the Ricardian equivalence theorem, the evidence cited is drawn largely from the United States where the assumptions of the theorem are perhaps most likely to hold. As Pierre-Richard Agénor and Peter Montiel (1996, 127) suggest, "In developing countries where financial systems are underdeveloped, capital markets are highly distorted or subject to financial repression, and private agents are subject to considerable uncertainty regarding the incidence of taxes, many of the considerations necessary for debt neutrality to hold are unlikely to be valid." Hence, the assumptions on which Ricardian equivalence rests (Barro 1989, 39–48) are almost bound to be violated sufficiently to negate the theorem in these countries. Indeed, Agénor and Montiel (1996, 127) conclude: "the empirical evidence [from developing countries] has indeed failed to provide much support for the Ricardian equivalence proposition." The empirical evidence presented in Part II of this book confirms the Agénor-Montiel position.

Voluntary private sector purchase of government debt is the fourth and final way of financing government deficits. Although government deficits are generally not conducive to economic growth, this way of financing them appears to reduce the damaging effects of any given deficit. Both economic and social efficiencies are improved not only though the use of the market-pricing mechanism but also through the transparent presentation of the costs of government expenditures. When the costs of borrowing are borne openly by the public and not hidden through the use of captive buyers, the true resource costs of government spending can be properly incorporated into both economic and social choices. Even politicians' choices can change when they are properly informed.

Hence, a move towards developing voluntary domestic markets for government debt appears to offer benefits in terms of lower inflation and higher saving and growth. High growth, in turn, alleviates the deficit. There is, therefore, some hint of a virtuous circle in which greater use of voluntary domestic markets lowers inflation and raises growth, both of which reduce the government's deficit. In general, developing countries make too little use of voluntary private sector lenders. Hence, Part III of this book concentrates on some of the practical issues involved in developing voluntary domestic markets for government debt.

While government deficits have various negative effects on an economy, this book is concerned with the *differential* impacts of financing a given deficit in alternative ways. A primary question here, therefore, is what are the effects on economic growth, saving and inflation of financing a deficit through central bank credit, reserve and liquid asset ratio requirements imposed on commercial banks, interest rate ceilings and captive buyers, loans from abroad and voluntary lending by the private sector?

One point that must be stressed at the outset is that the impact of borrowing from abroad or from voluntary domestic lenders will depend on the amount previously borrowed. In other words, the level of debt accumulated from past borrowing affects the impact of additional borrowing. Just as a household finds it increasingly difficult and expensive to borrow as its debt/equity ratio rises, so too does a government because, at some point, voluntary lenders may perceive further debt accumulation to be unsustainable. While a household may declare bankruptcy, a government can renege by resorting to inflation to erode the real value of its domestic debt and by defaulting on its foreign debt obligations.

The next chapter sets the stage by discussing the government's intertemporal budget constraint and debt-deficit dynamics. These principles are illustrated with data drawn from 111 countries for which data on deficits, economic growth and inflation are available. However, only for a smaller group of these countries are data on real interest rates and debt (both domestic and foreign) available.

Part II of this study examines the interactive effects of deficits, debts and the way deficits are financed in a large sample of developing countries. Chapter 3 examines government recourse to its central bank and the effects of the inflation tax. Chapter 4 turns to financial repression as a source of government revenue, again concentrating on its effects. Chapter 5 covers foreign borrowing and the effects of foreign debt accumulation. Part II of this book, summarised in the next section of this chapter, provides evidence that inflationary finance, financial repression and government borrowing from abroad are associated with higher inflation, lower saving ratios and lower growth rates.

Part III, summarised in sections 3 and 4 of this chapter, focuses on some of the practical issues involved in establishing a functional market for government debt in countries that have not so far developed one. Developing a voluntary market for government debt involves a fundamental change in the approach to financing the government deficit. Typically, the change occurs from a system in which most institutional interest rates are fixed and the government is financed at favourable fixed rates by unwilling captive buyers of its debt. Privileged access and captive buyers are now eschewed in favour of a level playing-field philosophy. Government now competes on the same terms and conditions as private agents for available saving. The economic principle behind the change is that a level playing field maximises the efficiency with which scarce

Table 1.1. Government Deficits as Percent of GDP, 1979–1993

Statistic	All	OECD	Developing
Mean	4.0	3.7	4.0
Median	3.5	3.3	3.6
Maximum	33.3	11.9	33.3
Minimum	−24.6	−1.9	−24.6
S.D.	5.5	3.1	5.9

resources are allocated throughout the economy.

In order to obtain a better understanding of this dramatic and possibly traumatic change to voluntary market financing, it seemed sensible to choose a relatively small number of case studies. Hence, the Bank of England asked the eight central banks in Ghana, India, Jamaica, Malaysia, Mexico, New Zealand, Sri Lanka and Zimbabwe, countries that had recently developed voluntary domestic markets for government debt, to answer some questions about the process of change; all eight central banks responded.[2] Much of the material in Part III is based on these questionnaire responses.

1.2 The Case Against Inflationary Finance, Financial Repression and Government Borrowing from Abroad

1.2.1 Deficits, Inflation and Growth

For my quantitative analysis, I took a sample of 111 countries consisting of 21 richer OECD countries and 90 developing countries. Somewhat surprisingly, Table 1.1 shows that average OECD and developing country government deficits expressed as percentages of gross domestic product (GDP) have been virtually identical over the period 1979–1993. However, dispersion has been much greater in the developing countries.

The first empirical observation presented in Chapter 2 concerns the relationships between government deficits, inflation, growth rates and saving ratios. I find a highly significant positive relationship between inflation and government deficit/GDP ratios. Conversely, I find signif-

---

[2] The questionnaire itself is reproduced as Appendix 1.

icant negative relationships between ratios of national saving to gross
national product (GNP) and deficits as well as between economic growth
and deficits in these 111 countries.

1.2.2   The Central Bank and Inflationary Finance

While deficits are bad, they are worse when financed by the central
bank. The typical developing country financed about 30 percent of
its deficit from its central bank since 1979. Excessive government
borrowing from the central bank inevitably results in faster expansion
in reserve money. And by causing higher inflation, rapid growth in
reserve money reduces economic growth.

One way of examining the *differential* impact of financing a deficit
from the central bank is to specify a relationship in which the impact of
the deficit is itself dependent on the form of its financing. Doing this
in Chapter 3, I find that, for any given deficit, inflation is *higher* the
greater the proportion that is financed by the central bank. Conversely,
saving ratios and growth rates are *lower* the greater the proportion of the
deficit that is financed by the central bank. In conclusion, inflationary
finance or the inflation tax is not a good way of financing government
deficits.

1.2.3   Financial Repression

Governments in many countries force captive buyers, mainly commercial banks, to hold their debt at below-market yields. Indirectly, banks
also lend at zero interest to governments through reserve requirements.
Directly, banks lend at below-market rates through liquid asset ratio
requirements or other balance sheet constraints.

While Chapter 4 considers several indicators of financial repression,
I use the ratio of the commercial banks' reserves to their deposits as an
indicator of the captive-buyer source of government finance for illus-
trative purposes in this introductory summary. First, higher government
deficits are associated with significantly higher reserve/deposit ratios;
we detected this in Fry, Goodhart and Almeida (1996, 5). Second,
inflation and reserve/deposit ratios are *positively* and significantly associated, again as we found in Fry, Goodhart and Almeida (1996, 5).
This positive relationship still holds after controlling for the deficit.
Finally, higher reserve/deposit ratios are associated with significantly
lower saving ratios and *lower* growth rates.

My interpretation of this negative relationship between growth and the reserve/deposit ratio is that the more the government takes from the financial system at below-market rates, the lower is the return to depositors and so the less willing is the public to hold deposits. This produces a doubly destructive effect on the ability of the banking system to lend for productive investment. First, its resource base in the form of deposits is reduced. Second, the government takes a larger share of the smaller pie.

Again, therefore, I conclude that captive buyers and financial repression are bad ways of financing government deficits.

1.2.4 Foreign Debt Accumulation

As an alternative to inflationary finance or financial repression, government borrowing from abroad might seem benign. Certainly, developing countries have continued to accumulate foreign debt, here defined as government plus government-guaranteed foreign debt. Data presented in Chapter 5 show that the average foreign debt ratio for a sample of 79 developing countries doubled between 1979–1983 and 1989–1993.

Research in the mid-1980s indicated that when government plus government-guaranteed debt exceeds 50 percent of GDP, further accumulation of this type of debt does more harm than good (Fry 1989). This conclusion is supported in Chapter 5 by the facts that foreign debt accumulation is associated with higher inflation after the debt ratio exceeds about 50 percent, that national saving starts to decline after the debt ratio exceeds about 50 percent, and that the growth-inhibiting effect of foreign debt accumulation is greatest when the debt ratio exceeds about 50 percent.

I conclude that foreign borrowing by the government is not the panacea that it might have seemed in the early 1970s.

1.3 The Case for Voluntary Domestic Markets

As mentioned above, developing countries make little use of voluntary domestic markets to finance government deficits. However, such markets appear to be benign. First, regressions in Chapter 6 show that greater reliance on nonbank private sector domestic government borrowing is associated with *lower* inflation for any given deficit. Second, saving ratios and growth rates are reduced less, for any given deficit, when more of the deficit is financed in this way.

With this, I rest the statistical case in favour of voluntary domestic markets as the best alternative for financing government deficits. I turn now to some of the practical issues involved in establishing a functional market for government debt in developing countries that have not so far developed such a market.

1.3.1   Essential Elements

Two key points on the development of voluntary domestic markets for government debt emerge from the questionnaire responses of the case study countries reported in Chapter 6:

1. Success is critically dependent on the implementation of any required concomitant fiscal reform.

2. Real as opposed to illusory success is critically dependent on taking the plunge and really letting market forces determine the price of government debt. Emancipating all captive buyers is essential.

The first point constitutes an essential prerequisite when starting the market development process with a deficit that would be unsustainable without reliance on the inflation tax and financial repression. In Fry, Goodhart and Almeida (1996, 34–36), we reported that the typical developing country obtained over 2 percent of GDP from the inflation tax and about the same amount from financial repression in the form of borrowing at below-market interest rates. Relinquishing these two sources of quasi-tax revenue must be taken into account at the outset of the market development process. To prevent debt from rising inexorably, it may well be necessary to find alternative sources of revenue producing at least 4 percent of GDP or to cut the government's noninterest expenditures by a similar magnitude. Chapter 2 contains the mathematics required to calculate such necessary fiscal changes.

The second point emerges from the setbacks that have occurred during the market development process. When the government says "Yes, but not at *such* high interest rates," the delicate process of building market confidence can easily be stalled or reversed as witnessed, for example, by Jamaica and Mexico. The lessons of experience indicate that governments must be prepared to accept the rough with the smooth, with more of the rough-going likely during the early stages. In other words, strong commitment to this market development policy at the outset is a prerequisite for success in the longer run.

One of the best litmus tests of commitment and acceptance of the principle of the market determination of the price of government debt lies in the way the treasury bill auction market works. Specifically, market development is likely to take root and flourish only when the authorities resist the very strong temptation to set a reserve price. There are four advantages of a "clean" auction in which all bills are sold at whatever price the market offers:

1. It informs the government of the true opportunity cost of its borrowing.

2. It avoids recourse to the central bank and so avoids the road back to inflationary finance.

3. It provides important feedback signals from the market for use in monetary policy making.

4. The treasury bill yield can and soon will be used as a crucial reference rate for the pricing of other financial claims in new markets.

1.3.2 Persuasion

One of the questionnaire's first questions asked how the main political actors were persuaded that voluntary domestic markets for government debt would be a good thing. *Ab initio,* ministers of finance and other cabinet ministers are likely to see the increased price of financing government deficits as a costly certainty, while viewing the benefits as vague and uncertain.

Central banks may well become involved in the debate, since they stand to benefit on at least three counts:

1. Getting the government out of the central bank clearly reduces the inflationary threat of deficits.

2. Developing voluntary domestic markets for government debt enables the central bank to use indirect market-based instruments of monetary policy.

3. By divorcing fiscal and monetary policy in this way, the central bank is bound to attain more independence regardless of any legal provisions.

Both the UK and the US pursued cheap money policies with central bank support of government debt prices in the immediate postwar period. Both attempts at fixing prices and hence setting low interest rates were abandoned when their inflationary consequences were recognised. In the US, this recognition was, perhaps ironically, more evident on the part of the Treasury than the Federal Reserve.

In any event, persuasion and education are typically needed, as evinced for example by India's case considered in Chapter 6. After some years of public cajoling by the Reserve Bank of India, the Minister of Finance finally acknowledged the case against automatic monetisation of the government's deficit through the issue of *ad hoc* treasury bills. In September 1994, he signed an agreement with the Reserve Bank to phase out this method of financing over a three-year period. This document is strikingly similar to "The Accord" between the US Treasury and the Federal Reserve System in March 1951.

The only obvious exception to the typical process of persuasion and education, usually spearheaded by the central bank, is New Zealand. Here, the new government that assumed power in 1984 was already committed to market mechanisms and had already recognised the benefits accruing from adopting market-based mechanisms of government finance and monetary policy implementation.

1.3.3 Macroeconomic Prerequisites

The questionnaire responses, together with other sources, suggest that successful development of voluntary domestic markets for government debt hinges on four key elements:

1. Macroeconomic stability, involving

   - monetary control;
   - fiscal discipline;
   - consistent monetary, fiscal and exchange rate policies.

2. Coordination, necessitating

   - establishing a coordinating committee including the central bank and ministry of finance;
   - sharing information;
   - limiting central bank credit to the government;
   - promoting secondary market development.

3. Supervision and regulation. Here it is essential to establish confidence in the market, to ensure that weak financial institutions are detected early, and to prevent Ponzi-type borrowing that escalates real interest rates to pathologically high levels.[3]

4. Sequencing the reforms, among which some of the more important measures that require initial planning for the subsequent market development process include

   - auctioning treasury bills;
   - reducing reserve and liquid asset requirements;
   - lengthening the maturity of debt offered at auction;
   - opening up the market to foreign buyers.

Chapter 6 discusses all these prerequisites and processes in more detail.

1.3.4 Microeconomic Prerequisites

At the microeconomic level, there seem to be five essential elements:

1. Market-clearing yields on government paper.

2. Relatively stable money market conditions.

3. A predictable or preannounced schedule of issues.

4. Some market-making arrangement.

5. Financial infrastructure ensuring transparency, low risk and low cost.

Chapter 7 covers these prerequisites at greater length.

---

[3] A Ponzi game is a type of swindle named after Charles Ponzi who promised extraordinarily high returns to investors which he was able to deliver for a time by using funds collected from new investors. It can also refer to a situation in which an insolvent enterprise continues to borrow in order to pay the interest on old debts in the knowledge that it will never be able to repay its debts.

1.3.5   The Players

Chapter 7 identifies three key groups of players that need to be considered at the start of any market development programme:

1. The ministry of finance needs to

   - acquire expertise in treasury management;
   - forecast its cash flow;
   - plan the maturity structure of its debt;
   - determine an optimal menu of debt types;
   - announce an issue schedule;
   - simulate costs of alternative funding strategies.

2. The central bank may have to assume tasks such as

   - the responsibility for the smooth and efficient functioning of the government debt market;
   - vetting and regulating market participants;
   - providing depository, registry and electronic delivery-versus-payment systems;
   - implementing monetary policy to avoid excessive short-term interest rate volatility;
   - implementing monetary policy to allow a normal degree of short-term interest rate fluctuation.

3. Financial institutions require the central bank's attention in at least three areas:

   - facilitating the acquisition of treasury expertise and the expansion of treasury activities;
   - dismantling or at least controlling any bank cartel;
   - selecting, where appropriate, primary dealers.

   As primary dealers, financial institutions are typically obliged to

   - act as market maker;
   - support auctions.

   In return, they may receive various privileges such as

- exclusive right to bid at auction;
- exemption from prepayment with bids;
- right to make telephone or electronic bids;
- access to borrowing from the central bank;
- tax breaks.

Although there can be large benefits in terms of secondary market development from giving primary dealers various privileges in return for certain obligations, are they worth the costs? Privileges necessarily violate the level playing-field principle. Furthermore, the vested interests created by these privileges can impede subsequent change. For example, privileges held by gilt-edged market makers (GEMMs) in the UK appear to have stalled the introduction of a market for repurchase agreements (a 'repo' market) by the Bank of England until the beginning of 1996. Experience suggests, therefore, that privileges should be granted only for a fixed time period at the end of which they may or may not be renewed depending on the new cost-benefit balance that is then perceived.

One of the early 1984 reforms in New Zealand consisted of disenfranchising official short-term money market dealers. The level playing-field philosophy ensured that, in their words, "no serious consideration was given to introducing preferred primary dealers. Our general approach was to encourage as wide, and competitively neutral, access to the market as possible."

1.3.6 Primary Markets

There are of course innumerable issues that must be addressed when initiating, say, an auction market for treasury bills. Eight of them considered in Chapter 7 involve choices with respect to:

1. Participants.

2. Bid screening and dealing with risks of noncompliance.

3. Central bank participation.

4. Competitive bids.

5. Price determination and a mechanism for allocating competitive bids.

6. Noncompetitive bids and post-auction sales.

7. Scheduling auctions.

8. Advertising.

Perhaps most important is ensuring that the system adopted works smoothly and efficiently. This suggests that an off-the-peg system rather than mix-and-match may be preferable, particularly in very small countries. In fact, none of the case study countries reported that their auction mechanisms had caused any specific problem.

Nevertheless, setting a reserve or cutoff price can have and has had major adverse consequences, as in Jamaica and Mexico. If a reserve price is to be set at all, it might best take a relative form such as excluding bids one standard deviation or more below the mean bid at either the current or previous auction or the average of mean current and previous auction bids. When competition is weak or nonexistent, however, the central bank will have to devise more sophisticated strategies to simulate competitive outcomes.

1.3.7 Secondary Markets

While many countries have developed primary markets for government securities through auctions, developing active secondary markets has been much more difficult, as detailed in Chapter 7. Among the case study countries, only in New Zealand were there no problems in attracting a sufficient number of competitive players to develop active secondary markets in government bonds.

Experience in developing countries indicates that secondary market development is not automatic or easy; it takes time and patience. Although it is recognised as a *sine qua non* of a strong primary market, the secondary market in India is still virtually nonexistent because of the preponderance of captive buyers in the market for government debt. As all the players are final investors, a secondary market of adequate depth has failed to develop. Malaysia has faced the same problem for exactly the same reason.

Plans to develop the Indian secondary market include improving institutional infrastructure and the payment and settlement system. Among various recent measures, the establishment of the Securities Trading Corporation by the Reserve Bank in 1994, approval of six primary dealers under the Guidelines for Primary Dealers issued in 1995, accounting requirements to mark to market and the introduction of an electronic delivery-versus-payment system in July 1995 are expected to promote secondary trading.

In Jamaica, use of the standard accounting practice of *not* marking to market is also cited as one of the deterrents to the development of a secondary market. In Zimbabwe, lack of interest and skill among stockbrokers as well as the lack of appropriate legislation are held responsible for the nonexistence of secondary markets there.

1.3.8 Spillover to Markets for Private Sector Debt

One anticipated effect of developing voluntary domestic markets for government debt is the encouragement of markets for private sector debt. After presenting evidence from the case study countries, Chapter 7 concludes that developing markets for government debt does appear to have encouraged markets for private sector debt in Ghana, at least to a limited degree. More generally, it has increased the public's financial awareness, e.g., the banking habit and investment culture.

The deregulation of corporate debenture rates is expected to stimulate the private sector bond market in India. Already, several innovative corporate bonds have been issued, with government security yields used as reference rates. Establishing a reference rate for pricing in the markets for commercial paper, certificates of deposits, interbank claims and other repo markets is also one of the benefits accruing from the development of the government debt market in Jamaica. There has also been increased trading in new financial instruments. However, the Bank of Jamaica suggests that an active interbank market is a prerequisite for developing markets for government debt.

In Malaysia, the infrastructure and procedures established for the government debt market have acted as models for markets in private sector debt. The development process for the government debt market has also provided market participants with the skills needed to trade in other debt instruments.

Specialised Mexican financial institutions such as brokerage houses that started operations only in government securities have expanded activities using the same techniques and facilities to develop markets for private debt. The Banco de México concludes: "Thus, economies of scale in the development of a government paper market have facilitated the introduction and evolution of a sound and solid private sector debt market."

Liberalised markets in New Zealand led to rapid financial innovation with big Euro and Yankee kiwi bonds in the early years followed by futures and options on domestic bonds, domestic interest rate swaps, fixed-rate mortgages and some strips.

1.3.9   Summary of Developing Markets for Government Debt

Experience in the case study countries indicates that developing a voluntary domestic market for government debt involves major changes in both outlook and activities on the part of ministries of finance, central banks and the financial institutions.

Although no questionnaire response doubted the advantages that could accrue from the successful development of a market for government debt, they all indicated many of the practical difficulties encountered during the development process. Interest in this topic has produced a wealth of detailed research over the past few years, as evinced by this book's bibliography. James Duesenberry (1995, vi) stresses the point that "the devil is in the details." While Chapters 6 and 7 do go into considerably more detail, I turn now in this introductory chapter to the specific roles that a central bank might play in this process.

1.4   Roles for the Central Bank?

One view of the appropriate conduct of central banking holds that the central bank should confine its activities as narrowly as possible to the primary objective—price stability—of monetary policy. Here, government debt management, auctioneering, registry, payment and settlement systems, electronic delivery-versus-payment mechanisms, and prudential supervision and regulation of financial institutions are seen to be outside the proper scope of central banking. These activities should therefore be conducted by other public or private sector institutions.

Since monetary policy must be coordinated with fiscal and exchange rate policy, however, the central bank cannot, in practice, stand aloof from policies in these areas. Dialogue is essential and the central bank's influence on appropriate and coordinated macroeconomic policies will usually depend, at least in part, on the expertise that it can proffer. As we suggested in Fry, Goodhart and Almeida (1996, 108–110), central bank independence may well be more a matter of possessing the necessary expertise to argue its case than of any formal legal arrangements. Furthermore, implementing monetary policy to achieve price stability may be most efficiently pursued through the use of indirect market-based techniques of monetary control. If this is impossible because of the lack of appropriate markets, then the central bank may perforce be obliged to play a role in creating these markets.

The process of developing voluntary domestic markets for government debt requires not only conducive macroeconomic conditions and appropriate market structures, but also financial infrastructure. This infrastructure is being developed and improved continuously even in the most sophisticated financial markets of the world. But the appropriate financial infrastructure is highly country specific. It depends on the legal system, the ways fiscal and monetary policy are implemented, the structure of the financial system, as well as accounting conventions, geographical characteristics, the state of telecommunications, etc.

Chapter 8 identifies seven possible roles for central banks in the process of developing voluntary domestic markets for government debt. These appear not only to be particularly important at the early stages of this process but also to yield comparative advantage for central bank involvement. Issues such as tax treatment and contract enforcement, despite their obvious importance, are not discussed here because they do not appear to offer scope for such comparative advantage. Nonetheless, some central bankers may well feel that they do have a comparative advantage in proffering advice on tax matters, particularly when government deficits are undermining monetary policy or specific taxes on financial transactions are seriously impeding market development.

Here I pose some of the questions that were raised at the Bank of England's 1996 Central Bank Governors' Symposium. Some tentative answers emanating from the debate at this Symposium are presented in Chapter 8.

1.4.1 Information Provider

Information is an essential ingredient for market development. Given that it is a public good, i.e., its use by someone else does not remove it from one's own use, its provision will be suboptimal in perfectly competitive markets. Hence, there is economic justification for allocating some public funds to improve information systems. Among the case study countries, lack of adequate information was mentioned specifically as an impediment to development of the market in Ghana.

To the extent that the central bank collects much information from financial institutions as part of its supervisory role, the central bank may well have a comparative advantage in operating various types of information systems for financial markets. In some countries, central banks have provided trading systems for government securities in conjunction with clearing and settlement facilities. For example, the National Bank of Poland has developed a special information network for primary dealers in the money markets. In other countries, central banks have been instrumental in developing trading systems rather than in providing the networks themselves. Transparency and efficiency improvements have been noted.

Here I would simply ask the question:

- Starting *de novo* in the mid-1990s, how might a central bank design an ideal system both for obtaining and disseminating information?

1.4.2 Issue Manager

In some countries, e.g., Germany, Italy, Spain, Denmark and the UK among OECD countries, the central bank manages the issue of government debt, but in others this task is done by the ministry of finance or by a specialised semi-independent government debt management agency, as in Ireland, New Zealand and Sweden. While it may be largely a matter of historical accident as to who does what in this regard, I pose the questions:

- Is it possible to specify criteria that could be used to determine the best location of this activity, given particular country characteristics?

- In addition, what are the advantages and disadvantages, if any, of separating management of treasury bill issues from issues of longer-term government debt?

1.4.3 Market Maker

In the OECD countries, primary dealers rather than the central bank act as market makers. If a viable system of primary dealers already exists, the central bank might only undermine it by intervening as a market maker as well.

In many developing countries, however, no system of primary dealers or its equivalent exists. Several developing country central banks have established secondary market windows during the initial stages of market development.

Outstanding questions here include:

- Is there a case for the central bank to act as market maker in the early stages of the market development process?

- If so, to what extent could or should the central bank act as a market maker?

- How can the central bank be prevented from impeding market development by preventing essential price fluctuations or from becoming a residual buyer again?

- Do the potential costs outweigh any perceived benefits?

1.4.4 Auction Participation

It has been suggested that, where the central bank does participate in auctions of government debt as a buyer, it should be a noncompetitive buyer taking up debt at the weighted average auction price. Preferably, the maximum quantity of the central bank bid should be preannounced together with the total offer, so providing the market with the net minimum quantity on offer for competitive bids. In any event, central bank participation should not lead back down the path to inflationary deficit finance.

Among others, this brief introduction raises four questions:

- Should the central bank participate in auctions of government debt at all?

- Should it be involved in setting and administering a reserve price?

- How should unsold bills be handled?

- If the central bank does acquire bills at auction, should there be any rules or understandings about the extent to which it should subsequently sell its holdings on the secondary market, effectively as a tap stock?

1.4.5 Clearing and Settlement Systems

As lender of last resort, the central bank has an obvious interest in ensuring that clearing and settlement systems for government debt are well designed to minimise credit, liquidity and operational risks.

One can identify four key elements in the clearing and settlement system:

1. Trade comparison and clearing arrangements.

2. A depository that handles securities and maintains a book-entry transfer system.

3. A money transfer system.

4. A custodial/safekeeping arrangement where members of the depository can safely keep securities on behalf of clients.

In China, the cost of poor clearing and settlement systems can be measured because the quality of depositories varies between trading centres. Identical bonds fetch higher prices in Shanghai than elsewhere because Shanghai has the best depository and so the least delivery risk.

Among the case study countries, a Committee on Electronic Funds Transfer (EFT) and Other Payments submitted its proposals to the Reserve Bank of India in January 1996. It recommended the introduction of a national EFT system for interbank and intrabank credit transfers which will require an amendment to the Reserve Bank of India Act.

In 1994 the Banco de México initiated a reform of the national payment system. The three major elements of this reform are:

1. Limits and penalties on commercial banks' daylight and overnight overdrafts with the central bank.

2. Reform of the clearing and settlement system, including the introduction of a large-value transfer system.

3. Introduction of an electronic delivery-versus-payment scheme for transactions in bank securities.

This delivery-versus-payment system will soon be expanded to include secondary market transactions in government debt as well as other stock market transactions.

In primary markets, auction participants in some countries must deposit cash before the auction, while in others this is not required. Clearly, full cash deposits ensure that bids are honoured, but such a requirement is costly and can deter some agents from participating at all. The problem of nonpayment, however, is far more serious in the secondary markets. In the primary market, the worst that can happen is that the sale is not consummated with the resulting minor pricing distortion. In the secondary market, nonpayment could produce major systemic problems.

Among the OECD countries, an electronic assured payment system is provided by the Bank of England to ensure simultaneous transfer of title and payment for government debt at the end of each day.[4] Similarly, in New Zealand the government securities registry system is operated by the Reserve Bank. Among the case study countries, the absence of a central registry for securities delays transactions in Jamaica. Because treasury bills are bearer instruments in Jamaica, this creates an additional risk. The absence of a central depository system in Zimbabwe has impeded market development there too; Zimbabwean debt securities are also issued in bearer form. The introduction of a registry for a book-entry system run by a reputable organisation would apparently be welcomed by most Zimbabwean market participants.

The Banco de México operates a centralised depository for government securities and performs all the necessary custodial and book-entry operations. The advantage of this book-entry system is that it "significantly reduces operating and transaction costs as there is no need for the physical transfer of titles among market participants." Most participants in the market for government debt can access the Bank's electronic communications system (*Siac-Banxico*), which is equivalent to the US Fedwire. In this way, participants can conduct direct purchases and sales or repo agreements. Repayment on maturity is also effected through this electronic system. The delivery-versus-payment system already used for bank securities will be adopted for government debt in the near future.

Several questions remain:

- Are there any particular aspects of clearing and settlement system development that a central bank should recognise?

- What particular problems have been encountered and what remedies have been used to tackle them?

- Is there any advantage in bearer instruments as opposed to a book-entry registry?

- Given that the central bank administers the country's payment system, are there large economies in having the central bank run the registry for government debt?

- What are the practical problems that have been encountered in establishing a modern electronic delivery-versus-payment system for transactions in government debt?

---

[4]This system will be replaced by a true delivery-versus-payment system as soon as the Central Gilts Office system has adapted to encompass a real-time gross settlement system.

- Does the requirement of cash deposits prior to bidding exert a serious deterrent on auction participation that noticeably weakens competition?

- Should registration be confined to the name of the beneficial owner or is nominee registration, e.g., for brokerage houses, feasible and desirable?

1.4.6   Regulation and Supervision

Among OECD countries, government debt markets are supervised by the central bank in Italy, Spain, Netherlands and the UK. Since central banks in other OECD countries do not supervise government debt markets, one might ask:

- Is central bank supervision good practice or should central bank supervisory responsibilities be confined to commercial banks?

- In particular, which agency should be responsible for supervising primary dealers?

1.4.7   Secondary Market Development

Even if the central bank does not act as market maker, it can play a role as market developer. In particular, it can offer its expertise to the government on steps needed for this development. Active and efficient secondary markets in government securities are generally associated with the following seven features:

1. No price or tax distortions or other inefficient portfolio regulations that produce market segmentation and captive buyers.

2. An efficient primary market in which the authorities are prepared to sell government debt at true market-clearing prices to voluntary buyers.

3. A sufficient volume of government debt and widespread holdings among diverse agents.

4. Active liquidity management by the central bank, on the one hand to ensure adequate interest-rate flexibility and, on the other hand, to avoid excessive interest-rate volatility or instability.

5. Strong interbank and money markets supported by an efficient clearing and settlement system.

6. A well-defined microstructure for secondary market trading.

7. A transparent and equitable regulatory and supervisory framework.

In this connection, two questions emerge:

- Are these all measures that the central bank could and should promote?

- Finally, are there any other measures for secondary market development in which the central bank could be usefully involved?

1.5 Conclusion

The path followed in the development of a voluntary domestic market for government debt is highly dependent on initial conditions. This is exemplified by the contrast between the experiences of New Zealand, on the one hand, and Ghana and Zimbabwe, on the other; their starting points were entirely different. Size is another crucial factor; small countries face very different problems from large ones. It follows, therefore, that each country will learn much from its own experience as it develops its own markets for its own government debt. Nevertheless, it may also benefit from the experiences of the eight case study countries, which are described in Part III of this book, as well as from other lessons of experience.

Chapter 2

Debts, Deficits, Inflation and Growth

2.1 Introduction

THIS CHAPTER ANALYSES THE DYNAMIC relationship between persistent government deficits and the consequent accumulation of government debt. Here I make use of three definitions of the government deficit. The first, measured on a cash basis, is the overall or conventional deficit reported by the media and published in *International Financial Statistics* (*IFS*), the main data source used in this book.[1] It is defined as government expenditure minus government revenue. Here debt repayment is excluded from but interest costs included in government expenditure, while borrowing is excluded from government revenue. This definition measures the gap to be covered by *net* borrowing (Tanzi, Blejer and Teijeiro 1988, 5). When the government runs a conventional deficit, its *nominal* debt increases.

The second definition of the government deficit is the operational deficit. It excludes the part of nominal interest payments the government pays to service its debt that constitutes an inflation premium (Tanzi, Blejer and Teijeiro 1988, 12). For example, with an inflation rate of 10 percent and a nominal interest rate of 15 percent, interest costs in the operational deficit are reduced by the 10 percent inflation premium that exists in the 15 percent nominal interest rate.

The reason for excluding this cost is that it represents, in effect, principal repayment. The 10 percent inflation reduces the real value of

---

[1] Unless otherwise stated, all data used in this book are taken from *International Financial Statistics*, CD–ROM, March 1996, and World Bank, *World Data 1995*, CD–ROM, September 1995.

the government debt by 10 percent. When everyone understands what is going on, the interest rate compensates for this erosion in the real value of the principal and then includes a real or inflation-adjusted interest rate as the return to lenders. It is the real interest costs that are included in and the nominal interest costs that are excluded from the operational deficit. When the government runs an operational deficit, the *real* or inflation-adjusted value of its debt increases.

Finally, the third definition of the government deficit is the primary deficit. It excludes all interest costs, both nominal and real, from the definition of the deficit. The primary deficit is a useful concept when analysing the government's budget constraint. For example, the government may realise that the rising interest cost of its increasing debt is leading to an unstable, explosive situation. In such case, the *only* solution is for the government to reduce its primary deficit. With a constant interest rate, its interest costs are fixed in the short run and can be reduced only by a reduction in its debt. This can be achieved only by running a primary surplus, i.e., by ensuring that current revenue exceeds noninterest expenditures.

All three deficit concepts are cash-based measures. As Miguel Mancera suggested at the Symposium, deficits measured on an accrual basis might provide better indicators; Andrew Sheng made the same point in comments on an earlier draft of the manuscript. Donald Brash noted that market confidence in New Zealand had been developed, in part, by the publication of an accrual-based budget together with detailed three-year projections of the fiscal position. Treating privatisation proceeds as current revenue also clearly distorts the deficit measure, as does private finance initiatives that mobilise private funds only by assigning the project risk to the government, so creating a contingent liability for the future. There is also a strong case for amalgamating central bank and fiscal deficits (Fry 1995, Ch. 17; Robinson and Stella 1988).

2.2 The Government Budget Constraint

In the simplest case of price stability and no seigniorage revenue, government debt follows a time path that can be expressed:

$$B_t = B_{t-1} + r \cdot B_{t-1} + X_t, \qquad (2.1)$$

where B is the government debt, r is the interest rate (nominal and real) expressed in proportion rather than percentage form and X is the primary deficit. Both sides of equation 2.1 can be divided by gross domestic product (GDP), which grows at a rate γ. Hence, equation 2.1 can be rearranged and expressed:

$$\Delta b = x + [\frac{(1+r)}{(1+\gamma)} - 1]b, \qquad (2.2)$$

where b is the ratio of the government debt to GDP and x is the government's primary deficit, which equals government expenditure on goods and services ζ minus tax revenue ξ, also expressed as a ratio to GDP. Finally, equation 2.2 can be expressed in continuously compounded form:

$$\frac{db}{dt} = x + (r - \gamma)b, \qquad (2.3)$$

where r is the real interest rate on government debt and γ is the economy's real growth rate, but both rates are now continuously compounded and still expressed in proportional rather than percentage form. With continuously compounded rates, the real interest rate r equals exactly the nominal interest rate i minus the expected inflation rate π^e.[2] Appealing to the theory of rational expectations, the actual inflation rate π can be substituted for expected inflation π^e, particularly with the 15-year averages used here.

Equation 2.3 indicates that, in the normal case where the real interest rate r exceeds the real growth rate γ, the debt/GDP ratio will rise unless the government runs a primary surplus, i.e., x is negative.[3] To avoid an explosive debt expansion, the present value of tax revenue ξ must equal or exceed the present value of government spending ζ plus the initial level of debt b_0 (Blanchard and Fischer 1989, 54–55). The government's intertemporal budget constraint is defined here as the requirement that its debt should not explode, which implies that the present value of $\xi - \zeta$ must equal or exceed b_0.

2.2.1 A Numerical Example

To illustrate the dynamics of government debt, I use equation 2.2. Suppose that the government's debt equals 100 percent of GDP, that

---

[2]Using simple interest rates, the real rate r equals $(1+i)/(1+\pi^e) - 1$ or $(i - \pi^e)/(1 + \pi^e)$, where r, i, and π^e are again all expressed in proportional rather than percentage form.

[3]However, James Barth, George Iden and Frank Russek (1986) dispute the view that the real interest rate has normally exceeded the real growth rate in the United States.

the real interest rate is 5 percent and that the growth rate is 4 percent. Under these assumptions, equation 2.2 shows that the debt/GDP ratio will grow by $100[(1.05/1.04) - 1]$ or 0.96 percent a year, provided government spending on goods and services exactly equals tax revenue, i.e., x is zero.

Another way of illustrating the same case is to assume that GDP is $100 and that debt is also $100 in year 0, with the real interest rate still 5 percent and growth 4 percent. In this case, government debt will increase to $105 in year 1 because the government must borrow $5 to pay its interest cost. Since GDP rises to $104, the debt/GDP ratio increases to 100.96 percent in year 1, which is 0.96 percent higher than it was in year 0. Borrowing $5.25 in year 1 to meet the interest bill on the debt of $105 raises debt to 110.25 or 101.93 percent of GDP in year 2.

In this example, the level of debt will explode over time if the government continues to finance the interest costs of its debt entirely by borrowing. This is the archetypal Ponzi game in which the borrower has no intention of ever repaying his or her debt but rather continues to borrow to meet rising interest costs. As soon as they suspect that they will never be repaid, lenders refuse to provide additional credit and the scheme collapses.[4]

2.2.2 Stability when the Interest Rate Exceeds the Growth Rate

In the numerical example above, the government must spend less on goods and services ζ than its tax revenue ξ to prevent its debt from exploding. Specifically, it can keep its debt/GDP ratio constant only by holding ζ below ξ. By setting $db/dt = 0$ in equation 2.3, the required primary deficit for long-run solvency can be expressed

$$x = (\gamma - r)b. \tag{2.4}$$

If debt is positive and the real interest rate exceeds the rate of economic growth, this primary deficit must be negative. Therefore, the corresponding required primary surplus can be expressed

$$-x = (r - \gamma)b \tag{2.5}$$

---

[4]The ageing populations in some countries make their unfunded state pension schemes appear perilously analogous to a gigantic Ponzi game.

or

$$\xi - \zeta = (r - \gamma)b. \tag{2.6}$$

Consider a slightly different numerical example using continuously compounded interest and growth rates with a debt/GDP ratio of 0.5 or 50 percent, r equal to 5 percent and ζ equal to 4 percent. Now equation 2.5 shows that the required primary surplus $-x$ for a steady state in which the debt/GDP ratio remains constant equals 1 percent of the debt or 0.5 percent of GDP. The reduced borrowing requirement resulting from this primary surplus now increases debt exactly in line with the increase in GDP.

2.2.3 Recapitulation

The upshot of the mathematics presented in this section is that the relationship between debt and deficit ratios is dependent on growth rates and real interest rates. Furthermore, its debt will explode with concomitant economic instability unless the government constrains its expenditures or raises tax revenue sufficiently to remain solvent in the long run. By definition, solvency means that debt does not become infinitely large. In a steady state or long-run equilibrium situation, the ratio of debt to GDP will be constant.

For any given positive rate of economic growth, there is a unique debt/GDP ratio consistent with any constant operational deficit ratio. For example, a growth rate of 5 percent and an operational deficit equal to 4 percent of GDP will eventually produce a level of government debt equal to 80 percent of GDP. Suppose debt is $80, GDP is $100, so the deficit is $4. The growth rate increases GDP to $105, while the deficit increases debt to $84, leaving the debt/GDP ratio constant at exactly 80 percent.

If debt is rising towards this 80 percent ratio, however, interest costs will also be rising. Hence, a constant operational deficit necessitates a reduction in government spending on goods, services and transfer payments during the period of rising debt. More and more of its expenditures will be absorbed in debt service costs. This raises a question as to how the government will be able to maintain a constant operational deficit when its debt ratio is rising.

An alternative approach is to ask the question: what adjustment is required to maintain the present debt/GDP ratio constant? The answer depends on the rate of economic growth, the real rate of interest and the current debt ratio. Given the level of tax revenue, however, adjustment can take the form of changing noninterest expenditures on goods, services and transfers only because interest costs are fixed by the outstanding debt. The government can afford to spend more on these nontax expenditures without raising taxes, i.e., run a larger primary deficit, the higher is the growth rate and the lower is the real interest rate. If the real interest rate exceeds the growth rate, the government must run a primary surplus in order to hold any positive debt ratio constant. Conversely, when growth exceeds the real interest rate, the government can continue to run some primary deficit without its debt ratio necessarily increasing. For any given primary deficit, conventional deficits will be larger, the larger is the government debt. Operational deficits will also be larger if the real interest rate is positive.

2.3 The Fiscal Approach to Inflation and Financial Repression

In practice, many governments find it virtually impossible to satisfy their intertemporal budget constraint with conventional tax revenue. Indeed, this may be possible only by relying on revenue from the inflation tax or reducing interest costs through financial repression. For example, if the inflation tax yields 2 percent of GDP then the primary deficit can still be positive (at 1.5 percent of GDP in the previous numerical example) despite positive debt. Alternatively, if financial repression is used to reduce the real interest rate from 5 to 1 percent so reducing interest costs from 2.5 to 0.5 percent of GDP, the primary deficit can again remain positive at 1.5 percent of GDP. These examples of inflation tax revenue and interest saving from financial repression correspond quite closely to their average values estimated for a sample of 43 developing countries over the period 1979–1993 (Fry, Goodhart and Almeida 1996, 36).

Since the early 1970s, there has been increasing recognition of the costs associated with both the inflation tax and financial repression. As a result, many governments have attempted to move away from these two methods of satisfying their intertemporal budget constraints. *Ceteris paribus*, this involves increasing conventional tax revenues ξ or reducing expenditures on goods and services ζ as proportions of GDP.

The higher the growth rate, the easier it is to implement either or both these alternatives. Furthermore, equations 2.3 and 2.4 show that a higher growth rate γ eases the budget constraint itself. Conceivably, policies of price stability and financial liberalisation could pay for themselves. If it raised the growth rate by 4 percentage points, abandoning an inflation tax that produced revenue equal to 2 percent of GDP would exactly pay for itself and still allow a positive primary deficit of 1.5 percent in the previous example: $b(\gamma - r) = 0.5(0.08 - 0.05) = 0.015$. Were financial liberalisation also to increase the growth rate by 4 percentage points, exactly the same result could occur even if the real interest rate increased from 1 to 5 percent.

These examples are undoubtedly wildly optimistic in most cases. As will be shown in subsequent chapters, inflation and financial repression certainly damage growth. However, only in countries experiencing extraordinarily high and volatile inflation or seriously negative real interest rates could one hope that price stability and financial liberalisation would increase economic growth by 4 percentage points. But in such countries, government deficits are typically in double digits. Unless additional measures are taken concomitantly to reduce the primary deficits in these countries, abandoning these two distortionary tax-like revenue sources may well lead to worse instability involving excessively high real interest rates. Real interest rates may soar to stratospheric levels as they have in a number of developing countries since the mid-1970s. Such pathologically high real interest rates are just as damaging to economic growth as are strongly negative real rates.

2.4   Government Deficits and Debts in 111 Countries

Table 2.1 lists the 111 countries, 21 richer members of the Organisation for Economic Co-operation and Development (OECD) and 90 developing countries, for which government deficit and real GDP data exist. To avoid distortions from outliers, Table 2.2 reports values for the median rather than for the mean country in each group. It shows that the median country posted an average deficit (GDY) equal to 3.5 percent of GDP over the 15-year period 1979–1993.[5] The median period-average

---

[5] While the 15-year period 1979–1993 is used for all the averages discussed here, not all countries report data for the entire period. In the majority of these cases, the mean for the available data is used. To provide as much consistency as possible without decimating the data set, I estimated means for years in which all data existed within the following groups: (a) deficit GDY and government plus government-guaranteed foreign debt $DTGY$; (b) GDY, growth rate of real GDP YG and consumer price inflation INF; (c) GDY, government domestic debt $DTDY$, government foreign debt $DTFY$ and total government debt DTY; and (d) GDY and the real interest rate RR. Appendices 2 to 12 provide period-average data on all variables used in the analysis presented in this book for individual countries.

Table 2.1. The 111 Countries with Deficit and Growth Data

Richer OECD	Africa	Asia and Pacific	Middle East and Europe	Western Hemisphere
Australia	Botswana	Bhutan	Bahrain	Argentina
Austria	Burundi	China	Cyprus	Bahamas
Belgium	Cameroon	Fiji	Egypt	Barbados
Canada	Chad	India	Greece	Belize
Denmark	Ethiopia	Indonesia	Hungary	Bolivia
Finland	Gabon	Korea	Iran	Brazil
France	Gambia	Malaysia	Israel	Chile
Germany	Ghana	Myanmar	Jordan	Colombia
Iceland	Guinea-Bissau	Nepal	Kuwait	Costa Rica
Ireland	Kenya	Pakistan	Malta	Dominican
Italy	Lesotho	Papua New	Oman	Republic
Japan	Madagascar	Guinea	Poland	Ecuador
Luxembourg	Malawi	Philippines	Portugal	El Salvador
Netherlands	Mauritius	Singapore	Romania	Guatemala
New Zealand	Morocco	Solomon	Syria	Guyana
Norway	Namibia	Islands	Turkey	Haiti
Spain	Nigeria	Sri Lanka	United Arab	Honduras
Sweden	Rwanda	Thailand	Republic	Mexico
Switzerland	Seychelles	Tonga		Netherlands
United Kingdom	Sierra Leone			Antilles
United States	South Africa			Nicaragua
	Swaziland			Panama
	Tanzania			Paraguay
	Tunisia			Peru
	Uganda			St Kitts
	Zaire			and Nevis
	Zambia			St Lucia
	Zimbabwe			St Vincent and
				Grenadines
				Trinidad
				and Tobago
				Uruguay
				Venezuela

deficit is 3.3 percent for the 21 OECD countries and 3.6 percent of GDP for the 90 developing countries. Table 2.2 presents period-average deficit data because the thrust of the argument presented in this book is that excessive and persistent government deficits rather than small and temporary deficits damage the economy.[6]

---

[6] Indeed, I concur with Miguel Mancera who made the point at the Symposium that "not all government deficits are necessarily evil. A moderate-sized deficit, combined with

Table 2.2. Government Debts and Deficits, 1979–1993

Variable	Country Group				
	All	*OECD*		*Developing*	
	Median	*Median*	*Worst*	*Median*	*Worst*
GDY	3.5	3.3	11.9	3.6	33.3
DTY	37.6	35.3	93.7	39.1	304.3
YG	2.9	2.2	1.4	3.4	–5.5
RR	1.8	3.3	5.1	0.4	57.8

Key: GDY   Government deficit as percent of GDP.
   DTY   Total government debt as percent of GDP.
   YG   Rate of growth in GDP (constant prices, continuously compounded).
   RR   Real interest rate (continuously compounded).

Note: "Worst" implies highest deficit and debt ratios, highest interest rate, but lowest growth rate.

While these medians are remarkably similar, their dispersions differ considerably. For the OECD countries, Italy recorded the maximum average deficit over the period 1979–1993 of 11.9 percent of GDP, while Guyana posted the maximum average deficit equal to 33.3 percent of GDP among developing countries. Figure 2.1 provides an indication of the dispersion in annual deficits, where data are available, over the period 1970–1995.

Not surprisingly, countries with large deficits over a 15-year period inevitably generate greater debt/GDP ratios than countries running budget surpluses or only small deficits over the same period.[7] The median ratio of government debt to GDP is 38 percent of GDP.[8] Again, the median values for OECD and developing countries do not differ significantly.

Among the OECD countries, Belgium recorded the highest average debt ratio at 94 percent of GDP. Among the 42 developing countries for

---

economic growth, is hardly a source of concern."

[7] When stock variables like debt are expressed as percentages of flow variables like GDP, the geometric mean of the stock variable at the beginning and end of the year is divided by the flow variable. When one stock variable is expressed as a percentage of another stock variable, the arithmetic average of the beginning- and end-of-year values is given.

[8] The problem here is that only 59 of the 111 countries record total government debt DTY data and only 56 provide a disaggregation between domestic $DTDY$ and foreign $DTFY$ debt. However, the World Bank publishes government and government-guaranteed foreign debt $DTGY$ for 79 of the developing countries in this sample.

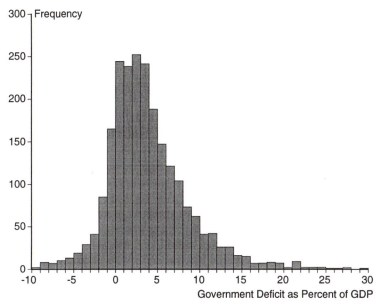

Figure 2.1. Dispersion in Government Deficits, 1970–1995

which data are available, the highest average government debt figure for the period 1979–1993 is Guyana's at 304 percent of GDP. For government and government-guaranteed foreign debt, Guyana also recorded the highest average at 213 percent of GDP.

The average rate of economic growth over the period 1979–1993 in the median country was 2.9 percent; 2.2 percent in the OECD countries and 3.4 percent in the developing countries. The highest OECD growth rate was Japan's 3.9 percent, while the highest developing country growth rate was Botswana's 9.6 percent. The lowest growth rate in the OECD countries was Sweden's 1.4 percent, while the lowest growth rate in the developing countries was Zaire's –5.5 percent.

The final variable required for the analysis of government debt dynamics is the real interest rate. Ideally, of course, one would use interest rates on government debt. Here, however, I use the geometric average of commercial bank deposit and loan rates, since these are the most prevalent interest rate data reported in *IFS*. The continuously compounded nominal interest rate is then subtracted from the continuously compounded inflation rate. The average real interest rate over the period 1979–1993 in the median country was 1.8 percent, with medians of 3.3 and 0.4 percent for OECD and developing countries, respectively. Among the developing countries, average real interest rates ranged from a low of −153 percent in Zaire to a high of 58 in Argentina. In the OECD countries, the range of real interest rates was much narrower, with Australia recording the highest average of 5.1 percent and Iceland recording the lowest average of −5.0 percent.

2.5   The Intertemporal Budget Constraint in Practice

The Maastricht Treaty stipulates a maximum debt/GDP ratio of 60 percent and a maximum overall or conventional deficit of 3 percent for member countries of the European Union that wish to join the Single Currency. These would be consistent steady-state values for a growth rate of 5 percent. With a growth rate averaging only 2.5 percent, however, a constant conventional deficit of 3 percent would produce a steady-state debt/GDP ratio of 120 percent of GDP. Alternatively, the Maastricht Treaty can be interpreted as setting a maximum operational deficit of 1.3 percent of GDP, implying an inflation premium in the conventional deficit of 1.7 percent. If government debt equalled 50 percent of GDP, this would imply an inflation rate of 3.4 percent.

When the values from Table 2.2 are inserted into equation 2.5, the result shows that the median OECD country needed to run a primary surplus averaging 0.39 percent of GDP in the steady state to satisfy its intertemporal budget constraint. Given that its real interest payments equalled 1.16 percent of GDP, the corresponding operational deficit in this situation is 0.78 percent of GDP. Indeed, the corresponding steady-state operational deficit for any given debt ratio b and growth rate γ is simply γb (0.022 multiplied by 0.353 in this case) since the operational deficit equals $x + rb$. Adding rb to both sides of equation 2.4 gives

$$x + rb = \gamma b. \tag{2.7}$$

The situation for the median developing country is better than it is for the median OECD country because its growth rate is higher and its real interest rate is substantially lower. Here the government can run a primary *deficit* equal to 1.17 percent of GDP and an operational deficit of 1.33 percent of GDP in the steady state.

Because of the relatively low levels of government debt in the median OECD and developing country, a steady-state situation in which the debt ratio remains constant requires both primary and operational budgets that are almost balanced, i.e., required surpluses or deficits are under 1.5 percent of GDP. Suppose, however, that the debt/GDP ratio starts at 100 percent. Now the OECD country with median characteristics for all other variables must run a primary surplus of 1.1 percent of GDP which implies a corresponding operational deficit of 2.2 percent of GDP.

2.6 The Italian Case

In part, the relatively low steady-state deficit figures produced with the median debt ratios arise from the assumption of price stability and hence the equality of real and nominal interest rates. In fact, of course, the conventional government deficit figures presented in Table 2.2 include nominal rather than real interest payments. Italy provides a clear example of how a steady state can accommodate much higher conventional deficits when inflation is not zero.

Inflation averaged 10.1 percent annually in Italy over the 1979–1993 period. Therefore, with a debt/GDP ratio averaging 72 percent, the inflation-adjusted or operational deficit is reduced from 11.9 to 4.6 percent of GDP; the inflation premium of 10.1 percent in nominal interest rates added 7.3 percentage points to the conventional deficit. At the same time, however, inflation of 10.1 percent eroded the real value of the Italian government's debt by 7.3 percent of GDP: $\pi b = 0.101 \cdot 0.72$, where π is the inflation rate and therefore also the inflation premium in the nominal interest rate.

Given an average real interest rate in Italy of 1.9 percent and debt equal to 72 percent of GDP, Italy's real debt service ratio was 1.4 percent of GDP. Hence, Italy must have been running a primary deficit equal to 3.2 percent of GDP (4.6 minus 1.4 percent). With an average growth rate of 2.5 percent and a real interest rate of only 1.9 percent, equation 2.5 indicates that Italy can maintain its 72 percent debt ratio while running a primary deficit equal to 0.6 percent of GDP. Running a primary *surplus* when the real interest rate lies below the rate of economic growth necessarily reduces the debt/GDP ratio over time. Given that Italy ran a primary deficit of 3.2 percent of GDP on average over the period 1979–1993, it is inevitable that Italy's debt ratio increased from 51 in 1979 to 110 percent of GDP in 1993.

Unfortunately for the Italian government, recent financial liberalisation has raised the real interest rate to about 4 percent in recent years which, with government debt equal to 110 percent of GDP and growth of 2.5 percent, necessitates a primary surplus of 1.65 percent of GDP to prevent the debt ratio from rising still further.

Table 2.3. Government Debts and Deficits in Six Countries, 1979–1993

Variable	USA	Belgium	Guyana	Nigeria	Sierra Leone	Zimbabwe
YG	2.2	1.8	–1.8	2.2	–0.8	5.1
RR	3.9	4.5	1.1	–8.4	–25.3	–1.2
INF	5.3	4.2	14.1	20.7	46.1	12.7
DTDY	n.a.	79.2	131.9	27.4	20.8	33.8
DTFY	n.a.	14.6	172.5	45.5	42.6	18.3
DTY	37.5	93.7	304.3	73.0	63.4	52.1
GDY	3.9	8.8	33.3	5.2	8.0	8.7
IPR	2.0	4.1	27.7	8.1	11.8	5.3
ODY	1.9	4.7	5.6	–2.9	–3.8	3.4
IC	3.5	8.2	35.9	7.6	8.2	5.6
PDY	0.5	0.6	–2.6	–2.4	–0.2	3.1
x	–0.6	–2.4	–13.6	2.1	3.1	2.3

Key:		
	YG	Rate of growth in GDP (constant prices, continuously compounded).
	RR	Real interest rate (continuously compounded).
	INF	Rate of change in consumer price index (continuously compounded).
	DTDY	Government domestic debt as percent of GDP.
	DTFY	Government foreign debt as percent of GDP.
	DTY	Total government debt as percent of GDP.
	GDY	Government deficit as percent of GDP.
	IPR	Inflation premium on debt service.
	ODY	Operational deficit as percent of GDP.
	IC	Nominal debt service cost as percent of GDP.
	PDY	Primary deficit as percent of GDP.
	x	Primary deficit required for constant debt/GDP ratio.

2.7   Six Country Studies

For a more general examination of debt-deficit dynamics in practice, Table 2.3 provides debt breakdowns and other relevant macroeconomic statistics for six countries chosen for their differing deficits and debt ratios, as well as their differing growth and interest rates. After providing the data required for the various adjustments, row 8 gives the estimated inflation premium on the debt service cost (IPR). For the United States, this is simply the inflation rate multiplied by the debt/GDP ratio, 0.053·0.375, which equals 2 percent of GDP. For all the other countries in Table 2.3, the inflation premium on debt service is estimated as the domestic inflation rate times domestic debt plus US inflation times foreign debt. I assume that all domestic debt is unindexed and denominated in domestic currency, while all foreign debt is denominated in US dollars. I also assume that purchasing power parity holds, so that exchange rates adjust solely for inflation differentials. Subtracting the inflation premium IPR from the conventional deficit GDY gives the operational deficit ODY in row 9.

Row 10 estimates the nominal debt service costs as a percentage of GDP by multiplying debt by nominal interest rates. For the United States, this is simply $(RR + INF) \cdot DTY$. For all the other countries, it is the domestic nominal interest rate $(RR + INF)$ times domestic debt plus the US nominal interest rate time foreign debt. Subtracting the nominal interest costs of debt service from the conventional deficit gives the primary deficit PDY shown in row 11; it is identical to subtracting the real interest costs from the operational deficit.

Row 12 gives the steady-state primary deficit required to maintain a constant debt/GDP ratio. For the United States, it is calculated from equation 2.4 as $(YG - RR) \cdot DTY$. For the other countries, it is calculated as $(YG - RR)$ times the domestic debt ratio plus $(YG - USARR)$ times foreign debt, where $USARR$ is the US real interest rate.

The majority of government debt in high-inflation developing countries is denominated in US dollars; inflation has eroded domestic debt. Over the period 1979–1993, for example, 57 percent of Guyana's government debt took the form of foreign debt; it rose to 83 percent in the period 1989–1993. For Guyana, this implies reducing the conventional deficit which equalled 33.3 percent of GDP by the average value of external debt (172 percent) times the inflation premium (0.053), i.e., by 9.1 percent. Assuming that Guyana's domestic debt was all denominated in domestic currency, the inflation premium averaging 14.1 percent must be applied to the domestic debt/GDP ratio of 132 percent: 18.6 percent. Subtracting the total inflation premium of 27.7 percent from the 33.3 percent conventional deficit, Guyana's operational government deficit averaged 5.6 percent of GDP over this period.

Even an operational government deficit of 5.6 percent was unsustainable in Guyana's case. Its rate of economic growth averaged −1.8 percent annually over the period 1979–1993 and its domestic real interest rate was 1.1 percent. Using the average US nominal interest rate of 9.2 percent for the foreign debt ratio of 172 percent and the domestic nominal interest rate of 15.2 percent for the domestic debt ratio of 132 percent of GDP indicates that Guyana's nominal debt service costs equalled 35.9 percent of GDP. Hence, Guyana ran a primary deficit averaging −2.6 percent of GDP over the period 1979–1993.

Equation 2.4, however, indicates that Guyana could have prevented further debt expansion (expressed as a percentage of GDP) only by running a primary deficit of -13.6 percent of GDP: $(-0.018 - 0.011) \cdot 1.32 + (-0.018 - 0.039) \cdot 1.72$. In fact, its primary surplus averaged 2.6 percent of GDP (by subtracting 8.2 percent real debt service costs from the 5.6 percent operational deficit). Adding the inflation premium on domestic and foreign debt of 35.9 percent to the sustainable operational deficit of -13.6 percent indicates a sustainable or steady-state conventional deficit equal to 22.3 percent of GDP compared with the actual 33.3 percent deficit averaged over the period 1979–1993.

Evidently, debts and deficits in Guyana were far from approximating a steady state over the period of observation. It is precisely in such situations that governments explore alternative ways of dealing with a growing problem. The inflation tax and financial repression are two possibilities that may help to postpone or even avert a financial crisis. As Argentina found in the 1980s, however, there may be no steady-state inflation rate that prevents debt ratios from rising. In such case, hyperinflation eventually causes the economic collapse that would otherwise have been produced by an unsustainable level of debt.

To illustrate the use of inflation taxes and financial repression as ways of restoring a sustainable budgetary situation, consider the cases of Nigeria, Sierra Leone and Zimbabwe. Table 2.3 shows that in all three countries growth was substantially higher than domestic real interest rates. In such a situation, equation 2.4 indicates that it is unnecessary to run a primary surplus to achieve a steady state.

Despite the facts that growth in Nigeria was lower than the US real interest rate and foreign debt was larger than domestic debt, the real interest rate on domestic debt of -8.4 percent should have enabled Nigeria to run a primary deficit equal to 2.1 percent of GDP without increasing its debt ratio. In fact, while financial repression was successful in holding the ratio of domestic debt to GDP constant, it led to an increase in foreign debt from 5 percent of GDP in 1979–1983 to 88 percent of GDP in 1989–1993. Total government debt rose from 26 to 115 percent of GDP between these periods.

Even with falling real GDP, financial repression in Sierra Leone prevented a dramatic rise in its debt/GDP ratio. While foreign debt increased from 27 to 63 percent of GDP between 1979–1983 and 1989–1993, domestic debt fell from 32 to 7 percent. Hence, total government debt rose from 60 to 70 percent of GDP between these two periods. Zimbabwe benefited from a growth rate that exceeded the US real interest rate, so ensuring that a primary deficit was compatible with a

Table 2.4. Trends in Median Government Debts and Deficits

Variable	All Countries			
	1979–93	*1979–83*	*1984–88*	*1989–93*
GDY	3.5	4.2	3.3	2.7
DTY	37.6	27.8	41.3	44.8
YG	2.9	2.4	3.4	3.4
RR	1.8	–0.8	3.2	2.8
Variable	OECD Countries			
	1979–93	*1979–83*	*1984–88*	*1989–93*
GDY	3.3	4.3	3.3	2.9
DTY	35.3	27.1	38.6	40.6
YG	2.2	1.7	3.3	1.8
RR	3.3	1.0	4.4	4.0
Variable	Developing Countries			
	1979–93	*1979–83*	*1984–88*	*1989–93*
GDY	3.6	4.1	3.2	2.7
DTY	39.1	29.0	45.6	49.5
YG	3.4	2.9	3.5	4.1
RR	0.4	–1.6	1.8	2.1

Key: See Table 2.2.

constant debt/GDP ratio whatever the composition of its debt. However, because Zimbabwe's primary deficit averaged 3.1 percent of GDP over the period 1979–1993, both its domestic and foreign debt ratios rose: domestic debt from 33 to 37 percent and foreign debt from 12 to 23 percent of GDP between 1979–1983 and 1989–1993.

2.8 Time Trends

To examine changes over time for the full country sample, Table 2.4 splits the fifteen-year observation period used in Table 2.2 into three five-year periods. Evidently, government deficits as a ratio of GDP have declined since 1979–1983. This is explained in large part by the fact that the early 1980s witnessed the last major worldwide recession. Rates of economic growth were lower in this first five-year period than in the two subsequent periods. Real interest rates were also considerably lower in the 1979–1983 period than they were in the more recent two periods. Indeed, the gap between growth rates and real interest rates narrowed considerably after 1979–1983.

While ratios of government deficits to GDP declined between 1979– 1983 and 1989–1993, debt/GDP ratios rose.[9] Since real interest rates were almost the same as growth rates over the past decade, equation 2.4 shows that balanced primary budgets were required to prevent debt/GDP ratios from rising. Evidently, the median country ran primary deficits over the period 1984–1993, so ensuring that the debt/GDP ratio rose. Indeed, among the richer OECD countries only Australia, Luxembourg, Norway and Switzerland reduced their debt/GDP ratio between 1979– 1983 and 1989–1993 and, among developing countries, this occurred only in Israel, Korea, Mauritius, Swaziland and Thailand.

Table 2.4 shows a worldwide rise in real interest rates since the early 1980s. The real interest rate in the OECD countries increased from 1 to 4 percent and in the median developing country from –1.6 to 2.1 percent between 1979–1983 and 1989–1993. While the real interest rate was well below the rate of economic growth in the median country during the period 1979–1983, growth and real interest rates differed much less in the later periods. Indeed, since 1984 the real interest rate in the median OECD country exceeded the growth rate. This required a primary budget surplus to prevent a rising debt/GDP ratio. For any given primary deficit, however, the debt/GDP ratio necessarily increases faster the greater is the positive gap between the real interest rate and the growth rate.

2.9 Deficits, Inflation, Saving and Growth

Olivier Blanchard and Stanley Fischer (1989, 513) and Pierre-Richard Agénor and Peter Montiel (1996, 128–137), among others, point out that government deficits are positively related, albeit weakly, to inflation. Figure 2.2 presents this period-average relationship for the 111 countries listed in Table 2.1. The relationship is significantly positive, but the scatter indicates considerable dispersion for period-average data for this

---

[9] While the European Commission (1994) estimates government debt averaging 105 percent of GDP for Italy over the period 1988–1994 and 137 percent for Belgium over the period 1990–1994, the *IFS* data used here produce an average of 120 percent of GDP for Belgium as the maximum OECD government debt/GDP ratio over the period 1979–1993.

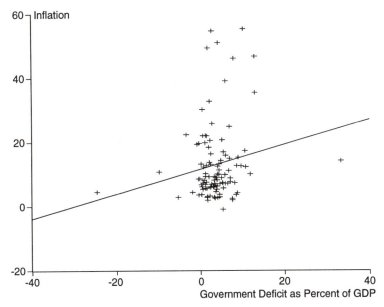

Figure 2.2. Inflation and Government Deficits in 111 Countries, 1979–1993

country group. Here, causality is likely to be bidirectional. While high deficits retard growth, low and particularly negative growth causes bigger deficits.

When all available annual observations for the period 1970–1995 are pooled in a fixed-effect model, however, this relationship becomes highly significant (2,166 observations, t values in parentheses):[10]

---

[10] Most of the regressions reported in this book are simple bivariate relationships estimated by ordinary least squares. A more sophisticated approach would have greatly reduced the number of countries and number of observations available for analysis, in large part because there are only a small number of paired observations for a substantial number of countries. Hence, issues of simultaneity, omitted variables and spurious correlations arise. Functional forms are generally chosen to maximise explanatory power, although in no case does the choice affect the direction of the reported effect. Some experiments with multivariate iterative three-stage least squares suggest that the basic relationships reported here remain but that t statistics and correlation coefficients can be substantially increased.

$$INF = 1.476(GDY)$$
$$(11.477)$$
$$\overline{R}^2 = 0.403$$

(2.8)

No intercept is reported because the fixed-effect model estimates separate constants for each country. There are therefore 111 intercepts estimated in this equation.

Agénor and Montiel (1996, 129–130) provide four possible reasons why only a weak relationship may exist between inflation and deficits: (a) bond finance rather than money creation;[11] (b) change in sources of financing over time; (c) unstable money demand or slow adjustment to inflationary pressures; and (d) differing and changing expectations about how the government's intertemporal budget constraint will eventually be satisfied. Specifically, in some circumstances individuals may anticipate accelerating inflation that would erode the debt whereas in other circumstances they may expect the government to run a primary surplus in the future. A fifth key reason for a weak link between inflation and deficits is that saving ratios differ considerably between countries. A 10 percent government deficit is likely to be much more inflationary when the national saving ratio is 15 percent than when it is 40 percent.

Figure 2.3 presents the period-average relationship between national saving ratios and government deficits for the 111 sample countries. When all available annual observations for the period 1970–1995 are pooled in a fixed-effect model, the relationship between the ratio of national saving to GNP *SNY* and the government deficit as a ratio of GDP *GDY* is highly significant (2,166 observations):

$$SNY = -0.291(GDY)$$
$$(-10.033)$$
$$\overline{R}^2 = 0.718$$

(2.9)

The period-average data for the 111 countries also indicate a significantly positive relationship between saving *SNY* and growth *YG*, as shown in Figure 2.4. The pooled fixed-effect estimate using annual data is (2,242 observations):

---

[11] Empirical analysis in the next chapter supports the proposition that for any given level of government deficit, inflation is higher the greater the proportion of the deficit that is financed from the central bank.

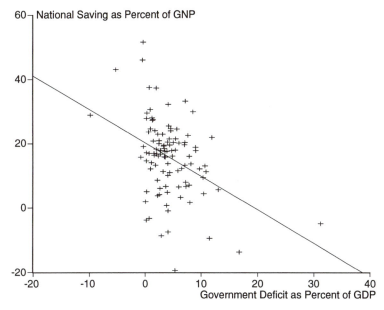

Figure 2.3. National Saving Ratios and Government Deficits in 111 Countries, 1979–1993

$$SNY = 0.230(YG) + 0.697(SNY_{t-1})$$
$$(11.278) \qquad (46.532)$$
$$\overline{R}^2 = 0.863$$
(2.10)

The period-average data for the 111 sample countries also indicate a negative relationship between the rate of growth in GDP at constant prices and the ratio of the government's deficit to GDP that is shown in Figure 2.5. This negative relationship is significant only at the 90 percent confidence level. Again, however, when all available annual observations for the period 1970–1995 are pooled in a fixed-effect model, the relationship becomes significant (2,160 observations):

$$YG = -0.069(GDY)$$
$$(-3.133)$$
$$\overline{R}^2 = 0.138$$
(2.11)

While a larger government deficit is associated with higher inflation, lower saving and a lower rate of economic growth, the effects of deficits

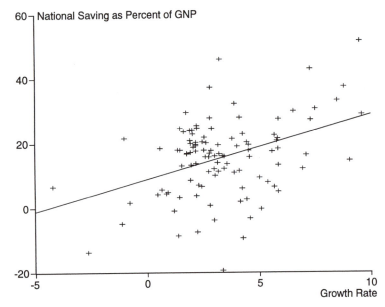

Figure 2.4. National Saving and Growth Rates in 111 Countries, 1979–1993

on inflation, saving and growth are likely to depend on the way deficits are financed. To the extent that they are financed through the inflation tax or financial repression, Chapters 3 and 4 demonstrate that any given deficit is associated with significantly higher inflation, lower saving and lower growth rates.

2.10   Conclusion

This chapter has explored the key macroeconomic relationships between government deficits, debt, inflation and growth. In 111 countries for which data exist in reasonably accessible and consistent form, deficits are associated with higher inflation, lower saving and lower growth. However, high recorded deficits, even over a 15-year period, do not necessarily produce high debt ratios. In part, the explanation for the lack of this anticipated relationship lies in the fact that the recorded deficits often include substantial inflation premia on nominal interest rates. In real terms, the inflation premium constitutes principal repayment that keeps the real value of the loan principal intact. Borrowing to pay

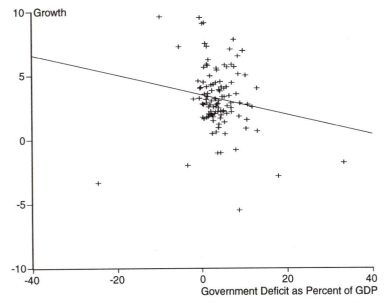

Figure 2.5. Growth and Government Deficits in 111 Countries, 1979–1993

the inflation premium does not, therefore, increase real indebtedness or therefore the ratio of debt to GDP.

What does emerge quite clearly from the data presented in this chapter is that more rapid economic growth eases the government's intertemporal budget constraint. Fast growth not only reduces the burden of a high debt ratio but also makes it easier to achieve a primary surplus. Hence any distortions, such as those created by the inflation tax or financial repression, that reduce growth necessarily worsen the fiscal position. Furthermore, Vito Tanzi (1977, 1989) shows that inflation erodes the real value of taxes that are collected with a time lag so creating a larger conventional deficit. The next chapter examines once again government recourse to its central bank and use of the inflation tax.

Part II

Captive and Foreign Markets

Chapter 3

The Central Bank and Inflationary Finance

3.1 Introduction

DEVELOPING COUNTRY GOVERNMENTS RELY considerably more than richer OECD governments on their central banks for financial support. Indeed, many have little alternative, given the nondevelopment of markets for government debt. The resulting inflation from such heavy reliance has led Kurt Schuller (1996) to ask whether developing countries would be better off without central banks. This chapter examines the effects of this greater reliance on central bank financing of government deficits in the developing countries.

There are in fact three distinct ways in which a government can appropriate seigniorage from its central bank. While they produce no fundamental difference in final outcomes, each has a distinct effect on the measured government deficit and central bank's profit-and-loss accounts.

In the first and simplest way, a central bank holds liabilities in the form of reserve money paying no interest and assets earning market interest rates; these assets might all be private sector bonds. In this case, the central bank profits should be comparable to the standard seigniorage revenue calculation (Fry, Goodhart and Almeida 1996, Ch. 3). Here seigniorage revenue becomes government nontax revenue when the central bank's profits are transferred to the government.

In the second way of appropriating seigniorage revenue, which makes the government accounts look better by reducing its conventional deficit, the government takes interest-free loans from the central bank.

All the assets of the central bank consist of such loans. In this case, central bank profits are always zero: no interest is earned on assets, no interest is paid on liabilities. Of course, however, seigniorage revenue now reduces government interest costs rather than raising its revenue.

In the third and final way, the government can reduce its recorded primary deficit by requiring its central bank to undertake various fiscal activities on its behalf. In this case, the first call on the seigniorage revenue is the central bank's own expenditures of a fiscal nature.

Not surprisingly, the greater extraction of seigniorage from money creation in developing countries than in OECD countries is reflected in higher inflation rates in developing countries. In 1990, for example, inflation averaged 5 percent in the industrial countries compared with 62 percent in the developing countries. In the same year, broad money (*M2*) grew by 8 percent in the industrial countries and by 79 percent in the developing countries (*World Economic Outlook,* October 1995, 102 & 110).

3.2   Central Bank Financing of Government Deficits

Table 3.1 provides statistics on the extent of government recourse to their central banks in both developing countries and the richer OECD countries. Again to avoid distortions from outliers, Table 3.1 gives the median values for each country group. These median values themselves represent the mean value of the variable over the period 1979–1993 in the median country.

3.2.1   Flow Variables

The first variable in Table 3.1 constitutes the increase in central bank net credit to the government (central bank loans to the government minus government deposits at the central bank) expressed as a percentage of the government deficit (*CBD*). The representative developing country government meets over 30 percent of its borrowing requirements from its central bank, while the median country in the richer OECD group has reduced net borrowing from this source (–5 percent) either by repaying loans or increasing deposits. Figure 3.1 presents the dispersion in annual borrowing percentages over the period 1970–1995.

Typically, government borrowing from the central bank is effected by an expansion in reserve money. Table 3.1 indicates that the median increase in reserve money over the period 1979–1993 was 1.6 percent

Table 3.1. Central Bank Financing of Government Deficits, 1979–1993

Variable	All Median	OECD Median	OECD Highest	Developing Median	Developing Highest
CBD	16.9	−5.3	183.8	30.4	3,678.9
CBCG	59.7	12.4	209.5	65.9	10,815.6
DHD	33.4	14.6	114.9	36.3	8,219.3
DHY	1.6	0.5	1.8	1.8	13.9
HM	30.2	11.6	26.1	38.3	110.3
RD	15.5	3.3	22.7	20.3	112.2
INF	9.3	6.1	25.8	11.3	175.4

Key:
CBD   Increase in central bank net credit to government as percent of government deficit.

CBCG   Central bank net credit to government as percent of net domestic credit to government.

DHD   Change in reserve money as percent of government deficit.

DHY   Change in reserve money as percent of GDP.

HM   Reserve money as percent of M2.

RD   Bank reserves as percent of bank deposits.

INF   Rate of change in consumer price index (continuously compounded).

of GDP (*DHY*); this is one commonly used measure of seigniorage revenue. In the median OECD country, seigniorage revenue constituted 0.5 percent of GDP compared with 1.8 percent in the representative developing country. Over the period 1979–1993, the highest average annual value for seigniorage revenue in the richer OECD countries was 1.8 percent of GDP (in Spain), while in the developing countries the highest average annual value was 13.9 percent (in Nicaragua).

3.2.2 Stock Variables

The greater reliance on central bank loans by developing country governments also shows up in a stock variable: central bank net credit to the government as a proportion of net domestic credit to the government from the banking system as a whole (*CBCG*).[1] The median value of this

---

[1] Net domestic credit to the government is defined as central and commercial bank loans to the government minus all government deposits with central and commercial banks.

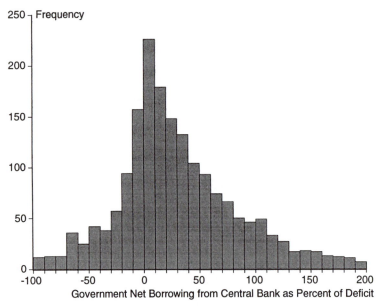

Figure 3.1. Dispersion in Government Central Bank Borrowing, 1970–1995

indicator for OECD countries is 12 percent compared with 66 percent for the developing countries.

To obtain two thirds of its bank borrowing from the central bank, the typical developing country government imposes high reserve requirements on the commercial banks. This ensures that the liabilities of the central bank are large compared with the liabilities of the commercial banks.[2] From the commercial banks' viewpoint, required reserves constitute a forced acquisition of an asset on which all interest is taxed away. Under competitive conditions, banks pass the reserve requirement tax on to depositors and borrowers, the incidence depending on relative demand elasticities, in the form of lower deposit rates and higher loan rates (Fry 1995, Ch. 7). In practice, however, banking systems in developing countries are often far from competitive.

Fiscal analysis of this tax is simplified for a small country in which businesses can borrow from the domestic banks or abroad at the world

---

[2]Greater reliance on currency transactions due to underdeveloped payment systems also increases the relative size of the central bank.

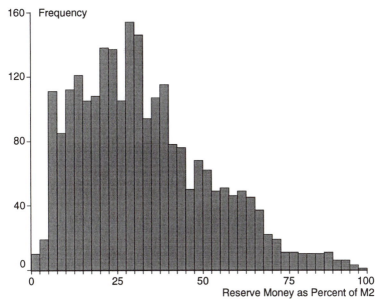

Figure 3.2. Dispersion in Ratio of Reserve Money to Broad Money, 1970–1995

interest rate; in other words, the demand for bank loans is perfectly interest elastic. In this case, the incidence of the reserve requirement tax is borne entirely by depositors. Similarly, currency holders bear the inflation tax on their currency holdings.

Two measures are used here to corroborate this proposition. The first is the ratio of reserve money to broad money (*M2* broadly defined to include savings and time deposits) (*HM*). It is 11.6 percent in the median OECD country and 39.1 percent in the median developing country. The second is the ratio of bank reserves to bank deposits included in the definition of money (*RD*), which is 3.3 percent in the median OECD country compared with 20.3 percent in the median developing country. The dispersions in these averages using annual observations over the period 1970–1995 are shown in Figures 3.2 and 3.3.

In fact, the reserve requirement tax, subsidised loan rates through selective credit policies and other types of political interference tend to decapitalise the commercial banks. In particular, state-owned banks may be discouraged from widening the spread between deposit and loan rates needed to pass the reserve requirement tax on to depositors or borrowers. Since the government usually bails out insolvent financial

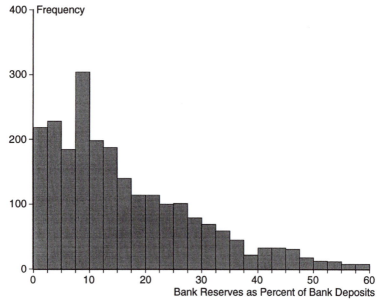

Figure 3.3. Dispersion in Ratio of Bank Reserves to Bank Deposits, 1970–1995

institutions, this decapitalisation produces a contingent liability for the government. Again, therefore, the lack of transparency in government finance exacts a price from the economy in terms of structural deficiencies in the financial sector and possibly financial crises as well.

3.2.3   Time Trends

Table 3.2 provides data on trends over time by splitting the 1979–1993 period into three five-year bands. Little change can be noticed in the first panel for all countries. The only noticeable trend here is the increase in the change in reserve money as a percentage of the government deficit. In the OECD country group, however, several trends appear. First, net borrowing from the central bank as a percentage of the government deficit has declined substantially from 4.6 percent in the first sub-period 1979–1983 to –11.2 percent in the last sub-period 1989–1993. This has been accompanied by a reduction in seigniorage revenue from 0.5 to 0.2 percent of GDP as well as a decline in the ratio of reserve money to *M2* from 14.2 percent to 10.2 percent. A similar decline from 3.6 to 2.7 percent can be observed in the ratio of bank

Table 3.2. Trends in Median Central Bank Financing of Government Deficits, 1979–1993

Variable	All Countries			
	1979–93	*1979–83*	*1984–88*	*1989–93*
CBD	16.9	25.3	16.8	24.2
CBCG	59.7	58.4	64.4	56.0
DHD	33.4	15.9	27.9	25.6
DHY	1.6	1.4	1.5	1.5
HM	30.2	30.9	30.4	30.0
RD	15.5	13.6	13.8	14.2
INF	9.3	11.0	8.2	9.2

Variable	OECD Countries			
	1979–93	*1979–83*	*1984–88*	*1989–93*
CBD	−5.3	4.6	−6.0	−11.2
CBCG	12.3	14.0	20.4	18.1
DHD	14.6	11.0	12.0	10.4
DHY	0.5	0.5	0.5	0.2
HM	11.6	14.2	11.9	10.2
RD	3.3	3.6	3.1	2.7
INF	6.1	9.3	4.5	3.8

Variable	Developing Countries			
	1979–93	*1979–83*	*1984–88*	*1989–93*
CBD	30.4	32.7	24.9	35.4
CBCG	65.9	67.2	71.3	68.6
DHD	36.3	27.4	30.0	30.4
DHY	1.8	1.5	1.9	1.9
HM	38.3	38.4	35.8	35.4
RD	20.3	17.7	17.7	19.5
INF	11.3	11.9	10.4	10.9

Key: See Table 3.1.

reserves to bank deposits. One consequence of this reduced recourse to central bank finance may be the decline in inflation from 9.3 to 3.8 percent in the OECD countries.

Rather different trends occurred in the representative developing country. The bottom panel of Table 3.2 shows increasing government borrowing from its central bank, increasing seigniorage revenue and an increasing ratio of bank reserves to bank deposits.[3] While the median inflation rate declined, the mean inflation rate for developing countries accelerated from 17.6 percent in 1979–1983 to 26.5 percent in 1989–1993.

The main inference of the data presented in Tables 3.1 and 3.2 is that developing country governments rely far more than OECD country governments on their central banks for financing their deficits. The next section examines the effects of such reliance.

3.3   Effects of Government Borrowing from the Central Bank

3.3.1   Deficits and Reserve Money Growth

Higher deficits (GDY) are associated with larger increases in reserve money (DHY), both expressed as ratios of GDP. This is shown by the following regression of average values over the period 1979–1993 (t values in parentheses):[4]

$$DHY = 0.013 + 0.244(GDY)$$
$$(4.068) \quad (5.053)$$
$$\overline{R}^2 = 0.191 \tag{3.1}$$

When all available annual observations for the period 1970–1995 are pooled in a fixed-effect model, the relationship is (2,107 observations):[5]

$$DHY = 0.154(GDY)$$
$$(10.750)$$
$$\overline{R}^2 = 0.307 \tag{3.2}$$

---

[3] While commercial banks in developing countries are likely to hold higher reserves than commercial banks in the OECD countries because of deficiencies in the payment system, higher required reserve ratios account for the lion's share of the difference (Fry, Goodhart and Almeida 1996, 29).

[4] Luxembourg and Panama are excluded from the initial 111 countries because of lack of data; Panama's currency is the US dollar, while Belgian and Luxembourg francs circulate interchangeably in Luxembourg.

[5] No intercept is reported because the fixed-effect model estimates separate constants for each country. There are therefore 109 intercepts estimated in this equation.

Evidently, higher deficits are associated with more rapid growth in reserve money. Although this relationship is statistically significant, only 30 percent of the variance in reserve money growth is explained by government deficits.[6] Another important source of reserve money growth in several countries arises from central banks' quasi-fiscal activities. These include allocating subsidised credit to agriculture, exports and development finance institutions through selective credit policies, providing explicit or implicit (below-cost) deposit insurance and bailing out insolvent financial (or even nonfinancial) institutions when necessary, and providing exchange rate subsidies or guarantees, particularly for debt service and essential imports. Interest rate ceilings imposed and enforced by central banks constitute both taxes and subsidies. The taxes are imposed on depositors/lenders, who subsidise priority borrowers (Fry, Goodhart and Almeida 1996, Ch. 3).

When central banks are obliged to conduct an extensive array of quasi-fiscal activities, monetary control is bound to be one casualty. Where quasi-fiscal expenditures exceed seigniorage revenue consistent with a stable price level, the central bank must either resort to the inflation tax or, if price stability is to be maintained, the government must make annual budgetary appropriations to keep the central bank afloat, as has happened in Chile.

3.3.2 Growth and Reserve Money Growth

Figure 3.4 shows the dispersion in reserve money growth rates over the period 1970–1995. This figure omits 13 observations below –40 percent and 40 observations above 130 percent. Over some range, rapid growth in reserve money is associated with lower rates of economic growth, as shown by this nonlinear fixed-effect estimate of growth in real GDP on reserve money growth (HG) using annual data for the period 1970–1995 (2,266 observations):[7]

---

[6] However, Ziba Farhadian and Robert Dunn (1986) find that for countries with the least developed financial systems the government deficit acts just as well as domestic credit expansion in a monetarist model of the balance of payments.

[7] Among several alternatives, this functional form produced the best fit.

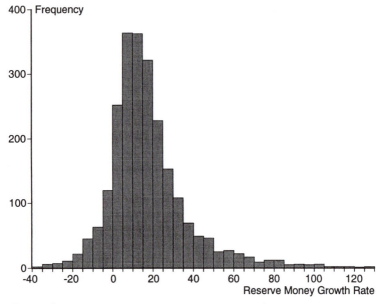

Figure 3.4. Dispersion in Reserve Money Growth Rates, 1970–1995

$$YG = -0.014(HG^2) + 0.002(HG^3)$$
$$(-3.425) \qquad (2.293)$$
$$\overline{R}^2 = 0.111$$

(3.3)

Figure 3.5 traces out this relationship. It indicates that economic growth is not impaired severely for moderate rates of growth in reserve money. Furthermore, when reserve money growth rates reach an annual rate of about 400 percent, higher rates again have little growth-reducing impact.[8] It is in the intermediate range from 50 to 300 percent that higher rates of growth in reserve money have their greatest growth-reducing effect.

---

[8] In fact, there are only five observations of reserve money growth rates exceeding 400 percent.

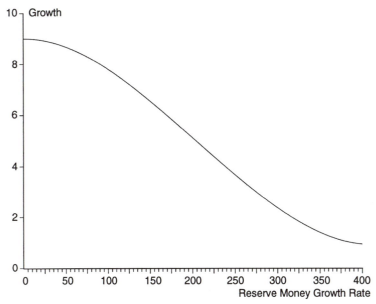

Figure 3.5. Annual Growth and Reserve Money Growth Rates, 1970–1995

3.3.3 Inflation and the Proportion of Central Bank Financing

One way of examining the effect of the government's source of borrowing on inflation and growth is to specify a functional form in which the effect of the deficit depends on the way it is financed. In this case, therefore, one might specify an equation of the form

$$INF = b_0 + (b_1 + b_2 CBD) \cdot GDY, \tag{3.4}$$

which can be simplified to

$$INF = b_0 + b_1 GDY + b_2 (CBD \cdot GDY). \tag{3.5}$$

In other words, the coefficient of GDY is variable and depends on the proportion of the deficit that is financed by the central bank CBD.

The estimate of equation 3.5 on average values from 110 countries over the period 1979–1993 is:[9]

---

[9] Kuwait is excluded because of lack of data.

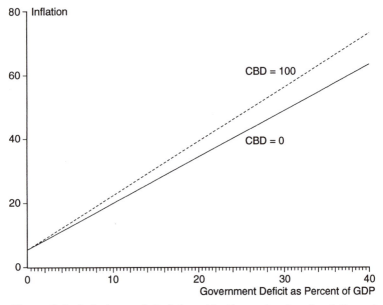

Figure 3.6. Inflation and Deficits with Alternative Levels of Central Bank Financing

$$INF = 0.128 + 1.634(GDY) + 0.076(CBD \cdot GDY)$$
$$(3.208)\quad(2.623)\qquad\quad(2.359)$$
$$\overline{R}^2 = 0.101$$

(3.6)

When all available annual observations for the period 1970–1995 are pooled in a fixed-effect model, the relationship becomes stronger (2,039 observations):

$$INF = 1.443(GDY) + 0.244(CBD \cdot GDY)$$
$$(10.530)\qquad\quad(2.742)$$
$$\overline{R}^2 = 0.442$$

(3.7)

Using equation 3.7, Figure 3.6 shows the differential impact of government deficits on inflation in two cases: the first when government net borrowing from the central bank is zero ($CBD = 0$) and the second when it is 100 percent ($CBD = 100$). Evidently, the greater the proportion of a given deficit that is financed by the central bank, the higher is the resulting inflation.

3.3.4 National Saving and the Proportion of Central Bank Financing

The effect of central bank financing on national saving ratios can be analysed in the same way as the effect of central bank financing of deficits on inflation by specifying a functional form in which the effect of the deficit depends on the way it is financed. Here, therefore, I specify an equation of the form

$$SNY = b_0 + (b_1 + b_2 CBD) \cdot GDY, \qquad (3.8)$$

which can be simplified to

$$SNY = b_0 + b_1 GDY + b_2 (CBD \cdot GDY). \qquad (3.9)$$

In other words, the coefficient of GDY is again variable and depends on the proportion of the deficit that is financed by the central bank CBD.

The estimate of equation 3.9 using all available annual observations for the period 1970–1995 in a fixed-effect model gives (2,039 observations):

$$SNY = -0.180(GDY) - 0.232(CBD \cdot GDY)$$
$$(-5.777) \qquad (-11.569)$$
$$\overline{R}^2 = 0.723 \qquad (3.10)$$

Evidently, the greater the proportion of a given deficit that is financed by the central bank, the lower is the saving ratio. A government deficit equal to 10 percent of GDP reduces the saving ratio by 1.8 percentage points but, if it is financed entirely from the central bank, the saving ratio is reduced by a further 2.3 percentage points. In other words, the overall reduction in saving when a 10 percent deficit is financed entirely by the central bank is 4.1 percentage points.

3.3.5 Growth and the Proportion of Central Bank Financing

The estimate of period-average rates of economic growth for the same countries with the functional form used for inflation and saving is:

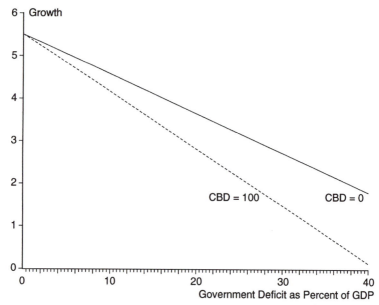

Figure 3.7. Growth and Deficits with Alternative Levels of Central Bank Financing

$$YG = 4.114 - 0.188(GDY) - 0.005(CBD \cdot GDY)$$
$$(14.055)\ (-4.093) \qquad (-1.967)$$

$$\overline{R}^2 = 0.163 \tag{3.11}$$

while the pooled fixed-effect estimate is (2,030 observations):

$$YG = -0.093(GDY) - 0.041(CBD \cdot GDY)$$
$$(-4.000) \qquad (-2.752)$$

$$\overline{R}^2 = 0.147 \tag{3.12}$$

Perhaps the most important finding reported in this chapter is that the greater the proportion of a given deficit that is financed by the central bank, the lower is the rate of economic growth. Using equation 3.12, Figure 3.7 shows the differential impact of government deficits on economic growth in two cases: the first when government net borrowing from the central bank is zero and the second when it is 100 percent. When the government's deficit reaches 25 percent of GDP, financing it entirely from the central bank reduces growth by about 1 percentage

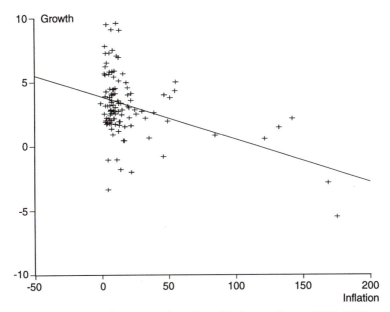

Figure 3.8. Period-Average Growth and Inflation Rates, 1979–1993

point more than it is reduced when there is no borrowing from the central bank.

While these results are hardly surprising, the explanatory power of these estimates is rather modest. This may be due to differing expectations, as suggested by Olivier Blanchard and Stanley Fischer (1989, 513) and Pierre-Richard Agénor and Peter Montiel (1996, 128–137). It may also be due to the distortions in measuring government deficits exclusive of central bank quasi-fiscal activities.

3.3.6   Growth and Inflation

Be that as it may, one relationship that has obtained increasing support in recent years is the negative relationship between growth and inflation. Figure 3.8 shows the period-average relationship for the country sample over the period 1979–1993, while the pooled time-series fixed-effect estimate using a nonlinear functional form on annual data over the period 1970–1995 is (2,322 observations):

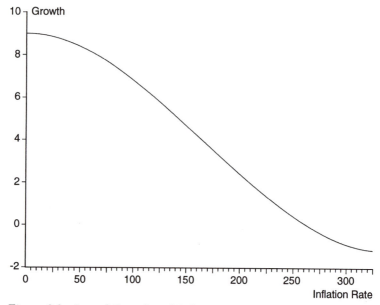

Figure 3.9. Annual Growth and Inflation Rates, 1970–1995

$$YG = -0.028(INF^2) + 0.006(INF^3)$$
$$(-3.994) \qquad (2.756)$$

$$\overline{R}^2 = 0.113$$

(3.13)

Figure 3.9 illustrates this nonlinear relationship between growth and inflation. As with the effect of reserve money growth shown in Figure 3.5, Figure 3.9 shows that inflation is not seriously damaging to growth at rates below 20 percent and has little incremental impact above about 300 percent annually. This result is consistent with Robert Barro's (1995) findings.

Evidently, the extent to which government deficits are financed by the central bank affects not only inflation but also economic growth. Far from there being any tradeoff between inflation and growth in the sense of having to accept higher inflation in order to obtain higher growth, recent evidence indicates that inflation is inimical to growth (Barro 1995; De Gregorio 1994; Fischer 1994; Fry 1995, Ch. 10; Fry, Goodhart and Almeida 1996, Ch. 2; Hoggarth 1996). These findings are corroborated here.

Various reasons have been suggested for this negative relationship. First, higher inflation is invariably more volatile inflation; the level and standard deviation of inflation rates are highly correlated (Fry, Goodhart and Almeida 1996, 15). The variability in inflation is also associated with variability in real exchange rates and real interest rates. Instability in nominal variables, money and inflation, is thus associated with higher variance in key real variables, another channel by which inflation may depress growth.

In developing countries, fixed nominal interest and exchange rates have been particularly harmful (Fry 1995, Ch. 8). As inflation rises, lower real interest rates resulting from fixed nominal rates reduce credit availability in real terms and distort resource allocation, while a fixed exchange rate prices exports out of world markets. Both effects reduce growth rates as well as saving ratios.

Inflationary finance reduces the base on which regular taxes are levied by lowering output growth. It also reduces the effective tax rate by lowering the real value of tax receipts collected with any lag. In such case, the tax is assessed on the basis of the lower prices that existed at some time in the past.

Tax theory suggests that the optimal tax structure should equalise distortions at the margin from alternative tax sources. To the extent that in practice all tax sources produce some distortion, it follows that the inflation tax should be used up to the point where its distortionary costs equal the distortionary costs of other tax revenues. The practical problem is that setting fixed tax rates on petrol or cigarettes is relatively easy, while setting a fixed tax rate on money through inflation is not. In practice, therefore, the choice may be between low and stable inflation on the one hand or higher and more variable inflation on the other. If so, fiscal policy that does not rely on inflation as a source of government revenue is surely preferable to one that does.

There is little disagreement that inflation impairs the domestic currency's attributes not only as a store of value but also as a means of payment. James Tobin (1992, 772) states: "A society's money is necessarily a store of value. Otherwise it could not be an acceptable means of payment." Inflation and the concomitant deterioration of money impede the financial system from performing its two basic functions of administering the country's payment mechanism and intermediating between savers and investors. Elsewhere, I suggest that the former effect may reduce income levels while the latter effect could reduce income growth (Fry 1995, 4).

3.4   Conclusion

This chapter has shown that the considerably greater recourse by developing country governments compared with OECD governments to their central banks for deficit finance has resulted quite predictably in far higher inflation in the developing world. It has also been associated with lower saving ratios and lower growth rates. More precisely, the evidence presented in this chapter indicates that, for any given government deficit, inflation is higher and saving and growth lower the greater the proportion of the deficit that is financed by the central bank.

The explanation for higher inflation is fairly simple. When $1 in reserve money is created to finance $1 of the deficit, the money supply multiplier ensures that the money supply increases by some multiple of the reserve money injection. Suppose that the money supply multiplier is 4 and velocity of circulation is constant at 2. In such case, a 1 percent deficit financed entirely by an increase in reserve money would increase the money supply by 8 percent and, under the assumption of constant velocity, would also increase inflation by 8 percent. In contrast, were the 1 percent deficit financed entirely by an increase in the money supply, the concomitant increase in inflation would be only 2 percent with velocity equal to 2.

Since lower growth causes lower saving, the explanation of lower growth is also likely to be the explanation for lower saving. Financing a deficit by increasing reserve money reduces growth because, as just demonstrated, it is more inflationary than any other method. Inflation reduces growth for reasons given in the previous section. Furthermore, financial intermediation is inhibited by high reserve requirements that typically accompany excessive inflationary finance. Higher reserve requirements increase the sustainable spread between the commercial banks' deposit and loan rates of interest.

The implicit tax imposed by reserve requirements rises with inflation. With stable prices, for example, a reserve requirement of 25 percent ensures that a competitive zero-cost, zero-equity, zero-profit banking system can offer depositors 7.5 percent when the loan rate is 10 percent: $d = \ell(1 - rrr)$, where d is the deposit rate of interest, ℓ is the loan rate of interest and rrr is the required reserve ratio. If inflation of 30 percent raises the loan rate to 40 percent, the sustainable deposit rate rises to only 30 percent, so reducing the real deposit rate from 7.5 percent to zero. The next chapter examines the effects of financial repression, including high reserve requirements, on inflation, saving and growth in the sample countries.

Chapter 4

Financial Repression

4.1 Introduction

ONE WAY GOVERNMENTS FINANCE EXPENDITURES in excess of tax revenue is to force private sector agents to buy government securities at below-market yields. Contractors may be required to hold government bonds as security when bidding for government contracts. Insurance companies and pension funds are often obliged to hold larger proportions of assets in the form of government securities than they would choose voluntarily to hold. But the largest captive buyers of government securities are commercial banks. By setting high liquid asset ratios and ensuring that government securities are the only eligible asset that satisfies this requirement, governments can borrow substantial amounts at below-market rates of interest. A second way of financing government deficits is to set high reserve requirements. In this way, the government can borrow indirectly from the banking system at a zero rate of interest. Finally, governments may set ceilings on institutional interest rates to limit competition from the private sector for loanable funds.

How damaging are these forms of financial repression in terms of higher inflation, lower saving and lower economic growth? This chapter answers this question both by examining the available evidence and by presenting new estimates of the relationships between inflation, saving and growth, on the one hand, and high reserve requirements, high proportions of domestic credit expropriated by government and distorted real interest rates on the other.

4.2   Real Interest Rate Distortions

The evidence from the 85 developing countries for which the necessary data exist suggests that financial repression in the form of distorted real interest rates retards economic growth. In particular, when real interest rates are well outside what one might consider a normal or tolerable range of −5 to +10 percent, the cost in terms of forgone growth appears to be considerable. In this sample of 1,429 real interest rates, 967 or two thirds lie within the range −5 to +10 percent. One third of the observed real interest rates, however, were either less than −5 percent or more than +10 percent.

While Table 2.3 shows median real interest rates for all periods and all country groups lying within the range −2 to +5 percent, Table 4.1 indicates that the dispersion in real rates increased considerably over the period 1979–1993. Again, I use the geometric average of commercial bank deposit and loan rates, since these are the most prevalent interest rate data reported in *IFS*. The continuously compounded nominal interest rate is then subtracted from the continuously compounded inflation rate. Table 4.1 shows that the standard deviation of real interest rates actually fell in the OECD country group, with Iceland's double-digit negative real rate in the 1979–1983 period rising to zero in 1989–1993. In the developing country group, however, the standard deviation of real interest rates rose from 9.5 in 1979–1983 to 39.8 in 1989–1993. Not only did some countries post larger negative rates in the last five-year period, but the incidence of pathologically high positive real interest rates also increased.

In the developing country group, the range of real interest rates was −38.5 to +15.8 percent in the 1979–1983 period compared with a range of −224.8 to +144.4 percent in the 1989–1993 period. On the one hand, the proportion of real interest rates above 10 percent in developing countries doubled from 5.2 percent in 1979–1983 to 10.9 percent in 1989–1993. On the other hand, however, the proportion of real interest rates below −5 percent in developing countries fell from 30.1 percent in 1979–1983 to 13.6 percent in 1989–1993. Note that this increasing dispersion is not influenced by the violent fluctuations in countries of the former Soviet Union. Among all economies in transition, only China, Hungary, Poland and Romania are included in this sample of developing countries.

Table 4.1. Real Interest Rates, 1979–1993

Statistic	All Countries			
	1979–93	*1979–83*	*1984–88*	*1989–93*
Mean	–2.6	–2.3	0.6	–0.5
Median	1.8	–0.8	3.2	2.8
Maximum	57.8	15.8	240.8	144.4
Minimum	–152.9	–38.5	–116.9	–224.8
S.D.	23.0	8.5	30.6	35.3
Statistic	OECD Countries			
	1979–93	*1979–83*	*1984–88*	*1989–93*
Mean	2.9	0.4	3.9	4.4
Median	3.3	1.0	4.4	4.0
Maximum	5.1	4.1	6.7	9.0
Minimum	–5.0	–11.8	–3.1	–0.1
S.D.	2.1	3.4	2.0	2.2
Statistic	Developing Countries			
	1979–93	*1979–83*	*1984–88*	*1989–93*
Mean	–4.0	–3.2	–0.3	–1.8
Median	0.4	–1.6	1.8	2.1
Maximum	57.8	15.8	240.8	144.4
Minimum	–152.9	–38.5	–116.9	–224.8
S.D.	25.5	9.5	34.6	39.8

4.3   Rationale for Financial Repression

Critics of capitalism place considerable emphasis on the pernicious role of the financial system that forms the hub of the capitalist economy (Hilferding 1910). Karl Marx recognised the importance of the financial system in the process of capitalist economic development over a century ago. Lenin, impressed by the powerful political and economic influence of the European banks in the eighteenth and nineteenth centuries, also understood the crucial role of the financial system. He nationalised all Russian banks immediately after the 1917 revolution as the fastest and most effective way of ending capitalism and assuming control over the entire Russian economy.

John Maynard Keynes was also wary of the potential damage that could be wrought by financial systems in capitalist economies. He believed that without careful management money could disrupt economic activity quite seriously. Keynes's liquidity trap sets a floor to the nominal rate of interest. When the trap is binding, the real interest rate exceeds its equilibrium level consistent with full employment. In a liquidity trap, planned saving at the full-employment level of income exceeds planned investment. This disequilibrium is resolved by a fall in real income that, in turn, reduces planned saving.

Keynes (1936, 351) argues that historically there has been a natural tendency for the real interest rate to rise above its full-employment equilibrium level:

> The destruction of the inducement to invest by an excessive liquidity-preference was the outstanding evil, the prime impediment to the growth of wealth, in the ancient and medieval worlds. And naturally so, since certain of the risks and hazards of economic life diminish the marginal efficiency of capital whilst others serve to increase the preference for liquidity. In a world, therefore, which no one reckoned to be safe, it was almost inevitable that the rate of interest, unless it was curbed by every instrument at the disposal of society, would rise too high to permit of an adequate inducement to invest.

The substitution of "developing world" for Keynes's "ancient and medieval worlds" seems natural.

James Tobin (1965) develops one of the earlier models linking financial conditions and economic growth using Robert Solow's (1956) neoclassical growth model. In Tobin's (1965) model of money and economic growth, economic units allocate their wealth between two assets, money M and productive capital K. In this economy, the economic units are all small household producers. Hence, the business sector is identical to the household sector. If the return on capital relative to money rises in Tobin's model, households increase the ratio of capital to money in their portfolios. This portfolio shift produces a higher capital/labour ratio, higher labour productivity and hence greater per capita incomes. The rate of economic growth accelerates during the transition from a lower to a higher capital/labour ratio that occurs after the relative yield on money falls. Hence reducing the return on money increases welfare. This can be accomplished either by reducing deposit rates of interest, or by taxing money as proposed by Silvio Gesell (1911, Ch. IV–1), or simply by accelerating the rate of growth in the money stock, thereby raising the inflation rate.

The writings of Marx, Keynes and Tobin have influenced monetary and financial policies pursued in many countries throughout the world. There are also well-known political and religious objections to high, usurious or even nonzero interest rates. Many industrialised countries have pursued low interest rate policies from time to time. Institutional interest rates in most developing countries have indeed been "curbed by every instrument at the disposal of society." However, the relatively low and uniform institutional interest rate structures found in many developing countries today do not replicate the experience of the industrialised countries in their early stages of development.

The prevalence of interest rate ceilings has a number of other economic justifications in addition to Keynes's liquidity preference and Tobin's monetary growth model. Development planning models based on fixed input-output coefficients constitute another economic rationale for low interest rate policies. Many developing countries use or have used selective or directed credit policies to implement planned sectoral investment programmes derived from an input-output matrix. Institutional loan rate ceilings are a key element of directed credit policies. The ceilings are set deliberately below the equilibrium interest rate so that credit can be allocated on nonprice criteria. In this way the private sector can be encouraged to undertake the planned investment even though these projects might well be unprofitable at the competitive free-market equilibrium rate of interest. In particular, loan rate ceilings have been used in conjunction with import restrictions to encourage industrialisation through import substitution. Perceived returns to scale, externalities and hysteresis may also provide rationales for encouraging investments that are unprofitable at market interest rates through subsidised or controlled rates.

Structuralists and neostructuralists argue that raising interest rates increases inflation in the short run through a cost-push effect and lowers the rate of economic growth at the same time by reducing the supply of credit in real terms available to finance investment. Hence, their models provide another intellectual justification for financial repression.

In practice, however, the predominant rationale for financial repression lies in its fiscal implications. Interpreted as a discriminatory tax on the financial system, financial repression comprises inflation, reserve requirements, liquid asset ratios, interest rate ceilings and exchange controls. If institutional constraints prevent the government from collecting enough normal tax revenue to finance the level of government expenditure it regards as optimal, financial repression may be justified as a second-best strategy. Given disadvantages of high inflation and high reserve requirements, the government may turn to interest rate ceilings. Government deficits can be financed at a lower inflation rate and a lower required reserve ratio the more the private sector is hindered from competing for available funds (Fry 1973, Giovannini and de Melo 1993, Nichols 1974).

The effectiveness of financial repression is likely to be eroded over time. On the one hand, disintermediation through curb markets or other informal credit arrangements and, on the other hand, evasion of credit ceilings through foreign borrowing as well as capital flight reduce the revenue produced for financing government deficits through financial repression. These reactions also increase the fragility of the domestic financial system.

4.4   Financial Restriction and Financial Repression

Many developing countries appear to have slipped into financial repression inadvertently. The original policy was aimed not at indiscriminate repression but rather at financial restriction (Fry 1973, Giovannini and de Melo 1993, Nichols 1974). Financial restriction encourages financial institutions and financial instruments from which government can expropriate significant seigniorage; it discourages others. For example, money and the banking system are favoured and protected because reserve requirements and obligatory holdings of government bonds can be imposed to tap this source of saving at zero- or low-interest cost to the public sector. Private bond and equity markets are suppressed through transaction taxes, stamp duties, special tax rates on income from capital and an unconducive legal framework, because seigniorage cannot be extracted so easily from private bonds and equities. Interest rate ceilings are imposed to stifle competition to public sector fund raising from the private sector. Exchange controls prevent competition from abroad. Measures such as the imposition of foreign exchange controls, interest rate ceilings, high reserve requirements and the suppression or nondevelopment of private capital markets can all increase the flow of domestic resources to the public sector without higher tax, inflation or interest rates (Fry 1973, Nichols 1974).

Successful financial restriction is exemplified by a higher proportion of funds from the financial system being transferred to the public sector and by three effects on the demand for money: a rightward shift in the function, a higher income elasticity and a lower cost elasticity. Successful financial restriction produces a low and falling income velocity of circulation. This allows a greater public sector deficit to be financed at a given rate of inflation and a given level of nominal interest rates.

Selective or sectoral credit policies are common components of financial restriction. The techniques employed to reduce the costs of financing government deficits can also be used to encourage private investment in what the government regards as priority activities. Interest rates on loans for such approved investment are subsidised. Selective credit policies necessitate financial restriction, since financial channels would otherwise develop expressly for rerouting subsidised credit to uses with highest private returns. For selective credit policies to work at all, financial markets must be kept segmented and restricted.

The following quotation referring to Portugal describes a typical case of financial restriction: "To finance its deficit, the government has largely preempted the supply of domestic savings by preserving a 'sheltered' market for its own bond issues. Recourse of the private sector to the domestic bond market was, moreover, effectively curtailed by maintaining the maximum interest rate for bond issues at 5 percent" (Lundberg 1964, 40). The ceiling on after-tax returns from private bonds in Portugal was lower than the rate offered on government bonds. Even with these interest rate ceilings on competitive financial instruments, returns on government securities were so low that virtually no voluntary purchases took place: "In actual fact, the vast majority of the public debt bonds were taken up by the welfare institutions, the commercial banks, the Caixa Geral de Depósitos and insurance companies" (Banco de Portugal 1963, 52). However, the seigniorage base in the form of the money supply (broadly defined to include currency in circulation, sight deposits and time deposits—*M2*) was large and growing. Velocity of circulation in Portugal fell smoothly from 1.46 in 1962 to 1.09 in 1973.

Financial restriction was also successful in Turkey during the 1960s. Velocity of circulation (again using *M2*) fell from 5.26 to 3.66 between 1963 and 1970, a period of price stability and rapid economic growth. Interest rate ceilings protected banking, the government's golden goose, from outside competition (Fry 1972, Chs 3 & 6). As soon as private bonds showed signs of becoming a serious competitive threat in the early 1970s, controls were tightened up. Similar phenomena have been detected in Korea (Min 1976).

Nominal interest rate ceilings established to limit competition under policies of financial restriction are highly destabilising in the face of inflationary shocks. Just as deposit rate ceilings in the United States and other industrial countries caused disruptive disintermediation in periods of rising inflation and rising free-market interest rates, so all-embracing interest rate ceilings in developing countries cause destabilising portfolio shifts from financial to tangible assets, as well as into capital flight, when inflation accelerates (Lee 1980, Shaw 1975). Clearly such reaction magnifies the initial inflationary shock. Typically, it seems, financial repression is the unintended consequence of low, fixed nominal interest rates combined with high and rising inflation.

4.5   The Financial Repression Paradigm

In their analysis of financially repressed developing economies, Ronald McKinnon (1973) and Edward Shaw (1973) argue that financial repression, indiscriminate "distortions of financial prices including interest rates and foreign-exchange rates," reduces "the real rate of growth and the real size of the financial system relative to nonfinancial magnitudes. In all cases this strategy has stopped or gravely retarded the development process" (Shaw 1973, 3–4).

The essential common elements of the McKinnon-Shaw model, in which financial institutions intermediate between savers and investors, are illustrated in Figure 4.1. Saving S_{g_0} at an output growth rate g_0 is a positive function of the real rate of interest (McKinnon 1973, 67; Shaw 1973, 73 & 77–78). The line FF represents financial repression, taken here to consist of an administratively fixed nominal interest rate that holds the real rate r below its equilibrium level (McKinnon 1973, 71–77; Shaw 1973, 81–87). Actual investment is limited to I_0, the amount of saving forthcoming at the real interest rate r_0.

If the interest rate ceiling applied only to savers' interest rates (only to deposit but not to loan rates of interest), the investor/borrower would face an interest rate of r_3, the rate that clears the market with the constrained supply of saving I_0, in Figure 4.1. The spread r_3-r_0 would be spent by a regulated but competitive banking system on nonprice competition (advertising and opening new bank branches). These nonprice services, however, may not be valued at par with interest payments; real money demand invariably declines with a decrease in the explicit real deposit rate of interest.

In fact, there are loan rate ceilings as well as deposit rate ceilings in most financially repressed economies. Furthermore, there are very few competitive banking systems in the developing world. Although private commercial banks can evade loan rate ceilings through compensating balances, they seem to be observed by some state-owned banks and for

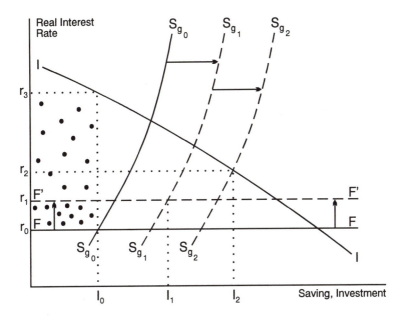

Figure 4.1. Saving and Investment under Interest Rate Ceilings

most public sector borrowing. To the extent that banks do observe loan rate ceilings, nonprice rationing of loanable funds must occur. Credit is allocated not according to expected productivity of the investment projects but according to transaction costs and perceived risks of default. Quality of collateral, political pressures, "name," loan size and covert benefits to loan officers may also influence allocation. The investments that are financed under such conditions are illustrated by the dots in Figure 4.1.

Even if credit allocation is random, the average efficiency of investment is reduced as the loan rate ceiling is lowered because investments with lower returns now become profitable. Entrepreneurs who were previously deterred from requesting bank loans now enter the market. Hence, adverse selection from the perspective of social welfare occurs when interest rates are set too low and so produce *disequilibrium* credit rationing of the type described here. Adverse selection also occurs when interest rates rise too high because *equilibrium* credit rationing is not working properly. Pathologically high positive real interest rates, possibly triggered by fiscal instability, indicate a poorly functioning financial system in which inadequate prudential supervision and regulation enable distress borrowing to crowd out borrowing for investment purposes (Fry, 1995, 305–306; McKinnon, 1993, 38–41; Rojas-Suárez and Weisbrod, 1995; Stiglitz and Weiss, 1981).

On the one hand, loan rate ceilings discourage financial institutions from taking any voluntary risks; risk premia cannot be charged when ceilings are binding and effective. This itself may ration out potentially high-yielding investments. On the other hand, financial institutions are typically forced to take risks that are unwarranted on commercial grounds through selective credit policies. Far from being potentially high-yielding but risky investments, investments dictated by selective credit policies may be risky because their potential commercial yields are too low. In the financially repressed economy there is, therefore, a tendency for the investments that are financed to yield returns barely above the ceiling interest rate r_0. These are shown in Figure 4.1 by the dots lying just above FF but below $F'F'$.

McKinnon (1973, 9) emphasises this dispersion in rates of return to investment in financially repressed economies: "In the face of great discrepancies in rates of return, it is a serious mistake to consider development as simply the accumulation of homogeneous capital of uniform productivity. Let us define 'economic development' as the reduction of the great dispersion in social rates of return to existing and new investments under domestic entrepreneurial control."

Interest rate ceilings distort the economy in at least six ways. First, low interest rates produce a bias in favour of current consumption and against future consumption. Therefore, they may reduce saving below the socially optimum level. Second, potential lenders may engage in relatively low-yielding direct investment instead of lending by way of depositing money in a bank. Third, bank borrowers able to obtain all the funds they want at low loan rates will choose relatively capital-intensive projects. Fourth, the pool of potential borrowers contains entrepreneurs with low-yielding projects who would not want to borrow at the higher market-clearing interest rate. To the extent that banks' selection process contains an element of randomness, some investment projects that are financed will have yields below the threshold that would be self-imposed with market-clearing interest rates. Fifth, interest rate ceilings encourage capital flight that may result in international misallocation of saving. Finally, Christophe Chamley and Patrick Honohan (1993) pinpoint another drawback of loan rate ceilings in that they tend to deter bank spending on loan assessments. Since even in an unrepressed situation banks are likely to underspend on screening, this additional deterrence may be worse for social welfare than another form of repression that affects the financial system at a margin which is initially undistorted.

Raising the interest rate ceiling from FF to $F'F'$ (from r_0 to r_1) in Figure 4.1 increases saving and investment. Changes in the real interest rate trace out the saving function in this disequilibrium situation. Raising the interest rate ceiling also deters entrepreneurs from undertaking all those low-yielding investments illustrated by the dots below $F'F'$. They are no longer profitable at the higher interest rate r_1. Hence the average return to or efficiency of aggregate investment increases. The output growth rate rises in this process and shifts the saving function to S_{g_1}.

Thus the real rate of interest as the return to savers is the key to a higher level of investment and as a rationing device to greater investment efficiency. The increased quantity and quality of investment interact in their positive effects on the output growth rate. Growth in the financially repressed economy is constrained by saving; investment opportunities abound here (McKinnon 1973, 59–61; Shaw 1973, 81). The policy prescription for the financially repressed economy examined by McKinnon and Shaw is to raise institutional interest rates or to reduce the rate of inflation. Abolishing interest rate ceilings altogether produces the optimal result of maximising investment and raising still further investment's average efficiency. This is shown in Figure 4.1 by the equilibrium I_2, r_2 and the higher output growth rate g_2.

4.6 Pathologically High Real Interest Rates

Several interest-rate liberalisation experiments have failed to produce the optimum results depicted at r_2, I_2 and g_2 in Figure 4.1. On the demand side, government borrowing requirements increase as its debt rises. This is compounded by the perverse reaction to the concomitant higher interest rates by insolvent and nonprofit-motivated firms. By definition, an insolvent firm is unable to repay its loans. Hence, it is not deterred from borrowing by a higher cost. It simply continues, if it can, to borrow whatever it needs to finance its losses. These inevitably increase with an increase in the interest rate which drives up the firm's cost of servicing its loans. The government too may be playing a Ponzi game when its borrowing costs rise.

In this situation, any initial interest rate rise increases demand for credit by those who will not be repaying their loans, so pushing interest rates up further. Higher real interest rates produce an epidemic effect by dragging down otherwise profitable and solvent firms. Some firms may be desperate and have virtually no option other than to borrow at rates they know will bankrupt them if sustained for any length of time. Other firms with little of their own capital at risk may simple gamble on riskier investments. Because the government and distress borrowers push real interest rates to levels at which virtually no economic activity can be profitable, solvent businesses start to face liquidity crunches which then force them to borrow at rates that they know are unmanageable. Hence, the accommodation of distress borrowing propagates more insolvency and more distress borrowing. The government's own budgetary situation disintegrates in this process which it may well have caused.

On the supply side, the basic problem is moral hazard. McKinnon (1993, 84–91) emphasises the adverse selection problem that arises with implicit or explicit deposit insurance under high and unstable inflation. When macroeconomic instability causes positive correlation between returns on alternative bank-financed projects, banks may no longer seek to reduce adverse selection through credit rationing. If deposit insurance protects depositors, banks may choose riskier lending strategies when macroeconomic instability produces strongly correlated outcomes. This is because favourable outcomes produce large bank profits, while unfavourable outcomes resulting in massive bank losses are borne mainly by the deposit insurance agency. Furthermore, as nonperforming loans rise, financial institutions must increase loan rates if they are to remain solvent, so increasing adverse selection. When banks become insolvent, then they too have every incentive to gamble for resurrection. When banks operate under conditions of macroeconomic instability with low or negative equity and deposit insurance protects depositors, effective prudential regulation and supervision are imperative. When macroeconomic instability increases, financial institutions should face an incentive to screen loan applications more rigorously. A second-best solution may be to reimpose a ceiling on loan rates of interest.

Newly liberalised financial sectors subject to inadequate prudential supervision and regulation have magnified the impact of exogenous shocks by accommodating distress borrowing by insolvent firms. In this way, financial sectors in these countries compound the problem of insolvency in the real sectors of the economy. Extraordinarily high real loan rates also appear when a substantial proportion of a country's commercial banks are insolvent or bank managements believe that shareholders as well as depositors are implicitly insured by the government.

Without proper financial incentives, bank managements may simply be unconcerned about the solvency of their state-owned institution. The supply of funds, therefore, is made available because of explicit or implicit deposit insurance. Demand rises because of firms' expectations that the government will eventually bail out nonfinancial as well as financial enterprises. When faced with insolvency, firms have every incentive to gamble on a government bailout in the future. The end result is financial and economic paralysis.

Financial distress of this kind results in reduced investment and worse resource allocation through the distressed financial sector. When government debt holdings and nonperforming loans increase, commercial banks have less resources for new lending. Furthermore, commercial banks often extend more loans to large firms unable to repay their old loans in an attempt to conceal their own losses, a practice known as "evergreening." Loss concealment is one manifestation of deficient accounting standards and bankruptcy procedures. In many developing countries, legal systems do not support the process of financial intermediation. Hence, loan demand rises, real interest rates increase and investment declines.

Attempts to lower interest rates by government decree in Argentina, Bolivia and Yugoslavia made matters worse by accelerating inflation and capital flight. The ensuing disintermediation and lower demand for domestic financial assets compounded the commercial banks' difficulties. An alternative solution, which is likely to accelerate bank insolvency, is to stop commercial banks from continuing to lend to insolvent borrowers. In any event, preventing bankruptcy at all costs can be highly destabilising and inefficient.

Distress borrowing and unstable government finances have both contributed to the phenomenon of excessively high real interest rates that has appeared in a number of countries since the mid-1970s. Experience indicates that, while financial repression may be growth-inhibiting, financial liberalisation in the absence of a sustainable fiscal balance, adequate prudential regulation and, where necessary, the restructuring of insolvent financial institutions may simply be a leap out of the frying pan into the fire.

4.7 Empirical Evidence

According to economists of almost all persuasions, financial conditions may affect the rate of economic growth in both the short and medium runs. Tobin's monetary growth model predicts a negative impact of a higher real return on money holdings in the medium run but has nothing to say about the short run. The McKinnon-Shaw school expects financial liberalisation (institutional interest rates rising towards their competitive free-market equilibrium levels) to exert a positive effect on the rate of economic growth in both the short and medium runs. The neostructuralists predict a stagflationary (accelerating inflation and lower growth) outcome from financial liberalisation in the short run. In the medium run, there is the possibility that the saving ratio will increase by enough to outweigh the negative influence of portfolio adjustments. In practice, neostructuralists, with the possible exception of Edward Buffie (1984), view a dominant saving effect as unlikely.

A simple way of discriminating between the McKinnon-Shaw school and others would be to examine episodes of financial liberalisation to see whether or not these were accompanied by higher or lower rates of economic growth. In practice, however, most clear-cut cases of financial liberalisation were accompanied by other economic reforms (such as fiscal, international trade and foreign exchange reforms). In such cases, it is virtually impossible to isolate the effects of financial components of the reform package. This is unfortunate, since causality can be inferred when financial conditions have been deliberately and substantially changed, as in the case of a discrete financial liberalisation. Examining the association between financial conditions and economic growth over time provides in itself no evidence of causality. With this caveat, I now examine the empirical evidence on the association between financial conditions and rates of economic growth.

4.7.1 Early Studies of Growth and Real Interest Rates

In one of the earlier studies of the effect of financial repression, Anthony Lanyi and Rüşdü Saracoglu (1983, Appendix III) implicitly address the causality issue by dividing 21 developing countries into 3 groups. Lanyi and Saracoglu give a value of 1 to countries with positive real interest rates, 0 to countries with moderately negative but "not punitively negative" real interest rates and -1 to countries with severely negative real interest rates. The regression reported by Lanyi and Saracoglu (1983, Table 4, 29) of the average rates of growth in real gross domestic product (GDP) YG on interest rate policies R for the period 1971–1980 is (t values in parentheses):

$$YG = 4.35 + 2.40(R).$$
$$(9.12) \quad (3.64)$$
$$\overline{R}^2 = 0.41$$

(4.1)

Lanyi and Saracoglu (1983, 28–30) conclude that this result

> seems to give some tentative support to the view that, in the longer run, positive real interest rates contribute to the growth of output. One possibility is that the principal effect of positive real interest rates is to raise the quality of investment, thereby increasing the growth rate of output and consequently that of financial saving. Another possibility is that the principal line of causation is, as suggested earlier, from interest rates to financial savings to growth of output. In either case, there does appear to be a relationship between interest rate policy and growth. Because of the administered nature of interest rates in these countries, a reversed direction of causation from either growth of output or growth of financial savings to interest rates has been ruled out in this analysis.

The World Bank (1989) uses the same methodology as Lanyi and Saracoglu for a sample of 34 developing countries. Over the period 1974–1985, the first group exhibited positive real deposit rates of interest, the second group posted moderately negative deposit rates (less than zero but greater than −10 percent) and the third group experienced strongly negative deposit rates (lower than −10 percent on average over this period). Given the fact that deposit rates were fixed by administrative fiat in all the countries posting negative deposit rates, one can argue that these rates are exogenous to the growth process.

The World Bank (1989, 31) presents its results in the tabular form shown in Table 4.2. Clearly, economic growth in the countries with strongly negative real deposit rates was substantially lower than growth in countries with positive real interest rates. Although the investment ratio was only 17 percent higher in the countries with positive real interest rates, the average productivity of investment, as measured by the incremental output/capital ratio, was almost four times higher.

The World Bank (1989, 30) also reports the following regression using period-average data over the periods 1965–1973 and 1974–1985 for 33 developing countries:

Table 4.2. Growth and Interest Rate Policies in 34 Developing Countries, 1974–1985

Indicator	Positive Real Interest Rates	Moderately Negative Real Interest Rates	Strongly Negative Real Interest Rates
Real interest rate	3.0	−2.4	−13.0
GDP growth rate	5.6	3.8	1.9
M3/GDP	40.3	34.0	30.5
Investment/GDP	26.9	23.2	23.0
Change in GDP/investment	22.7	17.3	6.2
Change in real M3/real saving	16.6	8.2	−0.9
Inflation rate	20.8	23.9	50.3

Source: World Bank (1989, 31)

$$YG = -0.12 + 0.20(R) - 0.02(D),$$
$$(-2.5) \quad (5.2) \quad (-3.4)$$
$$\overline{R}^2 = 0.45$$

(4.2)

where D is a dummy for the 1974–1985 period.

Several other studies present regression estimates showing positive and significant relationships between the rate of economic growth and the real deposit rate of interest (Asian Development Bank 1985; Easterly 1993; Fry 1978, 1991; Gelb 1989; Polak 1989; Roubini and Sala-i-Martin 1992). Defining the real rate of interest as RR, the ordinary least-squares (OLS) estimate of growth on the real deposit rate for pooled time-series data from seven Asian developing countries, 1961–1972, reported in Fry (1978, 470) is

$$YG = 0.033 + 0.405(RR).$$
$$(4.761) \quad (3.733)$$
$$\overline{R}^2 = 0.158$$

(4.3)

Another OLS fixed-effect estimate with country dummies on pooled time-series data for 14 Asian developing countries, 1961–1982, reported in Asian Development Bank (1984, Volume II, 70) is

$$YG = 0.044(RR).$$
$$(2.305)$$

$$\overline{R}^2 = 0.774$$

(4.4)

The empirical results reported in Fry (1978, 470; 1979, 132–134; 1980, 324; 1981, 87–88) suggest that on average a 1 percentage point increase in the real deposit rate of interest towards its competitive free-market equilibrium level is associated with a rise in the rate of economic growth of about half of a percentage point in Asia, i.e., the coefficient of the real deposit rate of interest averages 0.5. The World Bank (1989, 32) estimate reported above gives a coefficient of 0.2, Alan Gelb (1989, 20) estimates coefficients of 0.2 to 0.26 for his sample of 34 countries, while Jacques Polak (1989, 67) estimates coefficients of 0.18 to 0.27 when regressing the average annual rate of growth in real GDP on the median real interest rate for 40 developing countries. For 53 countries over the period 1960–1985, Nouriel Roubini and Xavier Sala-i-Martin (1992, 22) also find that countries with real interest rates less than –5 percent in the 1970s experienced growth rates that averaged 1.4 percentage points less than growth rates in countries with positive real interest rates. If the difference is approximately 10 percentage points, the implied interest rate coefficient is 0.14. The global evidence suggests that Asian developing countries may be more sensitive to real interest rate changes than other groups of developing countries.

4.7.2 Growth, Investment and Real Interest Rates

Mohsin Khan and Delano Villanueva (1991, 30–31) estimate the effects of real interest rates on growth for 23 developing countries using average data for the period 1975–1987 in equations that control for the ratio of private investment to GDP IPY:

$$YGN = -1.13 + 0.25(IPY) + 0.08(RR);$$
$$(-1.3) \quad (3.4) \quad\quad (2.4)$$

$$\overline{R}^2 = 0.55$$

(4.5)

$$YGN = -1.997 + 0.184(IPY) + 0.241(XKG) + 0.067(RR),$$
$$(-2.36) \quad (2.86) \quad\quad (3.37) \quad\quad (2.34)$$

$$\overline{R}^2 = 0.718$$

(4.6)

where *YGN* is the rate of growth in per capita real GDP, *IPY* is the private investment ratio and *XKG* is the rate of growth in exports at constant prices. They conclude that, "after allowing for changes in the rate of private investment, the real interest rate has a significant direct positive effect on per capita growth, suggesting that the direct favorable effects of real interest rates on the efficient use of capital, and thus on factor productivity, outweigh any possible negative impact on the rate of private investment such as found by Greene and Villanueva" (Khan and Villanueva 1991, 30).

4.7.3   Recent Studies of Growth and Real Interest Rates

Recent empirical work has tended to resort to far larger data sets than were used in studies before 1990. For example, Ejaz Ghani (1992) estimates growth equations for a sample of 50 developing countries following an approach used by Robert Barro (1991). The initial levels of human capital (as measured by years of schooling) and financial development (as measured by the ratio of total assets of the financial system to GDP or the ratio of private sector credit to GDP) in 1965 yield significantly positive coefficients, while the initial level of per capita real GDP produces a negative coefficient in an equation explaining average growth rates over the period 1965–1989 (Ghani 1992, 17). José De Gregorio and Pablo Guidotti (1995, 440) produce similar results for middle- and low-income countries using Barro's data set. Niels Hermes and Robert Lensink (1993) also find that growth in per capita real GDP is positively affected by the ratio of private sector credit to aggregate domestic credit in 14 Latin American countries over the period 1963–1989 using five-year averages for all variables.

Using financial ratios rather than real interest rates, Robert King and Ross Levine (1993a, 1993b, 1993c) examine links between finance and growth in a cross-section of 77 developing countries over the period 1960–1989. They construct four financial indicators: (a) liquid liabilities divided by GDP (usually *M2* divided by GDP);[1] (b) domestic assets in deposit money banks divided by domestic assets of both deposit money banks and the central bank; (c) domestic credit to the private sector divided by aggregate domestic credit; and (d) domestic credit to the private sector divided by GDP. King and Levine also construct

---

[1] To obtain mid-year estimates, beginning-of-year and end-of-year values of all financial variables are averaged.

four growth indicators: (a) average rate of growth in per capita real GDP; (b) average rate of growth in the capital stock; (c) the residual between (a) and 0.3 of (b) as a proxy for productivity improvements; and (d) gross domestic investment divided by GDP.

Using bivariate regressions, King and Levine (1993a, 725–727; 1993b, 530) show that each financial indicator is positively and significantly correlated with each growth indicator at the 99 percent confidence level. The same positive relationship is illustrated by dividing the 77 countries into 4 groups with respect to the growth indicators; countries are divided into those with average per capita income growth above 3 percent, greater than 2 but less than 3, greater than 0.5 but less than 2 and less than 0.5 percent. There are about 20 countries in each group. In each case, the average value of the financial indicator declines with a move from a higher to a lower growth group. Multivariate analysis produces much the same picture (King and Levine 1993c, 180–181).

De Gregorio and Guidotti (1995, 436–437) claim that real interest rates are not a good indicator of financial repression or distortion. They suggest that the relationship between real interest rates and economic growth might resemble an inverted U curve: "Very low (and negative) real interest rates tend to cause financial disintermediation and hence tend to reduce growth, as implied by the McKinnon-Shaw hypothesis. ... On the other hand, very high real interest rates that do not reflect improved efficiency of investment, but rather a lack of credibility of economic policy or various forms of country risk, are likely to result in a lower level of investment as well as a concentration in excessively risky projects" (De Gregorio and Guidotti 1995, 437).[2] Hence, De Gregorio and Guidotti abandon real interest rates in favour of domestic credit to the private sector divided by GNP.

4.7.4 A New Estimate of Growth and Real Interest Rates

In fact, the point made by De Gregorio and Guidotti (1995) holds up well with the data set prepared for this study. First, I divide the 15-year average real interest rates into two groups, one containing positive and the other negative real interest rates. Figure 4.2 shows a positive relationship between 15-year average growth rates and negative real interest rates and a negative relationship between average growth rates and positive real interest rates.

---

[2]This criticism is based on work by Guillermo Calvo and Fabrizio Coricelli (1992).

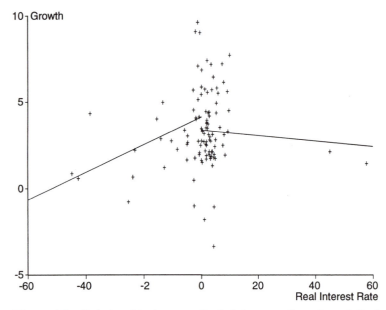

Figure 4.2. Relationship between Period-Average Growth and Real Interest Rates, 1979–1993

Second, using annual real interest data for 1970–1995 for 85 developing countries, I estimated the relationship between the annual rate of economic growth YG and the real rate of interest RR in an equation of the form $YG = \beta_0 + \beta_1(RR + \beta_2) \cdot (RR + \beta_2)$. Since the parameter β_2 was not significantly different from zero, although its negative value implies that growth is maximised at some positive real interest rate, I drop it from the estimate reported here. A pooled fixed-effect estimate including both the squared real interest rate and the absolute value of the cubed real interest rate gives the following result (1,296 observations):

$$YG = -0.033(RR^2) + 0.008(|RR|^3).$$
$$(-3.949) \qquad (3.598)$$
$$\overline{R}^2 = 0.163$$

(4.7)

Using equation 4.7, the effect of a rising real interest rate on growth is illustrated in Figure 4.3. Evidently, growth is maximised when the real interest rate lies within the normal range of, say, –5 to +10 percent.

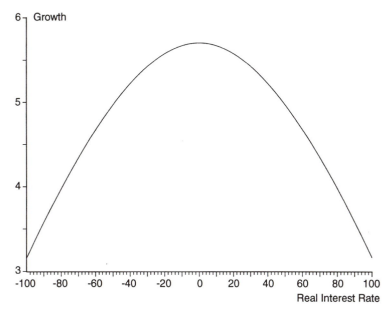

Figure 4.3. Relationship between Annual Growth and Real Interest Rates, 1970–1995

4.8 Domestic Credit Expropriation and High Reserve Requirements

As noted earlier, government expropriation of domestic credit through the imposition of liquid asset ratios and reserve requirements and represent two forms of financial repression. Denoting the ratio of domestic credit to government as a percentage of total domestic credit $DCGR$, the relationship between $DCGR$ and the government deficit as a proportion of GDP GDY using annual data in a fixed-effect model is (1,875 observations):

$$DCGR = 0.684(GDY)$$
$$(6.537)$$
$$\overline{R}^2 = 0.595$$

(4.8)

Evidently, a higher government deficit is associated with a higher proportion of domestic credit expropriated by government.

Given the government's deficit, the greater the proportion of domestic credit expropriated by the government the higher is the inflation rate (1,826 observations):

$$INF = 1.359(GDY) + 0.094(DCGR)$$
$$\quad\quad (9.342) \quad\quad\quad (2.908)$$

$$\overline{R}^2 = 0.428$$

(4.9)

The more the government expropriates from the banking system, the lower is the saving ratio for any given deficit (1,785 observations):

$$SNY = -0.086(GDY) - 0.183(DCGR \cdot GDY)$$
$$\quad\quad (-2.048) \quad\quad\quad (-2.474)$$
$$\quad - 0.038(DCGR)$$
$$\quad\quad (-5.046)$$

$$R^2 = 0.674$$

(4.10)

In this equation, deficits and credit expropriation by the government both reduce saving independently. They also exert a negative interactive effect similar to that produced in the case of central bank financing of the deficit.

Finally, higher $DCGR$ ratios are also associated with lower growth rates, even after controlling for the deficit (1,826 observations):

$$YG = -0.113(GDY) - 0.022(DCGR)$$
$$\quad\quad (-4.508) \quad\quad\quad (-2.908)$$

$$\overline{R}^2 = 0.132$$

(4.11)

An alternative indicator of the captive-buyer source of government finance is the ratio of the commercial banks' reserves to their deposits RD. First, higher deficits GDY are associated with significantly higher reserve/deposit ratios RD (2,041 observations):

$$RD = 0.364(GDY)$$
$$\quad\quad (6.431)$$

$$\overline{R}^2 = 0.593$$

(4.12)

Second, higher reserve/deposit ratios are associated with higher inflation after controlling for the government deficit (1,990 observations):

$$INF = 1.379(GDY) + 4.386(RD)$$
$$(10.164) \qquad (7.229)$$
$$\overline{R}^2 = 0.426 \tag{4.13}$$

Third, period-average (1979–1993) national saving ratios SNY and reserve/deposit ratios RD are negatively associated (103 observations):

$$SNY = 0.222 - 0.327(RD)$$
$$(12.594) \; (-4.524)$$
$$\overline{R}^2 = 0.160 \tag{4.14}$$

Finally, higher period-average (1984–1988) reserve/deposit ratios RD are associated with lower growth rates YG (96 observations):

$$YG = 0.044 - 0.046(RD)$$
$$(10.581) \; (-2.719)$$
$$\overline{R}^2 = 0.063 \tag{4.15}$$

My interpretation of the negative relationships between growth, on the one hand, and both the proportion of domestic credit expropriated by government and the reserve/deposit ratio, on the other hand, is that the more the government takes from the financial system at below-market rates, the lower will be the return to depositors and so the less willing will the public be to hold deposits. This produces a doubly destructive effect on the ability of the banking system to lend for productive investment. First, its resource base in the form of deposits is reduced. Second, the government takes a larger share of the smaller pie.

In fact, financial repression is usually even more damaging than this. Captive buyers receive below-market returns on their forced holdings of government debt. Typically, such a method of financing the government deficit is accompanied by a range of financially repressive measures that include interest rate ceilings on bank deposits, bank loans and various other financial claims. When interest rates are fixed under conditions of high inflation, the concomitant negative real interest rates produce growth-inhibiting effects that have been described earlier in this chapter and are examined in detail elsewhere (Fry 1995).

4.9   Saving, Growth and Financial Distortions

In this section, I extend the earlier empirical work on financial repression by estimating a simultaneous-equation system in which saving and investment ratios as well as export and output growth rates are affected by financial conditions. I also examine the effects of the excessively high real interest rates that have been experienced after several financial liberalisation experiments. These distorted financial conditions appear to be just as debilitating as financial repression. Hence, this section examines the role of financial distortions in inhibiting virtuous circles of high saving and investment ratios in conjunction with high output and export growth rates. The estimates indicate that financial distortions reduce investment ratios and export growth. In turn, lower investment ratios and export growth reduce output growth rates. Output growth is also reduced directly by financial distortions, possibly through an impact on investment efficiency. Because a major determinant of saving ratios is the output growth rate, this section concludes that saving ratios are influenced substantially, albeit *indirectly,* by financial distortions through their effects on investment ratios, export growth and output growth.

Following Shaw (1973, 3), I use both the real deposit rate of interest RR and the black market exchange rate premium $BLACK$ as proxies for financial distortions. Negative real interest rates generally reflect some government-imposed distortion in domestic financial markets (Fry 1995, Giovannini and de Melo 1993). Since governments using financial repression as a source of revenue attempt to prevent capital outflows that would erode their tax base, black market exchange rate premia also provide an indicator of financial repression.

High positive real interest rates indicate a poorly functioning financial system in which inadequate prudential supervision and regulation enables distress borrowing to crowd out borrowing for investment purposes. The De Gregorio-Guidotti effect discussed in section 4.7 could also apply to saving behaviour. Very high real interest rates reflecting increased risk and uncertainty could reduce measured national saving, particularly if the increased domestic risk encourages savers to remove their savings abroad through under- and overinvoicing. Again, I resolve the problem that both very low and very high real interest rates could deter saving not by abandoning real interest rates but rather by using the square of the real deposit rate. This ensures that large positive and negative values exert the same, presumably negative, effect on the saving ratio.

For the empirical work reported in this section, I use data from a sample of 16 developing countries—Argentina, Brazil, Chile, Egypt, India, Indonesia, Korea, Malaysia, Mexico, Nigeria, Pakistan, Philippines, Sri Lanka, Thailand, Turkey, and Venezuela—for the period 1970–1988.[3] The regression method used throughout this section is iterative three-stage least squares which is, asymptotically, full-information maximum likelihood (Johnston 1984, 486–492). I estimate the 16 individual country equations for saving, investment, export growth and output growth as systems of equations with cross-equation equality restrictions on all coefficients except the intercept. Hence, the estimates apply to a representative member of this sample of developing countries. The estimation technique corrects for heteroscedasticity across country equations and exploits contemporaneously correlated disturbances.

4.9.1 National Saving

My saving function is based on a life-cycle model (Mason 1987).[4] The estimate of the national saving ratio expressed as the ratio of national saving to GNP (both in current prices) SNY for this sample of 16 developing countries is (297 observations, hats denote endogenous variables):

$$SNY = 0.289\widehat{YG} - 0.038\,BLACK - 0.006\,RR^2$$
$$(123.359) \quad (-39.816) \quad\quad (-3.981)$$

$$- 0.198\,(\widehat{YG} \cdot BLACK) - 0.205\,(\widehat{YG} \cdot RR^2) \tag{4.16}$$
$$(-12.487) \quad\quad\quad (-5.696)$$

$$+ 0.812\,SNY_{t-1}.$$
$$(748.272)$$

$$R^2 = 0.861$$

It indicates that the national saving ratio in this sample of countries is increased by income growth YG. However, both the black market

---

[3] The ending date was determined by the availability of black market exchange rates taken from the World Bank's *World Development Report 1991: Supplementary Data* diskette. All other data used in this section are taken from *International Financial Statistics* CD-ROM and the World Bank's *Socio-economic Time-series Access and Retrieval System: World Tables* diskette.

[4] Paul Masson, Tamim Bayoumi and Hossein Samiei (1995) provide a recent comprehensive survey of both theoretical and empirical issues relating to saving behaviour.

exchange rate premium $BLACK$ and the squared real interest rate RR not only exert negative impacts on saving through the level effect but also reduce the rate-of-growth effect as shown by the negative interaction terms. Later I demonstrate that a higher black market exchange premium and a real exchange rate that diverges from zero also reduce the national saving ratio *indirectly* by reducing the output growth rate YG.

Because I compare saving performance in five Pacific Basin countries (Indonesia, Korea, Malaysia, Philippines and Thailand) with saving performance in the eleven remaining countries, I test the appropriateness of imposing coefficient equality constraints across all the equations. Relaxing this constraint by allowing the Pacific Basin country coefficients to differ from the coefficients of the eleven remaining countries produces an F statistic of 0.90, well below the 95 and 99 percent significance levels of 3.04 and 4.71 respectively. In other words, pooling is not rejected (Johnston 1984, 206–207 & 553).

4.9.2   Investment

The investment function specified here in terms of the ratio of investment to GNP is based on the flexible accelerator model. Mario Blejer and Mohsin Khan (1984, 382–383) describe some of the difficulties of estimating neoclassical investment functions for developing countries. Without data on the capital stock and the return to capital, there is little choice in practice but to use some version of the accelerator model; see Fry (1996) for a fuller discussion.

A simple specification search suggests that, for the 16 developing countries analysed here, the speed of adjustment is influenced by the real interest rate squared but not by the black market exchange rate premium. If the real deposit rate of interest is held below its free-market equilibrium level, the effective (albeit unobservable) real loan rate would rise as the real deposit rate falls. The lower the real deposit rate, the smaller is the volume of saving and hence the higher is the market-clearing loan rate of interest. In such case, the real deposit rate acts as an inverse proxy for the real loan rate and has a positive impact on the investment ratio (Blejer and Khan 1984, 386). In other words, changes in the real deposit rate trace out movements along the supply (saving) curve rather than along the demand (investment) curve.

In the absence of administrative ceilings, real interest rates are likely to be positive. In such case, a rise in real deposit rates could be produced by a leftward shift in the supply (saving) curve and a corresponding movement up the demand (investment) curve. The result is a reduction in investment. In other words, a zero real interest rate may maximise the investment ratio. Lower real rates imply ceilings that reduce the availability of investible funds. Higher real rates signal distress borrowing not for investment but for survival; loan demand for productive investment is crowded out. The real interest rate squared allows for these nonlinear or regime-shift effects on investment.

The estimated investment function derived from this flexible accelerator model is (297 observations):

$$IY = 0.251\widehat{YG} - 1.628\,RR^2 + 0.692\,IY_{t-1}.$$
$$(32.671) \quad (-11.661) \quad (43.998)$$

$$R^2 = 0.794$$

(4.17)

where IY is the ratio of gross domestic investment to GNP at current prices. Evidently, high negative or positive real interest rates do reduce the investment ratio.

4.9.3 Export Growth

For a small open developing economy, export demand is likely to be infinitely elastic. Therefore, export growth in this model is determined from the supply side. The first determinant of export supply, expressed as the rate of growth in exports at constant prices XKG, is the rate of growth in real GNP YG acting as the supply constraint. Since investment raises the capacity to export, the ratio of gross domestic investment to GNP at constant prices IKY is included as an additional supply constraint.

The basic price variable in the export equation is the real exchange rate or the relative price of exports to nontraded goods. However, the real exchange rate is itself determined by the saving-investment balance and foreign exchange restrictions. Hence I estimate a quasi reduced-form equation substituting the gap between national saving and domestic investment as a ratio of GNP SIY and the black market exchange rate premium for the real exchange rate.[5] Here the black market exchange rate premium squared yields somewhat better results than its level (290 observations):

---

[5] An estimate using the national logarithm of the real exchange rate produces virtually the same results.

$$XKG = 0.364(\widehat{YG}) + 0.179(\widehat{IY}) + 0.496(\widehat{SIY})$$
$$(5.797) \qquad (3.756) \qquad (11.941)$$

$$- 0.224(BLACK^2).$$
$$(-2.846)$$

(4.18)

$$R^2 = 0.153$$

As anticipated, the output growth rate, the investment ratio and the saving-investment balance increase export growth, while the black market exchange rate premium exerts a negative effect.

4.9.4   Output Growth

Following Gershon Feder (1982), my growth rate function estimates the effect of export growth on output growth. The assumption of constant marginal returns to capital in the early development models was regarded as a serious defect for most of the 1960s and 1970s. However, endogenous growth models developed since the mid-1980s provide a theoretical justification for assuming that the marginal product of capital does not diminish for the economy as a whole.

Although the marginal product of capital may not suffer diminishing returns, its value could be affected by financial distortions. As the World Bank (1989, 29–31) points out:

> Historically, the quality of investment has been at least as important for growth as the quantity. Although the fastest-growing countries had higher rates of investment than the others, empirical studies generally find that less than half the growth in output is attributable to increases in labor and capital. Higher productivity explains the rest. Faster growth, more investment, and greater financial depth all come partly from higher saving. In its own right, however, greater financial depth also contributes to growth by improving the productivity of investment.

An increasing body of evidence now suggests that qualitative differences in investment are far more important than quantitative differences in explaining different output growth rates across countries (Fry 1995, Ch. 8; King and Levine 1993a, 1993b; Roubini and Sala-i-Martin 1992). These productivity differentials may be caused by trade and financial distortions imposed on the economy by government policy (Dollar 1992, Roubini and Sala-i-Martin 1991). Therefore, I interact both the black market exchange rate premium *BLACK* and the domestic real interest rate *RD* squared with the investment ratio. In this case, the initial specification search indicated that the level rather than the square of the black market exchange rate premium produced better results.

The point made by De Gregorio and Guidotti (1995) that very high real interest rates can be as destructive as very low real rates again holds up well in this growth rate estimate. Initially, I estimated the relationship between the output growth rate YG, the investment ratio IKY, the real rate of interest RR and the rate of growth in exports at constant prices XKG in an equation of the form:

$$YG = \beta_1(IKY) + \beta_2[IKY \cdot (RR + \beta_3) \cdot (RR + \beta_3)] + \beta_4(XKG). \quad (4.19)$$

Since the parameter β_3 was again not significantly different from zero, although its negative value implies that growth is maximised at some positive real interest rate, I drop it from the estimate reported here. The three-stage iterative least squares estimate is (290 observations):

$$
\begin{aligned}
YG = \; & 0.226(\widehat{IKY}) \; - \; 0.999(\widehat{IKY \cdot BLACK}) \\
& (16.850) \qquad\quad (-9.786) \\
& - \; 0.354(\widehat{IKY \cdot RR^2}) \; + \; 0.098(\widehat{XKG}). \\
& (-11.389) \qquad\qquad (19.691)
\end{aligned}
\qquad (4.20)
$$

$$R^2 = 0.202$$

4.9.5 Direct and Indirect Effects of Financial Distortions on National Saving Ratios and Output Growth Rates in the Pacific Basin and Other Developing Regions

I now examine both the direct short-run and overall long-run effects of financial distortions on saving and output growth by comparing the estimated variations in the saving ratio and output growth rate caused by changes in the financial distortion variables in equations 4.16 and 4.20 with the estimated variations caused by changes in the financial distortion variables in the system of equations consisting of equations 4.16, 4.17, 4.18 and 4.20. The simulated changes in the financial distortion variables are confined to the observed range recorded for this country sample.

The five Pacific Basin developing market economies (Indonesia, Korea, Malaysia, Philippines and Thailand) in this sample experienced substantially less financial distortion than did the eleven remaining countries. Therefore, I indicate the range of values for each country

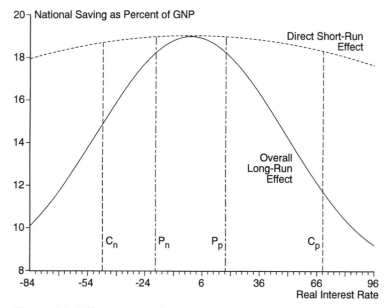

Figure 4.4. Effects of Real Interest Rates on National Saving Ratios

group in terms of standard deviations from respective mean values. For the real interest rate, standard deviations are calculated separately for negative and nonnegative rates.

Figure 4.4 illustrates both the direct effect from equation 4.16 and the overall effect from the joint simulation of equations 4.16, 4.17, 4.18 and 4.20 of a rising real interest rate on the national saving ratio. The simultaneous-equation model used to estimate the overall effect also contains identities defining the saving-investment gap and the equivalence of the nominal and real investment ratio. Figure 4.4 is produced using the mean values of all the explanatory variables with the exception of the real deposit rate of interest. The mean value of the real deposit rate for the entire country sample is zero with a standard deviation of 23 percent. Its minimum value is –83 percent and its maximum value 221 percent. Figure 4.4 shows that the relationship between the real interest rate and the national saving ratio resembles an inverted U. Both very low and very high real interest rates reduce national saving mainly through the effects of these interest rates on output growth.

The line P_n denotes two standard deviations below the mean of all negative interest rates in the Pacific Basin economies, C_n denotes two

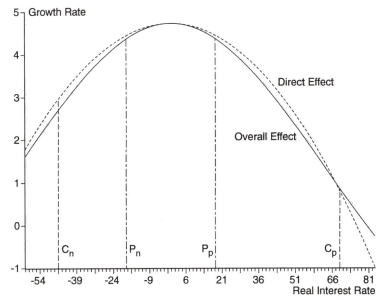

Figure 4.5. Effects of Real Interest Rates on Growth Rates

standard deviations below the mean of all negative interest rates in the remaining eleven countries (the control group), P_p denotes two standard deviations above the mean of all zero or positive interest rates in the Pacific Basin economies, while C_p denotes two standard deviations above the mean of all zero or positive interest rates in the control group countries. Evidently, real interest rates deviated from their saving-maximising level far more in the control group countries than they did in the Pacific Basin economies.

Figure 4.5 illustrates both the direct effect from equation 4.20 and the overall effect from the joint simulation of equations 4.16, 4.17, 4.18 and 4.20 of a rising real interest rate on output growth. Figure 4.5 shows that both very low and very high real interest rates also reduce output growth through their effects on investment productivity. Again, real interest rates deviated from their growth-maximising level far more in the control group countries than they did in the Pacific Basin economies. In contrast to the considerable differences between direct and overall effects of real interest rates on national saving ratios, Figure 4.5 indicates that the direct effects of real interest rates on growth rates are very similar to their overall effects.

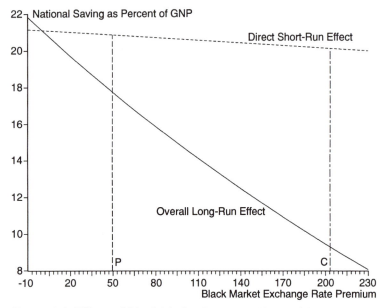

Figure 4.6. Effects of Black Market Premia on National Saving Ratios

Figure 4.6 illustrates both the direct effect from equation 4.16 and the overall effect from the joint simulation of equations 4.16, 4.17, 4.18 and 4.20 of a rising black market foreign exchange rate premium on the national saving ratio. The national saving ratio falls as the black market exchange rate premium rises, again mainly through the effect of the black market foreign exchange rate premium on output growth. For the complete country sample, the mean value of the black market exchange rate premium is 31 percent with a standard deviation of 63 percent. Its minimum value is −10 and its maximum value is 639 percent.

The line *P* denotes two standard deviations above the mean of all zero or positive black market exchange rate premia in the Pacific Basin economies, while *C* denotes two standard deviations above the mean of all zero or positive black market exchange rate premia in the control group of countries. Evidently, black market exchange rate premia tended to be considerably higher in the control group than they were in the Pacific Basin economies. The indirect effects of financial distortions on national saving ratios are far greater than the direct effects.

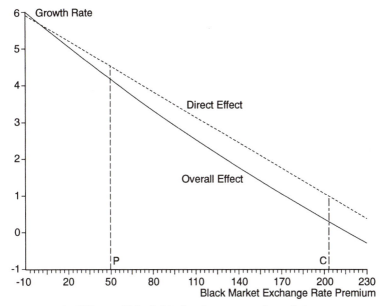

Figure 4.7. Effects of Black Market Premia on Growth Rates

Figure 4.7 shows the direct effect from equation 4.20 and the overall effect from the joint simulation of equations 4.16, 4.17, 4.18 and 4.20 of a rising black market exchange rate premium on output growth. Evidently, the growth rate falls as the black market exchange rate premium rises.

Over the period 1970–1988, the national saving ratio in the five Pacific Basin countries averaged 23.8 percent compared with 16.0 percent in the eleven countries of the control group, while the continuously compounded output growth rate in the Pacific Basin countries averaged 6.2 percent compared with 3.9 percent in the control group. Over the same period, the black market exchange rate premium averaged 6.2 percent in the Pacific Basin countries compared with 42.6 percent in the control group, while the square of the real interest rate was ten times greater in the control group than it was in the Pacific Basin.

The overall effects of both financial distortion variables are estimated by simulating the model consisting of equations 4.16, 4.17, 4.18 and 4.20, together with identities defining the saving-investment gap and the equivalence of the nominal and real investment ratio. These simulations indicate that differences in the average values of the financial distortion variables in each country group account for 3.7 of the 7.8 percentage point difference in the national saving ratios between the Pacific Basin and control group countries and for 1.7 of the 2.3 percentage point difference in their output growth rates. In other words, these two financial distortions explain approximately 50 percent of the difference in saving ratios and 75 percent of the difference in output growth rates between these two country groups.

This section has demonstrated that a reasonably large part of the above-average economic performance of the Pacific Basin developing market economies can be explained by their economic policies that ensured negligible levels of financial distortions, as measured both by the real rate of interest and the black market exchange rate premium. The macroeconomic policies that prevented seriously distorted financial and foreign exchange markets have stimulated investment and export growth. High investment and rapid export growth have accelerated output growth. Higher output growth rates and undistorted financial and foreign exchange markets raise both saving and investment ratios. The evidence suggests that financial conditions fostered by government policies played an important role in producing the virtuous circles of high saving, investment, output growth and export growth found in the Pacific Basin.

4.10 Conclusion

The evidence presented and reviewed in this chapter suggests that financial repression contributes to inflationary pressures, lowers saving and reduces economic growth. In practice, financial repression appears to have yielded government revenue in the order of 2 percent of GDP on average in samples of developing countries (Fry, Goodhart and Almeida 1996, 36; Giovannini and de Melo 1993). If government finances are just stable with this revenue from financial repression, the loss of such revenue requires higher revenue from alternative sources or expenditure cuts of a similar order of magnitude.

As a technique for reducing government borrowing costs, financial repression has adverse effects on saving and economic growth. But abandoning financial repression as a cost-reducing device for the government deficit may result in extraordinarily high real interest rates that can be just as damaging. Unless the government is committed to fiscal reform in conjunction with financial liberalisation, therefore, financial repression may be lesser of two evils. If government expenditure cannot be reduced or traditional tax revenue increased, abandoning financial repression as a source of government revenue may lead to an explosion in government debt, economic instability and lower economic growth.

Experience indicates that, to be successful, financial liberalisation must be accompanied by fiscal reform aimed at ensuring that government debt will not explode in the aftermath of the liberalisation. Successful financial liberalisation also requires sound prudential regulation and supervision, the restructuring of insolvent financial institutions, the profit orientation of state-owned financial institutions and the imposition of hard budget constraints on state-owned nonfinancial enterprises. "Good-bye financial repression, hello financial crash" is the verdict of Carlos Diaz-Alejandro (1985) on the Latin American experiments with financial liberalisation in the absence of these prerequisites in the 1970s and early 1980s.

Elsewhere I suggest that, since there is no question that financial repression inhibits growth, the debate among economists and policy makers should concentrate on the tricky problems of moving from the state of financial repression to a state of financial liberalisation (Fry 1997). Part III of this book aims to provide some guidelines for one aspect of this crucial transition.

Chapter 5

Foreign Debt Accumulation

5.1 Introduction

As AN ALTERNATIVE TO INFLATIONARY finance or financial repression, government borrowing from abroad might seem benign, at least in the initial stages. Inevitably, however, the government faces the same intertemporal budget constraint whether it borrows at home or abroad. The only difference lies in the possible solutions to debt buildup. Since the mid-1970s, a number of developing countries have faced serious difficulties in servicing their foreign debts. The typical foreign debt crisis has been accompanied by slower or even negative economic growth and accelerating inflation. This chapter examines the process of foreign debt accumulation in developing countries. Specifically, it considers the impact of excessive accumulation of government and government-guaranteed foreign debt on inflation, saving and growth.

Table 5.1 provides some statistics on the behaviour of government and government-guaranteed foreign debt in 79 developing countries for which at least some debt and deficit data are available over the period 1979–1993. While foreign debt as a percentage of GDP has increased over this period, so too has its standard deviation. The maximum debt ratio has risen from 117 percent in 1979–1983 to 346 percent in 1989–1993.

Rising foreign debt ratios are a cause for concern because earlier work on the effects of foreign debt accumulation suggests that when debt exceeds about 50 percent of GDP crises tend to occur unless decisive measures are taken at that point to stabilise or reduce the debt/GDP ratio (Fry 1989). The economic model from which this conclusion is drawn exploits one of the two alternative balance-of-payments identities:

Table 5.1. Trends in Median Government and Government-Guaranteed Foreign Debt as Percent of GDP in 79 Developing Countries, 1979–1993

Statistic	1979–93	1979–83	1984–88	1989–93
Mean	43.9	25.9	46.1	56.1
Median	32.9	20.7	39.7	37.9
Maximum	212.8	117.0	185.6	346.4
Minimum	1.3	0.6	1.1	0.5
S.D.	37.6	19.4	34.5	59.0

current account ≡ national saving − domestic investment. In this model, foreign debt is allowed to affect both saving and investment behaviour. If higher foreign debt reduces investment by more than it reduces saving or, alternatively, raises investment by less than it raises saving, the current account will eventually be brought into a steady-state equilibrium with sustainable (i.e., constant) debt/GDP and debt/export ratios. In such case, debt crises, like oil crises before them, are more illusory than real.

5.2 A Model of Foreign Debt Accumulation

5.2.1 Some Balance-of-Payments Accounting

The balance-of-payments accounts show that current account deficits are financed by capital inflows or decreases in official reserves. One way of presenting this identity is:[1]

$$CAY + KAY \equiv \Delta RY, \qquad (5.1)$$

where CAY is the current account as a proportion of GDP, KAY is the capital account ratio and ΔRY is the change in official reserves also expressed as a ratio of GDP. If the change in official reserves is unaffected, an increased capital inflow is matched by a smaller current account surplus or a larger current account deficit.

Capital inflows allow domestic investment to exceed national saving when they finance a current account deficit. Domestic investment equals national saving plus the current account deficit which is identical to

---

[1] This identity ignores errors and omissions.

foreign saving, as shown by the national income definition of the balance of payments on current account:

$$IY = SNY + SFY \tag{5.2}$$

or

$$CAY = SNY - IY, \tag{5.3}$$

where SFY is foreign saving, which equals the current account deficit and so is equal but of opposite sign to CAY, the balance of payments on current account, SNY is national saving and IY is domestic investment, all divided by GDP.[2] Hence, capital inflows that finance the current account deficit can increase investment and the rate of economic growth.

The current account ratio can also be defined as the export ratio XY plus the ratio of net factor income from abroad to GDP $NFIY$ minus the import ratio IMY:

$$CAY \equiv XY + NFIY - IMY. \tag{5.4}$$

If capital inflows increase capital formation in the host country, the increased investment could involve increased imports of raw materials or capital equipment. Alternatively, it could reduce exports by diverting them into the additional investment. In either case, the current account must deteriorate in equation 5.4 by exactly the same amount as it does in equations 5.1 and 5.3.

5.2.2   Stabilising Financial Effects

The extent and financing of a current account deficit depend both on a country's desire to spend more than its income and on the willingness of the rest of the world to finance the deficit from its saving. In other words, a current account deficit is determined simultaneously by both the demand for and the supply of foreign saving. My saving-investment model of a semi-open developing economy attempts to capture the essential determinants of this interactive process (Fry 1989; 1993; 1995, Ch. 12).

Based on the assumption that foreign saving takes the form of foreign loans to or guaranteed by the government, my model also permits

---

[2]This definition of the current account ratio is derived from the national income rather than the balance-of-payments accounts. It differs from the balance-of-payments definition by excluding unrequited transfers.

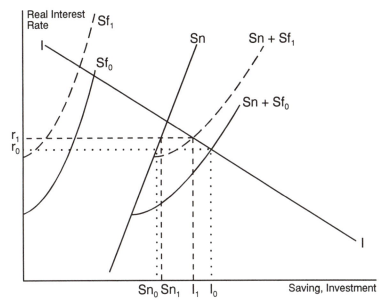

Figure 5.1. Saving, Investment and the Current Account Deficit

the ratio of foreign debt to GDP to converge to a constant and hence sustainable steady state. A steady state exists if a higher level of foreign indebtedness improves the current account. If foreign indebtedness reduces investment by more than it reduces saving or raises investment by less than it raises saving, rising foreign indebtedness improves the current account and so slows down the buildup of foreign debt. Hence, the model contains an informal error-correction process. The model also specifies a monetary policy reaction function, since domestic credit expansion usually worsens a current account.

The key components of this open-economy model are represented in Figure 5.1. This figure echoes Lloyd Metzler (1968) in viewing the current account deficit as the difference between domestic investment and national saving. It shows the planned levels of national saving, foreign saving and domestic investment at different levels of real interest rates r. The domestic investment function I slopes downwards indicating that there is more investment at lower interest rates. The national saving function Sn is nearly vertical indicating that changes in the domestic real interest rate have little *direct* effect on national saving.

Most developing countries face an upward-sloping supply curve of foreign saving Sf_0. However, the effective cost at which foreign saving begins to be supplied in any particular year depends on the country's foreign debt position inherited from past borrowing. In this model, the effective cost of foreign borrowing is also the effective domestic real interest rate. At an effective interest rate of r_0, domestic investment I_0 exceeds national saving Sn_0. Hence, the inflow of foreign saving is positive and the country runs a current account deficit on its balance of payments equal to I_0-Sn_0.

The accumulation of foreign debt resulting from the current account deficit in year 0 raises the foreign saving curve to Sf_1 in the next year. This change produces an effective cost of foreign borrowing of r_1 in year 1. In this case, foreign debt accumulation reduces domestic investment and raises national saving through a higher domestic real interest rate. As this process continues in subsequent years, the current account deficit declines until it reaches a steady-state equilibrium in which the foreign debt/GDP ratio is constant. This is the stabilising financial effect of foreign debt accumulation.

5.2.3   Destabilising Fiscal Effects

Much foreign debt in developing countries takes the form of government and government-guaranteed foreign debt. The level of this type of foreign debt accumulated from past current account deficits may itself affect the position of the saving and investment functions in Figure 5.1. Presumably the modern Ricardian equivalence view would hold that if households expect the existence of government-guaranteed foreign loans to necessitate government expenditure and hence higher taxation in the future, private saving would rise as more guarantees were extended. Hence, the Ricardian equivalence hypothesis suggests that more foreign debt could actually raise the national saving ratio, since this *future* contingent government liability does not reduce the *current* level of government saving.

While rising government and government-guaranteed foreign debts could well lead households to anticipate higher future tax burdens for debt service and repayment, they may respond in the alternative way suggested by David Ricardo (1817, 338):

> A country which has accumulated a large debt is placed in a most artificial situation; and although the amount of taxes, and the increased price of labour, may not, and I believe does not, place it under any other disadvantage with respect to foreign countries,

except the unavoidable one of paying those taxes, yet it becomes the interest of every contributor to withdraw his shoulder from the burthen, and to shift this payment from himself to another; and the temptation to remove himself and his capital to another country, where he will be exempted from such burthens, becomes at last irresistible, and overcomes the natural reluctance which every man feels to quit the place of his birth, and the scene of his early associations. A country which has involved itself in the difficulties attending this artificial system, would act wisely by ransoming itself from them, at the sacrifice of any portion of its property which might be necessary to redeem its debt.

Here Ricardo is clearly refuting the Ricardian equivalence proposition that the way governments finance their expenditures is immaterial.

Savers could also perceive that a high and rising foreign debt ratio may goad the government into stimulating exports, which would involve a devaluation in the real exchange rate. Indeed, a steady-state equilibrium necessitates a depreciation in the real exchange rate at some stage. In this case, the real returns on assets held abroad could be higher than the real returns on domestic assets.

Most developing countries prohibit capital outflows. Hence, the removal of capital abroad takes place through overinvoicing imports and underinvoicing exports (Cuddington 1986, 38; Dooley 1986, 1988; Khan and Haque 1985; Watson *et al.* 1986). Typically, an exporter submits an invoice for a smaller sum than that actually received for the exports when surrendering foreign exchange to the central bank; the difference can then be deposited in the exporter's bank account abroad. Conversely, an importer submits an invoice for an amount exceeding the true cost of the imports in order to siphon the difference into his or her foreign bank account.

This method of removing capital from a country reduces measured national saving, even in the unlikely event that the true level of saving remains constant. Hence, one might expect a higher value of government plus government-guaranteed foreign debt to reduce measured national saving, implying a leftward shift in the saving function in Figure 5.1. Here, therefore, is an explanation of a *negative* effect of foreign debt on the current account; an increase in foreign debt can worsen the current account. By raising the effective costs of foreign borrowing and shadow domestic real interest rates, higher foreign debt also reduces investment and growth. Lower growth reduces saving, implying another leftward shift in the saving function in Figure 5.1. This is the destabilising fiscal effect of foreign debt accumulation which may or may not outweigh the stabilising financial effect of foreign debt accumulation discussed in section 5.2.2.

The magnitude of capital flight caused by a buildup of foreign debt can be, and in several developing countries has been, destabilising. Instead of an increase in foreign debt *reducing* domestic investment and *increasing* national saving, the foreign debt buildup shifts the national saving function to the left; hence the current account deficit *increases*. Real interest rates can reach, and in several developing countries have reached, astronomical levels without reducing the current account deficit.

The variable representing this foreign debt factor $DTGY$ is the stock of government plus government-guaranteed foreign debt converted from dollars to local currency divided by GDP. In addition to its effect on the position of the national saving function, $DTGY$ also affects the supply of foreign saving. By reducing foreign saving from Sf_0 to Sf_1, a higher debt ratio produces a higher domestic real interest rate and hence a movement up the saving function in Figure 5.1. This financial or interest rate effect on saving (a movement up the saving function) can be of opposite sign to the fiscal effect of $DTGY$ (a leftward shift in the saving function). To allow for these conflicting and possibly nonlinear influences of debt on saving, the debt/GDP ratio is used in quadratic, cubic and level form.

5.2.4   Debt Effects on Investment

An increase in government and government-guaranteed foreign debt may also deter domestic investment because it raises the probability of higher taxes on domestic assets in the future (Ize and Ortiz 1987). This would shift the investment function in Figure 5.1 to the left. Anne Krueger (1987, 163) concludes: "When debt-service obligations are high, increasing public resources to service debt will be likely to reduce incentives and resources available to the private sector sufficiently to preclude the necessary investment response." Jeffrey Sachs (1986, 1989, 1990) documents the deleterious effects of the foreign debt buildup on investment in Latin America.

In its early stages, however, foreign debt buildup could actually stimulate investment. Entrepreneurs may perceive that there would be profitable investment opportunities in export activities as debt service mounts and the government is forced to intensify its drive to raise foreign exchange earnings. Again, therefore, the impact of foreign debt accumulation on investment and hence on growth need not be linear.

5.3 Empirical Evidence

5.3.1 Saving and Investment Behaviour

The estimates of saving, investment and growth functions for 28 heavily indebted developing countries reported in Fry (1995, Ch. 12) show that the national saving ratio is increased by higher growth YG and by terms-of-trade improvements. Income growth attributable to terms-of-trade improvements raises the saving ratio by more than income growth attributable to output growth. In a permanent income framework, this is consistent with the perception that terms-of-trade changes are more temporary than output changes. A higher world real interest rate and a higher ratio of net government credit to total domestic credit reduces the national saving ratio, as does higher foreign debt after foreign debt $DTGY$ exceeds 30 percent of GDP. The Ricardian equivalence hypothesis with respect to foreign debt is rejected; higher government plus government-guaranteed foreign debt reduces rather than raises national saving ratios in these countries.

The domestic investment ratio is raised by faster real growth YG, lagged improvements in the terms of trade and a higher real exchange rate that makes imported capital goods cheaper. Capital inflows allow domestic investment to exceed national saving, a movement down the investment curve from its intersection with national saving in Figure 5.1. They also stimulate domestic investment by appreciating the real exchange rate, so moving the investment curve itself to the right. Higher investment accelerates the rate of economic growth. However, a higher ratio of net government credit to total domestic credit reduces the investment ratio, as does a higher foreign debt ratio after foreign debt exceeds 50 percent of GDP.

Estimates of a five-equation model which includes these saving and investment functions indicate that capital inflows raise economic growth by allowing investment to exceed saving and by stimulating investment indirectly through the real exchange rate effect (Fry 1989).[3] However, a rising ratio of foreign debt to GDP eventually has three negative impacts on growth: it reduces the saving ratio, it deters domestic investment and it lowers the efficiency of investment (Fry 1989). These negative effects

---

[3] These estimates confirm a point made by Miguel Mancera at the Symposium that "within a certain range, borrowing from abroad should not be detrimental to growth. On the contrary, growth could be enhanced if total investment in the country is increased as a results of foreign loans."

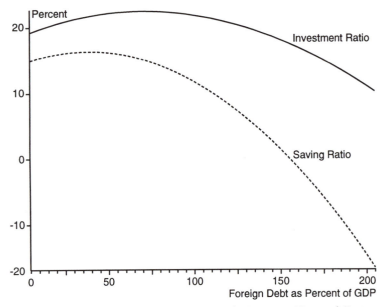

Figure 5.2. Effects of a Rising Foreign Debt Ratio on National Saving and Domestic Investment Ratios

of debt *stock* start to outweigh the positive effects of debt *flow* when the debt/GDP ratio reaches about 0.5; this corresponds to a debt/export ratio of about 2.4 for this sample of countries. In fact, debt/GNP ratios ranged from 0.02 to 1.28 in this sample of countries. The problem arises from the lack of any automatic deterrent to continued debt accumulation after its effects turn malign.

Figure 5.2 shows the direct and indirect effects of increasing foreign debt on the national saving and domestic investment ratios (Fry 1989, Figure 2, 328). These are short-run equilibrium effects, since the values of all lagged endogenous variables are held constant while $DTGY$ is increased from 0 to 200 percent. The gap between the saving ratio and the investment ratio increases monotonically as the debt ratio rises. The same result occurs whether the foreign debt ratio is entered linearly or to the third or fourth power with beginning- or end-of-year values in both the saving and investment ratio equations. Whether entered linearly or in quadratic form, the debt/export ratio also produces the same result but has a somewhat lower explanatory power than the debt/GDP ratio in both the saving and investment functions.

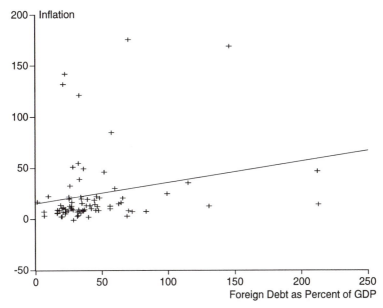

Figure 5.3. Period-Average Inflation and Foreign Debt Ratios, 1979–1993

5.3.2 New Estimates of Inflation, Saving, Growth and Foreign Debt Accumulation

Figure 5.3 shows the relationship between inflation and debt using 15-year averages for the period 1979–1993 for the 79 developing countries for which debt and deficit data are available. Using annual data for 69 developing countries with a minimum set of 10 observations, the best nonlinear estimate of inflation as a function of the foreign debt ratio is (1,494 observations, t values in parentheses):

$$INF = -0.318(DTGY) + 0.498(DTGY^2) - 0.098(DTGY^4)$$
$$(-3.457) \qquad (6.311) \qquad (-6.940)$$

$$\overline{R}^2 = 0.352$$

(5.5)

Figure 5.4 shows the effect of a rising foreign debt ratio on inflation produced by equation 5.5. In this case, debt accumulation lowers inflation initially, perhaps because it increases the aggregate supply of goods and services, before raising it as the debt ratio moves into the unstable region.

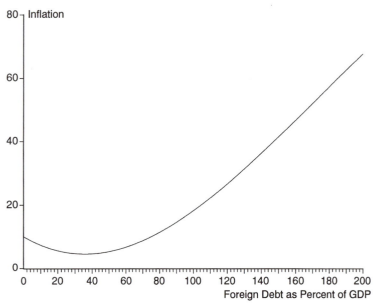

Figure 5.4. Annual Inflation and Foreign Debt Ratios, 1970–1995

Again using annual data for 69 developing countries with a minimum set of 10 observations, I estimated nonlinear fixed-effect models of the relationship between national saving ratios and foreign debt ratios. The most satisfactory functional form gives the following result (1,473 observations):

$$SNY = -0.082(DTGY^2) + 0.014(DTGY^3)$$
$$(-11.469) \qquad\qquad (8.258)$$
$$\overline{R}^2 = 0.677$$

(5.6)

Figure 5.5 shows the effect of a rising foreign debt ratio on the national saving ratio from equation 5.6. Consistent with the results reported earlier, the negative impact of foreign debt accumulation is not pronounced at small levels, but increases as the debt ratio itself rises.

Figure 5.6 shows the direct relationship between period-average rates of economic growth and government and government-guaranteed foreign debt for the 79 developing countries for which debt and deficit data are available. Using annual data for the 69 developing countries with a minimum set of 10 observations, the most satisfactory functional form gives the following result (1,495 observations):

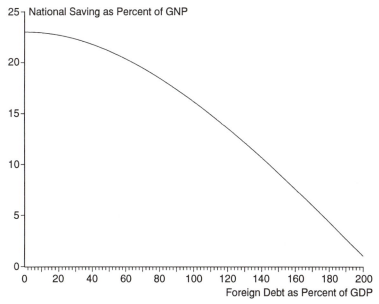

Figure 5.5. Annual National Saving and Foreign Debt Ratios, 1970–1995

$$YG = -0.015(DTGY^2) + 0.004(DTGY^3)$$
$$\quad\ \ (-2.587) \qquad\qquad (2.753)$$
$$\overline{R}^2 = 0.113 \tag{5.7}$$

Figure 5.7 shows the effect of a rising foreign debt ratio on growth. Consistent with the results reported earlier, the negative impact of foreign debt accumulation is not pronounced at small levels, but increases as the debt ratio itself rises.

5.3.3 Alternative Policy Responses

The tendency to overborrow can be countered by macroeconomic policies designed to stimulate saving (or to depress investment). Higher saving (or reduced investment) depreciates the real exchange rate which, in turn, increases exports and reduces imports. Foreign lenders might force a cold-turkey cure on a heavily indebted developing country by cutting off further net capital flows. In such case, the developing country could retaliate by repudiating its foreign debt.

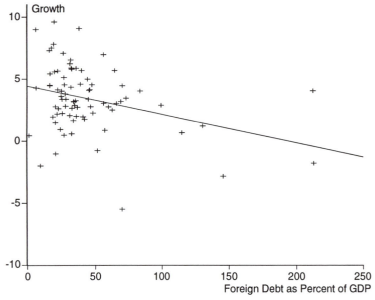

Figure 5.6. Period-Average Growth and Foreign Debt Ratios, 1979–1993

Alternatively, the necessary adjustments to saving (or investment) can be undertaken voluntarily and possibly more gradually. In either case, the five-equation model reported in Fry (1989) indicates that the growth rate should accelerate as the debt burden recedes. No alternative policy measure—stimulating exports, compressing imports and repudiating debt—seems capable of solving these countries' debt problem over the longer run.

5.4   Conclusion

That some developing countries have overborrowed (and some lenders have overlent) is certainly not a new finding. Among others, Michael Bruno (1985), Richard Cooper and Jeffrey Sachs (1985), Carlos Diaz-Alejandro (1985), Arnold Harberger (1986) and Ronald McKinnon (1991) provide explanations for why private sectors will borrow more abroad than is socially optimal unless restrained from so doing.

Bruno (1985, 868) and Harberger (1986, 157–158) show that the optimum tariff theory can be applied to the taxation of foreign capital

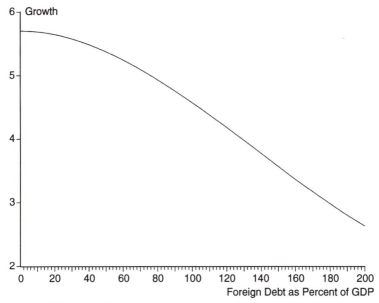

Figure 5.7. Annual Growth and Foreign Debt Ratios, 1970–1995

inflows when a country faces a rising supply schedule of foreign loans. In such case, a country's general welfare can be increased by reducing the incentives to borrow abroad through a tax on foreign indebtedness. Bruno (1985, 868) also argues that differential speeds of adjustment justify restrictions on capital inflows during a liberalisation programme. Cooper and Sachs (1985, 34–35) show that a *laissez-faire* policy towards foreign borrowing is justified only under very restrictive conditions. Specifically, the private sector must have rational expectations regarding the possibility of a liquidity crisis, the probability of such a crisis must not be a function of the overall level of foreign debt, the private sector must believe that the government will not bail it out and the liquidity crisis must not cause a wave of disruptive bankruptcies.

Diaz-Alejandro (1985, 18) and McKinnon (1991) pursue the bailout condition. They argue that government guarantees and deposit insurance in the lending countries combined with inadequate regulation have produced a strong incentive for the multinational banks to overlend to developing countries. In sum, government involvement in both borrowing and lending countries has contributed to foreign debt instability that has afflicted developing countries since the mid-1970s.

Part III

Developing Voluntary
Domestic Markets

Chapter 6

Prerequisites, Persuasion and Pitfalls

6.1 Introduction

PART II OF THIS BOOK DRAWS THE negative conclusion that excessive use of inflationary finance, financial repression and borrowing from abroad to finance government deficits reduces economic growth. Part III concentrates on the final source, voluntary lending by the domestic private sector, to which governments may turn. Over the period 1979–1993, the median OECD country financed over 50 percent of its government deficit from this source, while the representative developing country has financed only 8 percent of its government deficit in this way.

To start this Part, I report estimates of the association between inflation, saving and growth, on the one hand, and the proportion of the government deficit financed by the domestic private nonbank sector (NBD), on the other hand. Using average values for the period 1979–1993 for 89 countries for which some data are available, inflation INF is negatively related to the proportion of the deficit financed by the domestic private nonbank sector (NBD):

$$INF = 0.172 - 0.009(NBD)$$
$$(6.162)\ (-2.665)$$

$$\overline{R}^2 = 0.065$$

$$(6.1)$$

I now use the same method developed in Chapter 3 to examine the effect of the government's source of borrowing on saving and growth. The functional form makes the effect of the deficit depend on the way it is financed. In this case, therefore, I specify an equation of the form

$$SNY = b_0 + (b_1 + b_2 NBD) \cdot GDY, \tag{6.2}$$

which can again be simplified to

$$SNY = b_0 + b_1 GDY + b_2 (NBD \cdot GDY). \tag{6.3}$$

In other words, the coefficient of GDY is variable and depends on the proportion of the deficit that is financed by the domestic private nonbank sector. The estimate of equation 6.3 using annual data for the period 1970–1995 is (1,455 observations, t values in parentheses):

$$SNY = -0.332(GDY) + 0.177(NBD \cdot GDY)$$
$$(-8.335) \qquad (7.972)$$
$$\overline{R}^2 = 0.735 \tag{6.4}$$

Using a similar specification for growth with average values over the period 1979–1993 gives:

$$YG = 0.039 - 0.118(GDY) + 0.021(NBD \cdot GDY)$$
$$(12.762) \ (-2.362) \qquad (3.362)$$
$$\overline{R}^2 = 0.188 \tag{6.5}$$

Together with the results presented and discussed in Part II, this provides support for the premise that voluntary borrowing from the domestic private sector may be the least harmful way of financing any given government deficit. The remainder of this book turns to some of the practical problems of developing markets for such voluntary purchases of government securities.

Much of the material presented in this part of the book was provided by eight central banks from which the Bank of England requested information. The countries—Ghana, India, Jamaica, Malaysia, Mexico, New Zealand, Sri Lanka and Zimbabwe—were chosen on the grounds that their own experience in developing markets for government debt would be interesting and instructive to other countries that have not so far embarked upon any concerted programme along such lines.[1] While the questionnaire used for this purpose is reproduced in Appendix 1,

---

[1] These countries were chosen from among those invited to the Bank of England's 1996 Central Bank Governors' Symposium with a view to providing geographical spread as well as diversity in experience with respect to their market development process.

selected macroeconomic characteristics of these countries are presented in Appendices 13 to 24.

6.2 The Essential Elements

Developing markets for voluntary purchases of government debt involves a fundamental change in the approach to financing the government. Privileged access and captive buyers are eschewed in favour of a level playing-field philosophy. The government competes on the same terms and conditions as private agents for available savings and so faces the economy's opportunity cost of borrowing. It has to accept the interest cost consequences of its borrowing and this should exert fiscal discipline that may have been absent when borrowing was kept artificially cheap.

The economic principle behind the change is that a level playing field maximises the efficiency with which scarce resources are allocated throughout the economy. This change in approach necessarily involves many practical changes in the way government debt is sold.

Typically, the change occurs from a system in which most institutional interest rates are fixed and the government is financed at favourable fixed rates by unwilling captive buyers of its debt. In such a system, Bank Rate and all other institutional interest rates, including the treasury bill yield, are simply announced by the minister of finance. Captive buyers hold treasury bills and other government securities to fulfil their ratio requirements, etc., and the central bank takes up any shortfall.

6.2.1 Disequilibrium Pricing

Figure 6.1 illustrates this disequilibrium system. The government has fixed the price of treasury bills or bonds at P_f and needs to sell Q_s to meets its borrowing requirements. Hence, supply is T^s. Demand is determined inelastically by the various ratio requirements on financial institutions, etc., at T^d. The demand shortfall is made up by central bank monetisation of the deficit.

In the absence of captive buyers, the demand curve resembles T^d in Figure 6.2. At the fixed price P_f, the gap between demand and supply is larger than in Figure 6.1. There is therefore greater monetisation of the deficit by the central bank.

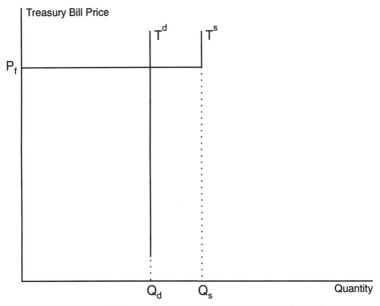

Figure 6.1. Disequilibrium Pricing of Government Debt under Financial Repression and Inflationary Finance

6.2.2   Equilibrium Market Pricing

When the government accepts the level playing-field concept that it should borrow under the same terms and conditions as the private sector, the situation resembles that portrayed in Figure 6.3. The equilibrium market price of treasury bills is P_m and the quantity Q is bought voluntarily. Here the government realises that increased borrowing can be achieved only at higher interest rates, i.e., lower prices. Here some fiscal discipline is introduced. It is depicted by the upward-sloping supply curve that implies reduced borrowing at higher interest costs. Under the liberalised market-based system illustrated in Figure 6.3, there need be no fixed interest rate at all. In Mauritius, for example, even Bank Rate is set automatically at a small markup over the latest treasury bill auction yield.

6.2.3   Illusory Equilibrium Pricing

Even in Mauritius, however, the situation is not that depicted in Figure 6.3 because captive buyers have not been emancipated. In Mauritius

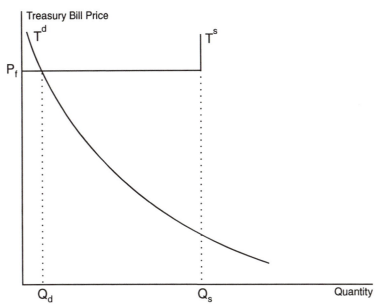

Figure 6.2. Disequilibrium Pricing of Government Debt under Inflationary Finance

and in many other countries, the situation resembles that shown in Figure 6.4. Under favourable conditions, the free interplay of market forces seems to produce a market-determined price P_m at quantity Q. However, this price is inflated artificially by the existence of intramarginal captive buyers illustrated by the vertical part of the demand curve T_0^d in Figure 6.4. The authorities fear that lowering the liquid asset ratio requirement would shift the demand curve to T_1^d, in which case the price of treasury bills falls substantially. To prevent an "unreasonable" increase in treasury bill yields, a reserve price is imposed which ensures that the quantity supplied exceeds the quantity demanded exactly as it did in the disequilibrium situation shown in Figure 6.1. As recently as 1995, one observer commented that yields on Indian government debt in primary markets were still set by moral suasion rather than by the market.

In fact, this endemic fear that treasury bill yields will rise to unreasonable rates with the abolition of liquid asset ratios is typically unfounded. If loan rates of interest are not freely determined by the interplay of market forces for all private sector bank borrowing, a first

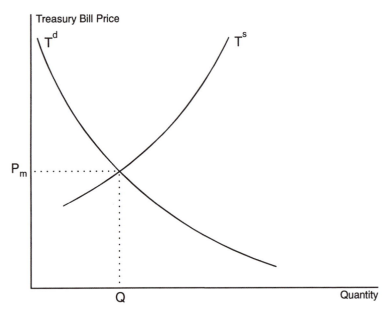

Figure 6.3. Noninflationary Voluntary Financing of Government Deficits

step would be to abolish loan rate ceilings. This immediately provides the authorities with an upper bound for a freely determined treasury bill rate, provided government borrowing remains constant. In the many developing countries that do not impose loan rate ceilings on bank lending to the private sector but do retain liquid asset ratio requirements, banks already lend voluntarily to the private sector at freely determined rates. Provided banks perceive the government as no more risky than private sector borrowers, loan rates to the private sector again provide an upper bound for treasury bill yields. Indeed, since the reduction in reserve requirements and abolition of liquid asset ratios reduce the competitive spread between loan and deposit rates, the concomitant rise in deposit rates could increase bank resources and so produce a decline in private sector borrowing rates. This would imply that emancipation would raise the government's borrowing costs but to a level somewhat below private sector rates which would themselves fall in this process.

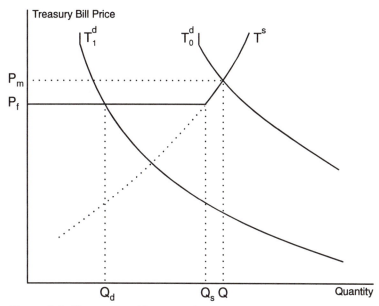

Figure 6.4. Illusory Equilibrium with Captive Buyers and Reserve Price

6.2.4 Unstable Equilibrium Pricing

If abandoning inflation and financial repression as sources of government revenue produces an unstable fiscal situation, however, the situation changes over time as shown in Figure 6.5. Starting at an equilibrium of P_{m_0} and Q_0, the government finds that it has to borrow more in year 1 to pay the increased interest cost on its Q_0 borrowing in year 0. The supply of treasury bills shifts to the right in year 1 to raise more revenue with which to finance higher interest payments. The equilibrium price falls to P_{m_1}. Price continues to fall as quantity increases in subsequent years. In this process, the real interest rate necessarily rises, the private sector is crowded out and a financial crises eventually ensues.

To the extent that lenders suspect that the government is playing a Ponzi game, the demand curve in Figure 6.5 will shift to the left. Figure 6.6 illustrates such movements in the demand curve. While these shifts will accelerate the interest rate rise facing the government, it may avoid crowding out of the private sector. This would be the case if the quantity lent to the government declined. A sufficiently large leftward shift in the demand curve would outweigh the rightward shift

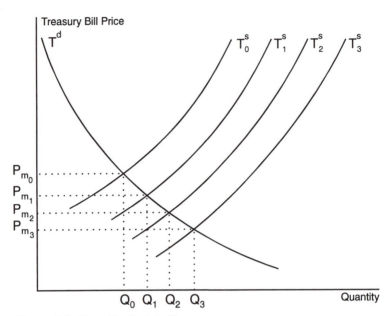

Figure 6.5. Unstable Deficit Finance

in the supply curve, so producing an equilibrium at a higher interest rate but lower quantity. In such case, the government's interest rate would incorporate a risk premium widening the gap between interest rates faced by the government and private sector. *Ceteris paribus,* the private sector's interest rate would decline because lenders would be increasing the amount supplied to the private sector as they steer away from lending to the government.

Even when the authorities claim that interest rates are determined by a free market, the actual situation may well resemble Figure 6.2 rather than Figure 6.3 simply because a reserve price is set below which treasury bills are not sold to those bidding at auction. The unsold bills may be either taken up by the central bank or withdrawn. The monetary consequences are identical because in the latter case the government draws down its balances at the central bank, so producing the same expansion in reserve money as would otherwise be injected by central bank purchases of treasury bills.

A "clean" auction in which all bills are sold at whatever price the market, as illustrated in Figure 6.3, yields four advantages: (a) it informs the government of the true opportunity cost of its borrowing; (b) it

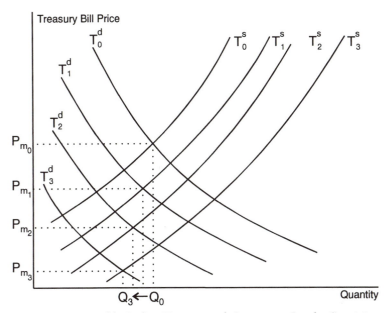

Figure 6.6. Unstable Deficit Finance with Increasing Lender Suspicion

avoids recourse to the central bank and so avoids the road back to inflationary finance; (c) it provides important feedback signals from the market for monetary policy purposes; and (d) the treasury bill yield can and soon will be used as a crucial reference rate for the pricing of other financial claims in new markets.

6.3   Perceived Benefits

The questionnaire's first question concerned the perceived benefits from developing voluntary domestic markets for government debt. In general, the responses elaborated both the negative effects of inflationary finance and financial repression as well as the positive externalities from developing voluntary markets for government debt.

6.3.1   Lack of Voluntary Markets

On the negative side, the absence of voluntary markets were perceived to:

- Divorce the cost of government borrowing from the opportunity cost of funds in the economy, thereby misallocating resources by encouraging larger government deficits.

- Be inconsistent with the aim of reducing the government's deficit.

- Impede monetary control.

- Exacerbate central bank losses.

- Cause distortions from the need to use credit ceilings, multiple reserve requirements, compulsory deposits at the central bank, interest rate ceilings and other direct methods of monetary control.

- Crowd out private sector borrowing through high reserve and liquid asset ratios on the banks.

- Impede monetary policy implementation; government debt yielding below-market returns could not be used for indirect market-based monetary policy implementation.

- Promote market segmentation and interest rate distortion.

- Produce high interest rate spreads.

- Prevent efficient price formation in the financial markets.

- Discourage secondary market trading in government securities.

- Prevent government securities from being used as collateral in financial transactions.

Several of these disadvantages have been substantiated in Part II.

6.3.2   Existence of Voluntary Markets

On the positive side, the existence of a voluntary market for government debt was perceived to:

- Finance government deficits in a less inflationary way.

- Impose fiscal discipline on the government and reflect the true market costs of government borrowing. Since 1990, for example, the rapidly rising interest costs of domestic borrowing in Zimbabwe have apparently squeezed Budget resources for other purposes.

- Widen the market beyond the captive segment, thereby reducing the extent of monetisation and inflationary impact of the government deficit.

- Provide a more competitive borrowing mechanism in the context of a market-orientated economic framework.

- Offer greater flexibility for government debt management in a less inflationary way.

- Increase liquidity of government debt instruments, so fostering savings.

- Reduce both the tax on the banking system and other financial market distortions thereby improving resource allocation.

- Reduce spreads between deposit and loan rates, so improving the efficiency of domestic resource allocation.

- Reduce compliance costs and disintermediation.

- Enable a shift from direct to indirect monetary policy techniques, thereby improving the efficiency and effectiveness of monetary policy implementation.

- Provide a reference rate in the form of the market-determined yield on treasury bills.

- Assist the development (broadening and deepening) and integration of money and capital markets as well as wider financial system reform and liberalisation.

- Develop new money market instruments.

- Enhance the country's attractiveness as an investment centre.

The extent to which such benefits actually accrue is examined in this and the next chapter. The finding that greater reliance on nonbank buyers of government debt reduces the inflationary impact of government deficits has already been reported above.

In combination, these perceived benefits suggest that voluntary market financing of government deficits provides, paradoxically, the cheapest form of financing for the government in the long run. Cheap finance from the central bank or through financial repression is a mirage. As

Leonard Tsumba remarked at the Symposium: "There are obvious economic costs when central banks validate budget deficits, when governments force purchases of government paper, when they rely too much on external borrowing as a means of financing budget deficits and when governments crowd out the private sector by making disproportionate and growing claims on domestic credit." In other words, the advantages of cheap credit disappear as soon as the costs of inflation, higher interest rate spreads for the commercial banks and lower central bank profits are recognised. Perhaps the most important benefit is that, by accelerating economic growth, a move to voluntary domestic financing reduces the deficit that has to be financed.

6.4   Persuading the Main Political Actors

While central bankers, civil servants and macroeconomists may be convinced of the efficacy of weaning the government from its central bank, ministers of finance and other cabinet ministers may see the increased price of financing government deficits as a costly certainty, while viewing the benefits as vague and uncertain. What persuades government to abandon cheap finance?[2]

Central banks may well become involved in the debate, since they stand to benefit on at least three counts:

1. Getting the government out of the central bank clearly reduces the inflationary threat of deficits.

2. Developing voluntary domestic markets for government debt enables the central bank to use indirect market-based instruments of monetary policy.

3. By divorcing fiscal and monetary policy in this way, the central bank is bound to attain more independence regardless of any legal provisions.

As Bernie Fraser pointed out at the Symposium: "Central banks have a vested interest in the smooth working of government debt markets for two reasons. Firstly, they usually conduct their policy operations in these markets and rely on them to transmit the effect of their policy

---

[2]Again, the evidence presented in Part II suggests that "cheap" finance is actually extremely costly in terms of high inflation and low growth.

actions as effectively as possible. Secondly, yields on government debt can provide information, such as expectations about inflation, which may be of interest to policy makers."

6.4.1 Two Historical Examples

One early example, mirrored by the 1994 agreement between the Reserve Bank of India and the Government of India, is the 1951 Accord between the US Treasury and the Federal Reserve System. Milton Friedman and Anna Schwartz (1963, 620–627) note that the Federal Reserve was committed to fixing the price of government securities during the Second World War and that monetary policy had been determined by the Treasury since 1933. The commitment was continued after the war in the interests of ensuring "the orderliness and stability of the Government securities market" (Board of Governors of the Federal Reserve System 1947, 3).[3]

The outbreak of the Korean War in 1950 produced, on the one hand, a speculative boom requiring monetary tightening and, on the other hand, the expectation of larger government deficits making the Treasury all the more anxious about the state of the government securities market. After failing to sell a new issue of five-year notes at $1\frac{1}{2}$ percent, the Treasury blamed the Fed for lack of cooperation. Conferences were then arranged in January and February 1951 attended by President Truman, Treasury and Federal Reserve officials, chairmen of the Congressional banking committees and the chairman of the Joint Committee on the Economic Report. An agreement, known as the Accord, was reached in early March 1951. It relieved the Fed from the obligation of supporting the government security market at pegged prices. After the support of government security prices was abandoned, two new criteria for monetary policy, "to restrict bank credit and monetary expansion to the growth needs of the economy" over the longer term and to "lean against the wind" in the short term, were adopted (Friedman and Schwartz 1963, 628–631).

Ironically, in this instance the US Treasury understood better than the Fed that supporting government bond prices jeopardised monetary control. Within a few years of the Accord, the Treasury fully endorsed the principle that the government should pay the market interest rate, whatever it might be, rather than hold down rates and thereby risk

---

[3] Rudiger Dornbusch (1996, 9) classifies this as a standard case of financial repression.

inflation. This principle had already been accepted by Italy in 1947 and Germany in 1948 (Friedman and Schwartz 1963, 626).

The UK also pursued a cheap-money policy in the aftermath of the Second World War. In 1946–1947, the Chancellor of the Exchequer embarked on a strategy of forcing down the long-term interest rate from 3 to $2\frac{1}{2}$ percent. This low rate, however, could be maintained only by huge purchases of government bonds by the Public Departments (the Post Office Savings Bank, the trustee savings banks, the social security funds and the Issue Department of the Bank of England). In the words of Richard Sayers (1967, 208):

> The 'unnaturally' high prices of securities—the prices that represented the $2\frac{1}{2}$ per cent. yield—could be held only by continued official buying of the long-term securities. As more and more holders of government securities came to believe that this was a mere juggling operation and that prices must fall, more and more unloaded their holdings and the official support began to involve an enormous pumping of money into the market [deposit money increased by 20 percent in just over a year]. In the months of disillusion that began in February 1947, the authorities took fright at the length to which they were having to go in support of the $2\frac{1}{2}$ per cent. line, and they withdrew their support. Gilt-edged prices promptly fell away, and the long-term rate was soon fractionally above 3 per cent., a level thereafter held for some considerable time by a free market, because people thought this a level that, given the various government controls, could reasonably be held.

6.4.2　The Case Study Countries

Turning to the case study countries, the benefits of abandoning the system of captive buyers for government securities in India's case were expounded in the Report of the Committee to Review the Working of the Monetary System in 1985, in the Presidential Address to the Indian Economic Association by the Deputy Governor of the Reserve Bank of India in 1988, in the Report of the Committee on the Financial System in 1991 and finally in the Kutty Memorial Lecture on Autonomy of the Central Bank by the Governor of the Reserve Bank of India in 1993. The Minister of Finance acknowledged the case against automatic monetisation of the government's deficit through the issue of *ad hoc* treasury bills in the Budget Speech of July 1994 and a formal agreement between the Reserve Bank and the Government of India to phase out this method of financing over a three-year period was signed in September 1994.

The Ghanaian government was made aware of the inflationary nature of central bank deficit financing and of the fact that captive buyers created distortions in the financial markets. In Jamaica, most of the disadvantages of captive buyers and the advantages of market-determined yields on government securities listed in section 6.3 were used to persuade the main political actors of the need for change. By the mid-1970s, both the Banco de México and Mexico's Ministry of Finance were convinced of the need to abandon interest-rate ceilings and the compulsory financing of government deficits. The belief that market mechanisms would reduce inefficiencies and increase the effectiveness of monetary policy was already widespread.

The new government that took power in New Zealand in 1984 was philosophically attracted to market mechanisms, it recognised the benefits accruing abroad from adopting of market-based mechanisms (particularly in Australia) and it felt that dramatic change was needed at home. Hence, this government was already convinced of the rationale for change and needed only advice on the technical details.

As in the case of India, the Central Bank of Sri Lanka initiated a dialogue with the Minister of Finance in which the indirect costs and distortionary impact of tapping captive buyers were discussed. At the same time, emphasis was placed on the economic benefits of developing a voluntary domestic market and how this was entirely compatible with the government's overall market-orientated economic philosophy.

In Zimbabwe's case, the planned reduction of the government deficit from double-digit levels to below 5 percent of GDP was used as an argument that captive buyers of government securities were no longer needed. The point was also made that liberalisation of financial markets was an integral part of the market-based structural adjustment process to which the government was already committed.

6.5 Macroeconomic Prerequisites

After a lengthy survey of financial systems and development, the World Bank concludes that there are four key prerequisites for successful financial liberalisation: macroeconomic stability, fiscal discipline, improved legal, accounting and regulatory systems for the financial sector, and a tax system that does not discriminate excessively against finance (World Bank 1989, 1). Financial liberalisation is itself a prerequisite for developing voluntary domestic markets for government debt.

6.5.1   Macroeconomic Stability

Price stability is a crucial prerequisite for developing markets for longer-term fixed-interest financial claims. High and variable inflation often destroys existing financial markets and prevents many potential financial markets from developing. In Jamaica, for example, continued high inflation has impeded development of the market for fixed-rate government bonds.

On the other hand, certain financial instruments such as indexed bonds can be and have been used to promote stability. Indeed, indexation has been used in Brazil, Chile and Israel to sustain financial markets in the face of ongoing inflation. Among the case study countries, Mexico developed markets for indexed bonds under inflationary conditions. But this can be only a short-term remedy or technique for assisting other stabilisation measures. In long-run equilibrium, indexation erodes the government's revenue from inflation. Hence, fiscal adjustment must be included as the major component of a stabilisation programme.

Containing inflation requires monetary control and fiscal discipline. Macroeconomic stability also necessitates consistent macroeconomic policies, in particular monetary and exchange rate policies that are consistent with the fiscal stance. Policy coordination is stressed repeatedly as essential for successful development of a market for government debt. Without coordination, real interest rates can rise, the private sector may be crowded out and government debt-servicing costs can become explosive.

6.5.2   Coordination

Coordination can take place within three alternative frameworks. In the first, the central bank determines the change in reserve money, which provides partial financing of the government's deficit, and the deficit is then set in the light of the feasible remaining financing possibilities. In the second, the deficit is predetermined and the central bank increases reserve money to finance it. In the third, the change in reserve money and the deficit are set independently, leaving the change in government debt as the residual. But debt can be residual only if interest rates are allowed to find levels at which it can all be sold.

If monetary policy is to be independent, the general level of interest rates must be treated as exogenous to the debt-management process, although there may be some play in the yield curve. Otherwise, monetary control and the development of financial markets are both undermined.

The challenge then is to adopt a debt management strategy that is compatible with the broader goals of monetary stability and the development of financial markets. Venkataraman Sundararajan, Peter Dattels, Ian McCarthy, Marta Castello-Branco and Hans Blommestein (1996) suggest that coordination within the third framework must involve:

- Limiting central bank credit to the government.

- Establishing a macroeconomic coordination committee that includes representatives of the central bank and ministry of finance.

- Sharing information.

- Agreeing rules for dealing with central bank profits and losses.

- Promoting secondary market development.

Lack of coordination in the case study countries is exemplified by the experiences of Jamaica, Sri Lanka and Zimbabwe. In Jamaica, a restrictive monetary policy confronted an expansionary fiscal stance. This was resolved partially by the issue of Bank of Jamaica paper and reverse repurchase (repo) agreements, actions that contributed to central bank losses. Reverse repos were also introduced by the Central Bank of Sri Lanka in November 1995 to counteract rising interest rates emanating from increased government borrowing. Earlier in 1995, the Central Bank had issued its own paper to mop up excess liquidity also caused by increased government borrowing. In Zimbabwe, the government's interest costs have remained unnecessarily high due to poor cash flow forecasting on the part of the Ministry of Finance as well as to the excessive deficit.

6.5.3 Tightening Monetary Policy

As Rudiger Dornbusch (1996, 14) points out, tightening monetary policy can worsen a government's debt problem in four ways:

- It raises the real interest rate so increasing debt service and, *ceteris paribus*, accelerating the growth in debt.

- It reduces the primary surplus by dampening economic activity, so reducing tax revenue and increasing unemployment-related expenditures.

- It slows the growth rate, so accelerating the rise in the debt/GDP ratio.

- It reduces seigniorage revenue by decelerating the rate of growth in reserve money, implying that a larger proportion of the deficit must be financed by increased debt.

To the extent that a tighter monetary policy reduces inflationary expectations, however, there may be an immediate decline in long-term interest rates that benefits the fiscal situation. Following Thomas Sargent and Neil Wallace (1981), Dornbusch (1996, 15–16) concludes that high government deficits and debt destroy credibility in conservative monetary policy. Facing either a big inflation in the future to erode the debt or oppressive taxation to service it,

> the monetary authorities face a dilemma in that they will be seen as contributing to if not creating single-handedly a major social problem. A fading confidence in the pursuit of hard money is therefore close at hand. The only resolution of the dilemma, as Sargent-Wallace note in their premonition of the Maastricht criteria, is low debt and low deficits.

In other words, it is not enough to persuade the main political actors that inflationary finance and financial repression are growth-reducing ways of financing deficits. It is also essential to persuade the main political actors that debts and deficits must be kept within sustainable bounds after inflationary finance and financial repression are abandoned. Hence, the primary macroeconomic prerequisite for developing voluntary domestic markets for government debt is a sustainable government deficit.

6.5.4 The Case Study Countries

Experience in the case study countries bears out Dornbusch's point. The need for improved budgetary positions was recognised explicitly in the questionnaire responses from India, Jamaica, Sri Lanka and Zimbabwe. However, the outcomes in these countries did not meet expectations. Over the period 1989–1993, India's average deficit of 7 percent, Sri Lanka's of 8.6 percent and Zimbabwe's of 7.8 percent are well above average. While the government deficit in Sri Lanka has been reduced from around 16 percent of GDP in the early 1980s to about 8 percent, it is well understood that this is still excessive. In 1995, the real yield on Sri Lankan treasury bills exceeded 10 percent. It is probably not coincidental that, in general, the highest deficit countries have been least successful in their attempts to liberalise their financial systems and to develop voluntary markets for government debt.

On the Maastricht criterion, Ghana, Jamaica, Malaysia, Mexico and New Zealand have posted deficits well below the 3 percent ceiling.[4] Although the Ghanaian government ran budget surpluses from 1986 to 1992, high inflation leading to high interest rates exerted substantial pressure on the government budget. The high interest rates also produced political pressure on the government to subsidise credit for priority sectors. The Malaysian government posted surpluses in the last two years, 1993 and 1994, for which data exist. To achieve its aim of reducing the debt/GDP ratio, the New Zealand government has run budget surpluses since 1987, except in 1992. In Mexico, the deficit was reduced from 14 percent of GDP in 1987 to zero by 1991; surpluses were posted in 1992 and 1993.

Turning to debt trajectories, New Zealand's government debt declined from a peak of 67 percent of GDP in 1986 to 54 percent in 1994.[5] The Indian government's debt has remained around 50 percent of GDP since the mid-1980s, Sri Lanka's has hovered around 90 percent of GDP since 1988, while Zimbabwe's debt ratio peaked in 1992 at 65 percent of GDP and has since fallen to 39 percent in 1995.[6]

While no data are available on total government debt for the other countries, government plus government-guaranteed debt ratios in Ghana (up from 7 percent of GDP in 1980 to 54 percent in 1993) and India (up from 10 percent in 1980 to 29 percent in 1993) have risen steadily. Over shorter periods, government and government-guaranteed debt ratios have fallen recently in Malaysia (from 55 percent in 1987 to 22 percent in 1993), Mexico (from 59 percent in 1987 to 20 percent in 1993), Sri Lanka (from 61 percent in 1989 to 55 percent in 1993) and Zimbabwe (from 48 percent in 1992 to 38 percent in 1994).

On the Maastricht criterion, therefore, Malaysia, Mexico and Zimbabwe are well under the 60 percent ceiling, while India is just under. Although debt ratios in Jamaica of over 100 percent and in Sri Lanka of around 90 percent have stabilised, their levels must give rise to concern. When compared to median debt ratios that have risen in

---

[4] Although government finance statistics for Jamaica have not been published in *IFS* since 1985, the Bank of Jamaica provided the relevant data up to 1993 for this study. They indicate government surpluses from 1988 to 1991 and deficits averaging only 1 percent of GDP in 1992 and 1993.

[5] Debt data for 1992–1994 were provided by the Reserve Bank of New Zealand; the data series published in *IFS* end in 1991.

[6] These figures were provided by the Reserve Bank of Zimbabwe; data for Zimbabwe's debt since 1990 have not been published in *IFS*.

all country groups since 1979, it seems reasonable to conclude that the main political actors in the case study countries were aware of the arithmetic behind the government's intertemporal budget constraint when they embarked on programmes to develop voluntary domestic markets for their government debt. In no case has government debt exploded in the aftermath of liberalisation.

6.5.5   Supervision and Regulation

Although some readers of his 1973 book may have assumed otherwise, Ronald McKinnon (1986, 326) states that "successful liberalisation is not simply a question of removing all regulations." There has been increasing awareness that a prerequisite for successful financial liberalisation is strong bank supervision. Financial liberalisation involving substantial increases in real rates of interest is bound to produce some casualties. Indeed, this must happen if resource allocation is to be improved by the liberalisation. Supervision is needed to ensure that weak financial institutions are detected early and liquidated or merged in an orderly fashion before their managements start engaging in perverse behaviour (Ponzi-type lending) of the kind observed in Chile in the mid-1970s that escalates real interest rates to pathologically high levels.

There exists, however, no analytical framework dealing with the relationship between financial liberalisation and financial regulation for prudential and monetary control (Darity and Horn 1986). First, there is the tricky theoretical issue of the relationship between financial liberalisation and adequate regulation, which revolves around the theory of the second-best. Then there are the practical problems of differentiating appropriate from inappropriate regulations, delineating appropriate regulatory frameworks, and examining on a case-by-case basis the most suitable supervisory systems to enforce the regulations (Caprio *et al.* 1994, Stiglitz 1994, Sundararajan and Baliño 1991, Tseng and Corker 1991).

Questionnaire responses highlighted the need for a proper regulatory and supervisory framework for securities' trading (Jamaica) and for strengthening the supervisory powers of the National Securities Commission to improve oversight and dissemination of information on traded securities (Mexico). Many other prerequisites relating to financial infrastructure were mentioned. Some of these are discussed in the subsequent two chapters.

6.6 Sequencing

Developing markets for government debt has never occurred overnight. As Bernie Fraser suggested: "The important first step for any country is to gain investor confidence in government debt and to build and maintain a good reputation for issuing and honouring debt." The process is necessarily one of learning-by-doing as much on the part of the authorities as on the part of the private sector. It is usually also a process of learning from one's mistakes.

David Cole, Hal Scott and Philip Wellons (1995, 19) identify four stages in the typical development process:

1. The controlled system.

2. Initial liberalisation.

3. Retrenchment after crisis.

4. More aggressive development.

The first step invariably takes the form of some interest rate liberalisation. The crisis can take various forms: exchange-rate or balance-of-payments problems, recession, excessive liquidity or fraud. The reaction is to "shoot the messenger" and reimpose controls. After the crisis abates, a second attempt is launched in the light of the previous experience.

In recent years, many developing countries have initiated strategies to develop financial markets by establishing auctions for treasury bills. For example, Ghana started auctioning 91-day, 180-day, 1-year and 2-year government and central bank paper in 1987. Later, 30-day, 3-year and 5-year maturities were offered. India also started an auction system for 182-day treasury bills in 1986; both shorter- and longer-term maturities were subsequently auctioned. While starting at the shorter end of the maturity spectrum seems obvious, particularly in countries that have recently suffered high inflation, this sequencing was not followed in New Zealand. There auctions of longer-term government debt had taken place for many years before the introduction of treasury bill auctions.

A typical element of sequencing has been the reduction in excessive reserve and liquid asset ratio requirements, although abolition has often been resisted on the grounds that such ratios still serve prudential purposes. In the case study countries, for example, India adopted a medium-term strategy of reducing the statutory liquidity ratio from

$38\frac{1}{2}$ percent to 25 percent in phases starting in 1992. To the extent that adoption of a capital-adequacy requirement is feasible, however, this should form a preferable alternative to most balance-sheet ratio constraints.

To the extent that they remain binding, liquid asset ratio requirements maintain captive buyers and so distort price signals emanating from treasury bill auctions and impede the market development process. In Malaysia, for example, maintaining a required liquid asset ratio increased demand in the primary market but hindered development of the secondary market (Cole, Scott and Wellons 1995, 35).

In the wake of the foreign debt crisis, Mexico liberalised interest rates in October 1982 in order to create a noninflationary source of government borrowing. The initial measure took the form of a weekly auction of *Cetes* at rates determined by the market. Because of continued high inflation, Mexico has introduced price- and exchange rate-indexed government securities. By 1994 the CPI- and exchange rate-indexed bonds had become by far the most popular form of government debt. From a minimal share in the early 1980s, marketable instruments constituted 100 percent of government debt by 1991.

Much of the basic infrastructure already existed when New Zealand instigated its dramatic measures of financial liberalisation in 1984. Its approach to sequencing was to do what could be done when it was possible to do it. All interest-rate controls, which had been in place for less than a year, were removed immediately. With a framework already in place for calculating required sales of government securities and by adopting a "clean" tendering system with no floor price from mid-1984, the old system of balance-sheet ratio controls quickly became redundant. These ratio controls were removed along with regulatory barriers on activities across all financial institutions over the following years.

Foreign participation in the New Zealand bond market became significant after withholding taxes were removed; 50 percent of New Zealand government securities are now held by foreigners. That there would be such a large shift in the government's borrowing from abroad to domestic currency-denominated debt had not been anticipated at the outset. While it reduced the fiscal cost of government debt, this capital inflow appreciated the exchange rate. At the Symposium, Donald Brash explained that "if inflationary pressure is intense in the nontradables sector and nonexistent in the tradables sector, this downward pressure on interest rates and upward pressure on the exchange rate may not be entirely helpful." This is New Zealand's monetary policy dilemma in the mid-1990s.

Donald Brash also pointed out that a switch from foreign to domestic borrowing could have unintended signalling effects. When New Zealand tightened monetary policy to achieve its announced policy target of low inflation, this implied an expected appreciation in the exchange rate. In fact, however, uncertainty about the government's commitment and ability to achieve this target kept domestic-currency yields much higher than yields on the New Zealand government's foreign currency-denominated debt. Under such conditions, a policy of switching from foreign to domestic currency-denominated debt could be interpreted by the market as a lack of credibility in its inflation target on the part of the government itself. With a low inflation outcome, the government would be paying higher real rates to borrow in domestic currency than it would pay to borrow in foreign currency. Therefore, a policy of reducing both domestic and foreign currency-denominated debt together with sales of shorter-maturity domestic debt might have been interpreted by the market as more consistent with a belief in its own inflation target. Indeed, the New Zealand government's funding strategy was revised in the light of this signalling problem.

Sri Lanka started a gradual process of financial liberalisation in the late 1970s as part of an overall economic reform programme; elsewhere I have identified 1978 as a year in which structural change took place (Fry 1990). Various legal changes were required before the development of a primary market in treasury bills was launched. Subsequently, a secondary market for treasury bills was developed. The authorities are now planning to develop markets for medium- and long-term government debt. However, the statutory reserve ratio has remained high at 15 percent, initially to counteract the expansionary impact of capital inflows caused by high interest rates, but in 1995 to counteract the considerable increase in the public sector's borrowing requirement.

Zimbabwe's market development programme starting in 1990 comprised the deregulation of interest rates, the reduction in the prescribed asset ratio for banks from 60 to 55 percent, the removal of the Reserve Bank's and discount houses' obligations to underwrite government debt issues, and the abandonment of the Reserve Bank's daily calculation and dissemination of government stock prices. The Reserve Bank stopped fixing interest rates in 1991 and exchange controls were relaxed in 1993 to enable foreigners to buy government securities in the primary market.

6.7   Risk Perceptions

In recent years, sovereign risk has been studied extensively in the aftermath of Mexico's default in 1982. However, sovereign risk preceded the Mexican crisis by many centuries. One example, revolving around Thomas Gresham, inventor of Gresham's Law, dates from the sixteenth century.

Gresham was the first of a new breed—the merchant prince. Born about 1518, he graduated from Cambridge University at the age of 16. In 1543 he received his first commission as Royal Agent; in this capacity he was to buy gunpowder for King Henry VIII. While living in Antwerp, Gresham established a highly successful commercial business and also devoted considerable time and effort as Royal Agent to negotiating foreign loans for Henry VIII, Edward IV, Mary and Elizabeth I.

As Gresham's private wealth increased, so did his concern over the Crown's mounting debts. He became determined to reduce the rate of interest on England's foreign loans. Gresham might well have become famous for his maxims on public finance. He put two of them successfully into effect while in Antwerp: it is better to borrow to repay debts than to reschedule them; interest must be paid punctually when due. As a result of Gresham's efforts, the Crown's credit standing rose, except in the first year of Mary's reign, when Gresham, a Protestant, was relieved of his official duties. He succeeded in reducing the interest rate on foreign loans from 14 to 10 percent compared with the prime rate in the mid-sixteenth century that remained a fairly constant 7 percent; sovereigns were not generally prime borrowers in those days.

After Queen Elizabeth I acceded to the throne in 1558, Thomas Gresham's influence at court rose. He wrote a long letter to the new monarch in which he explained England's contemporary monetary problems (Burgon 1839, Vol. I, 484):

> It may please Your Majesty to understand that the first occasion of the fall of the Exchange [rate] did grow by the King's Majesty, your late Father, in abasing his coin from six ounces fine to three ounces fine. Whereupon the Exchange fell from $26^s/8^d$ to $13^s/4^d$, which was the occasion that all your fine gold was conveyed out of this your realm.

The last sentence in this quotation was Gresham's statement of Gresham's law. The bad or abased (debased) money drives the good money out of circulation. Alternatively, the overvalued money drives out the undervalued money.

Henry VIII's expenses had invariably exceeded his regular tax revenue. One of his solutions was recoinage. The coins that came in as tax payments were melted down with some scrap metal. By adding an equal weight of scrap metal to the old coins, Henry VIII could produce twice the amount of money—just what he needed. However, the quantity of money increased as he spent these new coins. Doubling the money supply in this way guaranteed inflation. Prices of everything, including silver, rose. The value of silver in an old, undebased coin soon exceeded the coin's face value. The same happened to gold coins; gold coins had not been debased.

Thomas Gresham explained clearly the outcome of Henry VIII's currency debasements. The new, bad money drove the old, good money out of circulation and the exchange rate fell. Good money was melted down for its silver content, hoarded or, in the case of gold coins, used to buy goods abroad. Foreigners were unwilling to accept the debased currency, foreign trade was disrupted, and Gresham found it more difficult to raise foreign loans for Henry VIII. Potential lenders feared, with good reason, that they would be repaid in debased coins. Eventually, the rate of exchange fell from 180 old silver pennies to one gold sovereign to 360 new, debased pennies to the sovereign.

There are two ironic twists to the story of Gresham's law. First, Gresham persuaded Queen Elizabeth to restore England's silver coins to their traditional sterling fineness of 925 parts of silver in 1000. In other words, he was responsible for the substitution of good money for bad money—the opposite of Gresham's law.

The second twist is that Gresham's law had already been known for 2000 years. In *The Frogs*, first produced in Athens in 405 BC, Aristophanes (1964, 182–183) wrote:

> I'll tell you what I think about the way
> This city treats her soundest men today:
> By a coincidence more sad than funny,
> It's very like the way we treat our money.
> The noble silver drachma, that of old
> We were so proud of, and the recent gold,
> Coins that rang true, clean-stamped and worth their weight
> Throughout the world, have ceased to circulate.
> Instead, the purses of Athenian shoppers
> Are full of shoddy silver-plated coppers.
> Just so, when men are needed by the nation,
> The best have been withdrawn from circulation.

Just as it took time for Gresham to improve the track record of the English monarchy, so it takes time for any government to establish a new track record of sound finance. At the start of any initiative to develop voluntary domestic markets for government debt, the authorities are bound to face a suspicious and unwilling private sector. Their record is one of confiscation; the promise of attractive market yields is unlikely to be believed before some credibility has been earned. This implies that market yields on government debt will embody a significant risk premium, mainly taking the specific form of an inflation-risk premium. Once the debt has been sold, the private sector may reason, the government will have an incentive to inflate its way out of its obligations returning to the old confiscatory pattern, as did Henry VIII.

Initially, therefore, voluntary lenders demand a risk premium from government, just as they did in the sixteenth century. From the government's perspective, it is paying too high an interest rate immediately after the switch to voluntary domestic market financing. From the private sector's perspective, caution dictates the extraction of a risk premium before it can be enticed to lend.

One solution that can help reconcile the government's commitment to turn over a new leaf with the private sector's doubts that this has really happened is for the government to issue debt that is automatically adjusted for changes in the price level, i.e., index-linked debt, at the outset of its reform. Much of the literature on indexation (e.g., Dornbusch and Simonsen 1983, Gleizer 1995, McNelis 1988) concentrates on its role in a stabilisation programme rather than as a specific instrument for use in the process of developing voluntary domestic markets for government debt. For articles focusing more on the market-development and fiscal aspects of price-indexed debt in such countries as Australia, Canada and the United Kingdom, the interested reader may consult the Bank of England (1996b).

At the Symposium, Donald Brash said that, in retrospect, one of the important lessons learnt from New Zealand's reform experience was that index-linked debt could have been issued to great benefit at the start of the reforms in 1984. If one of the legacies of past inflation is a high risk premium embedded in nominal yields, then indexed bonds can offer large savings for the government in terms of lower interest costs so reducing the likelihood of igniting a Ponzi game, provided its new commitment to fiscal discipline and price stability is effective. An issue of index-linked debt can also enhance credibility in the new regime: the government can no longer benefit from surprise inflation to erode the real value of its debt, so has less incentive to renege in this way.

It is particularly noteworthy that the experience in New Zealand indicates the existence of a high risk premium after the 1984 reforms. Part of the reform package consisted of making price stability the only objective of monetary policy and in giving the Reserve Bank full independence to achieve this single objective. Furthermore, the Governor's emoluments are dependent on the achievement of this objective. Although these measures undoubtedly contributed to building credibility for low inflation and therefore facilitated the development of the voluntary domestic market for government debt, the erosion of this risk premium occurred only gradually. From levels of 18 to 19 percent in the mid-1980s, yields on 10-year domestic-currency government bonds have fallen to around $8\frac{1}{2}$ percent. For a few months in 1994, the New Zealand government was able to sell 10-year bonds at a slightly lower yield than the US government.

One problem is that consumer price indices in many developing countries are distorted deliberately through the maintenance of out-of-date weights that over-represent items whose prices are controlled. In other countries where there are no deliberate distortions to the price indices at present, governments may be tempted to tamper with them once they are used to adjust nominal values of government debt. Where there is suspicion about the quality of the price index, however, there may well be even more suspicion that the government may resort to the inflation tax to reduce the value of unindexed debt. Hence, indexation may reduce suspicion overall, even when the price index is dubious.

In some countries, the government statistical office is separated to a reasonable degree from the political process. In these countries, therefore, there would probably be greater confidence in the quality of the inflation data than in the integrity of future governments. Where the statistical office has established a track record for providing reliable and unbiased statistics, the case for issuing index-linked debt at the initial stages of the market development process is extremely strong.[7]

While it may be agreed that financial claims indexed to the price level can serve a useful role in the transition from inflationary finance and financial repression to voluntary domestic financing of government deficits, several participants at the Symposium were worried that this form of indexation could lead to other forms, such as wage indexation, that could easily induce or prolong inflationary pressures. Miguel Mancera noted the distinction between indexed securities, which had a

---

[7]I am most grateful to Donald Brash for discussion and correspondence on this issue.

limited life and need not be rolled over in the same form, and indexed wage contracts, which were open-ended and could create rigidities in the economy, e.g., by making it more difficult to achieve any downward adjustment in real wages. As pointed out by Eddie George, indexation could well provide a fruitful topic for a future Symposium.

6.8   Crowding Out?

One important question is whether or not developing a new source of government financing increases government deficits. The response to this question was invariably that primary deficits had been reduced as a result of higher interest costs of debt service. Indeed, for any given operational deficit, crowding out should be reduced. This is because higher interest rates under a liberalised system will elicit more saving in financial form and so increase the aggregate supply of credit in real terms. If the government takes a fixed amount from this aggregate, there must be more, albeit at a higher interest rate for some previously privileged and favoured borrowers, for the private sector as a whole.

Recognising that a large deficit fuels inflation which, in turn, increases interest rates and so raises the deficit even more, the Ghanaian government is now introducing specific measures to "eliminate" its deficit. The Bank of Ghana's questionnaire response claims that the higher interest rates increased the cost of private capital. Therefore, "government and central bank borrowing on the securities market has led to some crowding out of private sector borrowers." However, to the extent that credit was cheap but unavailable under the old disequilibrium interest rate system, higher equilibrium interest rates may not be synonymous with crowding out. Indeed, domestic credit to the private sector actually increased from 3 to 6 percent of GDP between 1984 and 1993.

The decision to pay market interest rates on its borrowing was designed in part to impose fiscal discipline on the Indian government by signalling the real cost of its borrowing. Rising interest costs have exerted pressure on the government to reduce its deficit. Particularly in 1995/96, tax reforms and expenditure controls were stimulated by the higher real interest rates for government borrowing.

In Jamaica, "it was felt that the higher cost would serve to constrain the size of the budget deficit." Developing the market for government debt in itself did not crowd out the private sector. Growth in private sector credit occurred together with growth in government debt. However, had tighter monetary policy been pursued to fight inflation, some crowding out might have occurred during the stabilisation process.

Since the mid-1980s, the Malaysian government has maintained a policy of fiscal prudence and consolidation in order to strengthen its overall financial position. Since 1993, the government has run overall budget surpluses enabling it to reduce its outstanding debt. Hence, no crowding out has been detected.

Between 1982 and 1987, a period of relatively high and volatile inflation, servicing its debt represented a considerable fraction of the Mexican government's current expenditures and increased the difficulties of controlling government finances. In conjunction with regulated deposit rates in the banking system, high free-market yields on government debt caused disintermediation and crowding out of private sector borrowers.

The reduction in inflation and the consequent decline in nominal interest rates in Mexico since 1987 have facilitated efforts to tighten fiscal discipline. With the liberalisation of bank interest rates in 1989 and the elimination of reserve requirements and other methods of compulsory financing of the government deficit, the private sector's share of domestic credit has increased. The experience of the early 1980s combined with "the existence of a well-developed market for government debt, in which government securities offer competitive yields, has contributed to imposing fiscal discipline on the fiscal authorities."

In New Zealand's case, the government was committed to reducing deficits and debt in conjunction with its market development programme. Therefore, although the voluntary system made it easier to finance larger deficits, use was not made of this facility.

The financial community in Sri Lanka became more aware of fiscal management when they found themselves competing with the government for domestic financial resources. Sectors that had previously benefited from subsidised interest rates faced higher interest costs as they now had to compete with the government in an open market. However, the government's rising interest bill constituted one of the major factors behind a major fiscal adjustment in Sri Lanka. By 1995, interest payment on domestic debt had reached almost 25 percent of the government's current expenditure. Despite the fiscal reform, there is fear that any continuation of high deficits could produce an unsustainable fiscal situation.

The anticipated reduction in the government deficit failed to materialise in Zimbabwe; it has remained in or close to double-digit levels. Here the situation depicted in Figure 6.5 seems to apply, with higher interest rates contributing to higher deficits. Real interest rates rose from around −5 percent in 1992 to positive double-digit levels in early 1995. High domestic interest rates have reduced lending to and encouraged increased foreign borrowing by the private sector. In the year to March 1995, domestic credit increased for the private sector by 18 percent (a decline in real terms), by 39 percent for public enterprises and by 106 percent for the government.

6.9 Implementing Monetary Policy

Developing markets for government debt provides the central bank with the opportunity to adopt indirect market-based techniques for implementing monetary policy. Abandoning direct controls in favour of indirect market-based techniques can be expected to improve efficiency: all agents face the same market constraint in the form of the market interest rate in their lending and borrowing decisions. This unified market system improves the efficiency with which investible funds are allocated. Formerly, this allocation took place under fragmented market conditions in which agents faced different price signals.

Among the case study countries, development of a market for government debt in Ghana has assisted monetary policy implementation through open-market operations.[8] It has also increased central bank independence in that the government now has access to nonbank sources of funds.

The agreement between the government and the Reserve Bank of India to phase out the automatic monetisation of government deficits by 1997–1998 has facilitated the adoption of indirect market-based methods of implementing monetary policy. Not only has the Reserve Bank been able to lower reserve requirements, but also it has increased interest rate flexibility. The Reserve Bank's ability to conduct open-market operations has been strengthened considerably. Major innovations in monetary policy implementation included the introduction of Reserve Bank auctions of repos in government long-term securities in December 1992 followed by reverse repo facilities in December 1994.

However, the Indian government's large borrowing requirements in 1995/96 combined with reduced capital inflows have recently circumscribed the extent to which the Reserve Bank could in fact implement

---

[8] Many developing country monetary authorities define treasury bill auctions as open-market operations.

open-market operations for monetary policy purposes. To prevent real interest rates from rising to even higher levels, the Reserve Bank acquired 17.3 percent of the government's primary issues during 1995/96, up from only 1 percent in 1994/95.

Typically, the use of indirect market-based instruments of monetary policy involves a transition from setting interest rates to adopting quantitative targets. For example, Zimbabwe adopted targets for both reserve money and domestic credit in late 1991. Realising that markets cannot develop if rediscount facilities are available without limit at a fixed interest rate approximately equal to the treasury bill yield, the Bank of Jamaica introduced penal rates at the rediscount window in order to discourage early encashment of government securities and hence also to promote secondary market trading. Development of the market for government debt has enabled the Bank of Jamaica to adopt indirect market-based techniques of monetary control through its acquisition of marketable government debt.

The Banco de México acts as financial agent of the government and so handles all the placing and redeeming of government debt. Cooperation with the Ministry of Finance has enabled the Bank to conduct open-market operations entirely with government securities in the secondary market rather than issuing its own paper. Until the Constitutional Reform in November 1993, however, the Banco de México's ability to implement monetary policy was constrained by the government's reluctance to pay market rates at auctions. After the Constitutional Reform, which granted autonomy to the Banco de México and prohibited the government from forcing the Bank to extend it credit, the government has rarely intervened in the auction process. Together with the full liberalisation of interest rates, the Bank has been able to conduct monetary policy through open-market operations using government securities. More recently, however, the reduction in government domestic debt has required the Bank to implement monetary policy through collateralised credit auctions using private sector claims as collateral.

In Sri Lanka, the development of a voluntary domestic market for treasury bills facilitated a move towards the use of indirect instruments of monetary policy, such as open market operations. It also helped the development of the money market and enabled the Central Bank to minimise the inflationary impact of the government's deficit.

The development of a market for government debt in Zimbabwe has enabled the Reserve Bank to adopt indirect market-based monetary policy techniques. It has also released the Bank from taking up government debt automatically as buyer of last resort.

6.10   Pitfalls

Questionnaire responses highlight two major pitfalls experienced by the case study countries.   The first was the failure of fiscal reform that seriously impeded the development of voluntary domestic markets for government debt.   On the one hand, high and rising deficits raise real interest rates that crowd out private sector investors while, on the other hand, keeping real rates artificially low implies a return to inflationary finance.   A continued commitment to fiscal discipline is therefore essential for the success of the lengthy process of developing such markets.

The second major pitfall lay in the pervasive mistrust of market mechanisms among officials steeped in nonmarket systems, the ubiquitous belief by the authorities that they knew better than the markets. On occasion, these gut reactions against market signals hindered market development.   For example, the Bank of Jamaica failed to conduct open-market sales of government debt because its selling price was above the market price for lengthy periods.   The belief in an "appropriate rate" also stalled development in Mexico where auctions were abandoned in 1985/86.   In Sri Lanka, some business groups exerted political pressure to limit the rise in interest rates.

The reluctance to let go and to rely on market forces also applies to balance sheet ratio requirements.   Maintaining the old system of ratio controls as a safeguard or fallback should things go wrong with the indirect market-based approach to implementing monetary policy has damaged or retarded market development.   For example, high liquid asset ratio requirements in Jamaica have distorted the pricing mechanism, particularly when the volume of government debt eligible as liquid assets fell short of the volume needed to satisfy the requirement.[9]   Jamaica's cash reserve requirement of 25 percent and liquid asset requirement of 50 percent are typical features of financial repression.   The 50 percent liquid asset ratio ensures a strong take-up of treasury bills and variable-rate bonds that are eligible liquid assets.

Nevertheless, too much innovation at too fast a pace may also be counterproductive.   For example, India's experience with the early introduction of repo markets in 1992 indicates that payment and settlement

---

[9]Shortages of eligible assets have occurred frequently in several other countries, e.g., Mauritius, that maintain high liquid asset ratio requirements after espousing indirect market-based monetary policy implementation.

systems may need to be streamlined and computerised before the introduction of such innovative instruments.

In some cases, incipient instability in the early stages of the transition process can be eliminated by installing various safety nets to act as stabilisers. For example, before reducing liquid asset ratio requirements, auctions might be aimed at producing voluntary holdings of treasury bills at the margin. In other words, banks would be persuaded to hold more treasury bills than the required minimum. Testing the water in this way could prevent violent swings in treasury bill yields as the liquid asset ratio requirement was subsequently phased out in, say, increments of 5 percentage points per month or per quarter. Various other direct controls, such as credit ceilings, can be made redundant through the application of appropriate market-based monetary policy actions before they are actually abolished. Not only do such procedures provide safety nets against unforeseen and unwanted market reactions, but also they can bolster confidence in those who view the whole transition as a perilous venture into uncharted waters.

The case study countries faced two other problems in developing markets for government debt that might be classified as subsidiary pitfalls. The first arises from pervasive vested interests created under controlled market conditions. As pointed out in Chapter 4, financial restriction involves protecting the commercial banks from which government can expropriate significant seigniorage and discouraging direct markets. Not too surprisingly, when the government develops direct markets not only for its own debt but for private debt as well, commercial banks face a competitive threat. Nonbank investors can be intimidated to some extent from participating in direct markets by fear of reprisals in some form or another from their banks. Aggressive competition among banks should prevent such behaviour, so measures to ensure vigorous competition may be needed at the start of the market development programme. At the same time, prudential supervision and regulation can play a vital role in maintaining stable rather than unstable competitive conditions.

To enhance competition, measures to broaden the investor base from the outset appear crucial. These may include advertising as well as improving access for nonbank participants at treasury bill auctions. Indeed, if the major investors remain commercial banks, portfolio adjustments by the banking system as whole in response to changing business conditions may be constrained or disruptive. If there are no other holders of treasury bills, the banking system will perforce have to hold the same volume even though it would now prefer to reduce such holdings in favour of loans to the private sector. In such case, treasury bill yields must adjust by possibly large amounts. With a broad and deep market for treasury bills, however, banks can use these assets as shock absorbers against fluctuations in both deposits and loan demand. Under such conditions, it is typical to find that banks decrease their holdings of government securities and increase their loans during economic upswings (Fry and Williams 1984, 92–93).

The second subsidiary pitfall concerns foreign participation. For example, India's continued sizeable fiscal deficit is held responsible for high real interest rates. These led to strong capital inflows in 1993/94 and 1994/95. In order to prevent a real appreciation of the rupee, the Reserve Bank of India intervened to buy foreign exchange and sterilised the monetary consequences through open-market operations. With the slowdown in capital inflows in 1995/96, however, it has become increasingly expensive to fund the government's borrowing requirements. The result has been a further rise in real interest rates. As Mexico can also attest, sudden and sizeable swings in capital flows increase volatility in both domestic interest rates and exchange rates. In New Zealand, foreign capital inflows produced an overvaluation of the real exchange rate after the 1984 liberalisation which may have raised the costs of disinflation. Sri Lanka's continued high government deficit also led to high real interest rates that crowded out domestic investment and encouraged excessive capital inflows.

6.11   Conclusion

Despite various unforeseen pitfalls, the general conclusion from the questionnaire responses is that the development of voluntary domestic markets for government debt has been beneficial in two distinct respects. First, it has imposed some fiscal discipline that was previously weak or nonexistent on government. Since 1979, deficits have been reduced substantially in Ghana, Jamaica, Malaysia, Mexico and New Zealand (Appendix 15). Second, it has given the central bank greater independence to pursue monetary policy more effectively through indirect market-based instruments.

In several respects, this group of countries appears to have increased macroeconomic stability. Since 1979, for example, inflation has declined substantially in Ghana, Mexico, New Zealand and Sri Lanka, while it has remained in single digits for most years in India and throughout this period in Malaysia. Only in Jamaica, where the ratio of government plus government-guaranteed foreign debt has remained over 100 percent of GDP, and in Zimbabwe, where government deficits have not been reduced noticeably, has inflation reached record levels in the 1990s.

While other countries have experienced increased ratios of government debt to GDP and many have also suffered accelerating inflation, debt ratios have fallen in Malaysia, Mexico, New Zealand and Zimbabwe, while they have stabilised in Jamaica, India and Sri Lanka, despite positive real interest rates in all countries since 1992.[10] However, in Jamaica and Sri Lanka debt ratios appear excessive at just under and just over 100 percent of GDP, respectively. Despite positive real interest rates in 1993 and 1994, Jamaica's debt ratio has actually declined since 1991.

Perhaps the most dramatic change produced by the development of domestic markets for government debt is the decline in net domestic credit to the government as a proportion of aggregate domestic credit in all eight countries: from 82 to 68 percent in Ghana, from 62 to 48 percent in India, from 59 to –30 percent in Jamaica, from 11 to 3 percent in Malaysia, from 60 to –6 percent in Mexico, from 38 to 5 percent in New Zealand, from 46 to 26 percent in Sri Lanka and from 45 to 23 percent in Zimbabwe. Such large declines are difficult to reconcile with any claims that government borrowing has crowded out the private sector, even in Zimbabwe.

As suggested earlier in this chapter, higher interest rates under a liberalised system elicit more saving in financial form, so increasing the aggregate supply of credit in real terms. If the government does not increase the amount it expropriates from this aggregate, there must be more, albeit at a higher interest rate for some previously privileged and favoured borrowers, for the private sector as a whole. In this country group, there is no evidence of Ponzi-type government behaviour or of any debt explosion.

---

[10] Jamaica is the sole exception in that it posted a strongly negative real interest rate in 1992.

Chapter 7

The Players and the Markets

7.1 Introduction

THIS CHAPTER FOCUSES ON ISSUES at the market level. While macroeconomic prerequisites have been considered in the previous chapter, I start here by examining microeconomic prerequisites. Not only
must prices be free to find their market-clearing levels, but also for an
efficient pricing outcome a sufficient number of market players must
be encouraged to compete. Efficient markets require efficient market
players who need skills that were probably not in great demand before
the financial reforms.

The main players, at least in the initial stages, are the ministry of
finance, the central bank and the financial institutions. A variety of arrangements exist for allocating government debt management responsibilities between the finance ministry and the central bank. In some OECD
countries, debt management is the responsibility of a semi-independent
government agency, e.g., the National Treasury Management Agency in
Ireland and the Swedish National Debt Office. In general terms, whatever institutional arrangements are adopted, the transition to market-
clearing asset pricing demands new skills in all three groups of players.

7.2 Microeconomic Prerequisites

The most obvious microeconomic prerequisite to developing markets
for government debt is the existence of market-clearing yields on government paper. Despite the prevalence of central bankers and finance
ministry officials who may believe that they know what the appropriate

market-clearing yields are, there is in fact no known substitute for a market-clearing mechanism such as an auction. As Bernie Fraser pointed out at the Symposium:

> For a government to establish itself successfully as a first-class borrower in financial markets, two basic conditions must be met:
>
> - the government must offer competitive yields on its debt instruments. It should not hinder the market's ability to reflect, though price signals, its demand for government debt; and
>
> - the government needs to establish a good track record in regard to its ability to pay and its capacity to honour its obligations.

Furthermore, to equate the cost of government borrowing with the opportunity cost of funds in the economy, all bids at auction must be voluntary rather than made by captive buyers. Emancipating such captive buyers is a *sine qua non* of market development. Nor can the market mechanism provide crucial feedback information if the central bank offers virtually unlimited fixed-price rediscount facilities.

The Malaysian authorities identified a number of other prerequisites:

- No tax deterrents.

- Sufficient number of well-capitalised dealers to act as market makers.

- Broad investor base.

- Relatively stable money market environment.

- Financial infrastructure ensuring transparency, minimum risk and low cost.

- Sustainable and regular issue of government debt on a predictable or preannounced schedule.

On the last item, Bernie Fraser indicated that the Australian authorities also found that "there are benefits in informing the market in broad terms of the government's funding requirements in the year ahead. The government provides information on the amount to be issued, the types of securities and, broadly, the timing of issues. This allows the market to plan its investment activities."

Regular and predictable issues of government debt may well be impeded by legislative provisions on deficit finance that are too restrictive. For example, in Romania government securities must be refinanced exactly as they mature. Not only is this unconducive to establishing a smooth and regular issuing calendar, but also it is unconducive to monetary policy coordination.

Early steps to reform the tax system may be vital because financial repression often involves distortionary taxes, such as tax duties, on direct financial instruments. Under financial repression, these taxes are usually imposed deliberately to deter the development of such instruments that might compete with indirect instruments from which seigniorage can be extracted more easily (Fry 1995, Ch. 2). In any event, a fixed-percent transaction tax expropriates a larger proportion of the interest earnings the shorter is the maturity of the financial claim. Hence, a tax of this type is inimical to the development of voluntary markets for short-term government securities and may completely stifle secondary market development.

The Mexican authorities regard legal reform taking the form of a new securities law (*Ley del Mercado de Valores*) in 1975, which institutionalised brokerage houses, reorganised securities exchanges and strengthened the supervisory powers of the National Securities Commission, as a key prerequisite for their rapid development of a market for government debt.[1] As soon as the Mexican government was able to issue new tradable financial instruments, the market expanded rapidly. In contrast, major legislative measures to strengthen central bank supervision, implement the Basle capital-adequacy guidelines, improve the market for government securities and to reduce government influence of state-owned banks were enacted only in 1995. At the Symposium, Miguel Mancera stressed two additional prerequisites in the Mexican case: (a) the willingness of the government to accept true market-clearing prices; and (b) the introduction of a book-entry transfer system for transactions in government securities.

7.3   The Players

In the early stages, the main groups of players in the market for government debt are the ministry of finance, the central bank and the financial

---

[1] Legal prerequisites are probably most acute in transitional economies such as Romania.

institutions. Most problems in the development of markets for government debt arise from one or more of these players failing to acquire the necessary skills, information systems and incentive structures required to interact successfully in a deregulated environment (Wilton 1996).

7.3.1 Finance Ministry

Arguably the ministry of finance faces the most difficult adjustment. Interacting only with captive buyers implies that the ministry did not require debt management and funding capabilities. With the transition to a voluntary competitive market, the ministry now needs treasury skills and some understanding of market mechanisms immediately. In order to develop an efficient funding strategy, the ministry will now have to forecast its cash flows, plan the maturity structure of its debt, determine the optimal menu of debt types to be issued, announce an issue schedule and simulate costs of different funding strategies under alternative macroeconomic scenarios (Wilton 1995).

Inability to perform these tasks raises funding costs, jeopardises monetary control and can easily hinder market development. For example, if the ministry fails to announce an issue schedule or funds in an erratic fashion, costs will be higher and market activity dampened. If the ministry plans and executes its funding programme to coincide with net cash outflows, however, it will automatically face buyers with excess reserves; *ceteris paribus,* the deficit increases bank reserves as a result of the transfer of government deposits from the central bank to the commercial banks.

One way to acquire the necessary expertise speedily may be to adopt a system of primary dealers. Where local expertise is lacking, nascent primary dealers may be able to recruit expatriates back from the large international financial centres at salaries above civil-service rates. To some extent, such dealers can be used as expert advisors while the ministry builds up its internal capabilities to ensure that its advisors are not providing merely self-serving recommendations.

Coordination between the ministry of finance and central bank is essential for successful market development. If the ministry cannot provide the central bank with cash flow forecasts, the central bank cannot take timely action to control the level of excess reserves in the banking system. This can then cause undesired volatility in short-term interest rates in the absence of reserve requirement averaging or nonpenal and unlimited access to the central bank's rediscount facility.

7.3.2   Central Bank

As Peter Dattels (1996) points out, the central bank is a key player in several respects in the development of voluntary markets for government debt. As the government's agent, the central bank will often be responsible for minimising debt-service costs by ensuring that the government debt market is functioning smoothly and efficiently. To implement indirect market-based monetary policy, one of the central bank's objectives is to ensure efficient price discovery as a key element in the transmission mechanism of monetary policy. Since intervention for monetary policy purposes is frequently conducted in the market for government debt, the central bank is again concerned with the organisation of that market. The central bank may also act as regulator responsible for sound and fair functioning of the government debt market. As a provider of financial infrastructure, the central bank may contribute to market development by providing depository, registry and electronic delivery-versus-payment systems.

Some modes of intervention in related markets impinge critically on the government debt market. First and foremost, if the central bank fails to control the level of excess reserves continuously, short-term interest rates may be excessively volatile. On the other hand, central bank rediscount practices can deter market development if virtually unlimited access at a fixed nonpenal rate is offered. Under such conditions, there will be no volatility in short-term interest rates. In this case, the central bank can encourage the process of developing treasury management capabilities by being less accommodative.

To ensure that interest rates fluctuate to some extent, a penal rate or limited rediscount tranches may be appropriate. Under one system, each bank has access to its first rediscount tranche calculated as the coefficient of variation of daily deposit values over the preceding six months at 1 percent over the latest treasury bill auction rate, a second rediscount tranche equal in size to the first at a rate approximately 50 percentage points above the first tranche's rate and a third unlimited tranche at 500 percentage points above the rate on first-tranche rediscounts. This system also constitutes part of a defence mechanism against turbulence on the foreign exchange market. Obviously, the authorities expect the second- and third-tranche facilities to be used only very occasionally and then only overnight.

Whatever rediscount system is adopted, one principle consistent with the development of markets for government debt might be considered: ensure that the central bank is never the lender of first resort, i.e., that it never presents profitable arbitrage opportunities for commercial bank borrowing. This necessarily involves access limits or costs of access continuously above market rates. Among the case study countries, the Reserve Bank of India manages both central and state government debt. In October 1992, the Reserve Bank of India established an Internal Debt Management Cell to improve debt management techniques. Commercial banks have also been improving their treasury capabilities, in some cases by establishing separate subsidiaries to reorganise their investment operations into a profit centre rather than an activity designed simply to maintain reserve requirements.

Initially, the Bank of Jamaica was not adequately prepared to undertake daily market intervention necessary to offset liquidity injections of relatively small magnitudes. At the outset, the Bank did not possess a sufficient inventory of marketable government debt and later did not possess mechanisms for conducting open-market operations. To remedy the latter problem, the Bank appointed primary dealers in 1994. Recently, however, the Bank of Jamaica established a trading room for government securities. Because treasury management staff in the Ministry of Finance were unable to predict monthly treasury requirements, a committee consisting of staff from the Bank of Jamaica, the treasury and the fiscal policy unit of the Ministry of Finance was established to forecast weekly, monthly, quarterly and annual cash requirements.

As the financial agent of the government, the Banco de México handles all the placing and redeeming of government debt. Cooperation with the Ministry of Finance has enabled the Bank to conduct open-market operations entirely with government securities in the secondary market rather than issuing its own paper. Since the Banco de México is the government's financial agent, the Mexican Ministry of Finance has not needed to develop treasury management capabilities.

The Reserve Bank of Zimbabwe manages the government debt. Recently, increased turnover volumes, with which it has been unable to cope, have swamped the stock transfer section.

7.3.3 Financial Institutions

Financial institutions can be categorised in various ways. From the market development perspective, the distinction between public and private is possibly the most relevant. Typically, private sector institutions respond quicker to changing market conditions. In Ghana, for example, private banks and other private financial institutions have been more responsive to the changes than have the state-owned banks. Many Ghanaian commercial banks recognised the need to begin or expand treasury activities. Most banks opened treasury departments to assume responsibility for the management of bills traded for themselves and their customers.

In India, altering the incentive structure for management and staff in the state banks to encourage active portfolio and risk management has been identified as critically important. In Indonesia, the state banks created barriers to market development through their lack of expertise and anti-competitive outlook.

Initially, the Mexican commercial banks viewed the emergence of markets for government debt as a competitive threat. To counter these anxieties, the authorities stressed that a voluntary domestic market for government debt would eliminate, as it eventually did, the need for the captive market. As Miguel Mancera stated: "The potential benefits for the banking system were obvious, as intermediation costs would be lower for both lenders and borrowers."

Improved treasury management in the Sri Lankan financial institutions was also required. Most financial institutions in Zimbabwe also found it necessary to establish active treasury departments after prices of government debt and other financial instruments became market determined. During the initial stages, most financial institutions were not interested in government debt simply because their treasury departments had not developed systems for dealing in these securities. The four major banks now possess treasury divisions that actively assess balance-sheet risk, despite the relatively low volume of market activity.

7.3.4   Primary Dealers

As Robin McConnachie (1996) points out, primary dealers in government debt receive various privileges in return for one or more obligation. The most common obligations are: (a) to act as market maker by providing continuous bid and offer prices in marketable government securities and (b) to support auctions of government debt by submitting reasonable bids or acting as underwriters. The precise nature of these obligations varies across countries from vague understandings to more precise requirements regarding maximum spreads on specific volumes or types of debt, etc. Criteria for appointing primary dealers usually include sound financial capacity, adequate management skills and an active market presence (McConnachie 1996, 8–9).

Although benefits in terms of secondary market development can accrue from giving primary dealers various privileges in return for certain obligations, the question arises as to whether they outweigh the costs. Privileges necessarily violate the level playing-field principle. Furthermore, the vested interests created by these privileges can impede subsequent change. For example, privileges held by gilt-edged market makers (GEMMs) in the UK appear to have stalled the introduction of a repo market by the Bank of England. When this market was launched on 2 January 1996, those affected included not only GEMMs but also Stock Exchange money brokers (SEMBs) (Bank of England 1996a, 142). Likewise, more frequent use of the repo market by the Bank of England for monetary policy purposes would jeopardise earnings of the discount houses.[2]

Experience suggests, therefore, that privileges should be granted, if at all, only for a fixed time period at the end of which they may or may not be renewed depending on the new cost-benefit balance at that time. But without primary dealers, the market development process may never occur. Establishing a primary dealership system at the outset may be a crucial factor in instilling the authorities with sufficient confidence to make the transition to a full market-based auction system.

Ceteris paribus, privileges that exclude others or provide privileged access to primary dealers discourage competition. Basically, primary dealers expect to make profits from their privileged position as intermediaries between government or central bank and the private sector. When there are only a few primary dealers, ideal conditions for forming a cartel are provided. The prevalent Antipodean view seems to be that primary dealers hinder competition, particularly when there are not many potential market participants. In circumstances where financial institutions are moving from a controlled and repressed environment, a primary dealer system offers scope for retaining old collusive habits that are inimical to the market development process. However, if more agents, possibly in the form of foreign firms, enter the market as a result of being offered primary dealerships, competition may actually be enhanced.

As McConnachie (1996, 13–15) notes, privileges granted to primary dealers include:

- Exclusive rights to bid at auctions of government debt.

---

[2]By merging with discount houses, some SEMBs may have jumped out of the frying pan into the fire.

- Exclusive rights to bid on a noncompetitive basis, effectively providing underwriting services.
- Exclusive right to bid for particular issues, e.g., tap issues in the UK.
- Exclusive access to inter-dealer brokers' screens.
- Exclusive access to inter-dealer brokers' secondary market trading system.
- Wider range of permitted operations than other traders, e.g., ability to borrow stock and to take short positions.
- Access to loans from the central bank.
- Access to repo facilities from the central bank.
- Certain tax exemptions.
- Exemption from the requirement to submit prepayment with the bid.
- Right to submit telephone or electronic bids.

The last two privileges listed above yield sufficient competitive advantages in the UK to effectively exclude nonprimary dealers from bidding at auctions for government debt. Hence, primary dealers usually act on behalf of major investing institutions, although the latter are not excluded and would bid were the primary dealers' commissions uncompetitive.

When it became clear that only banks bid at auctions for government debt in Mauritius because only banks were effectively exempt from submitting payment with their bids, brokers were offered the same privilege on the understanding that it would be withdrawn should payments not be made promptly on the settlement date. At the same time, banks were obliged to calculate interest on savings and time deposits based on average rather than minimum balances over each month as a way of encouraging bidding from individuals whose dealers required payment to accompany a bid.

Repos facilitate the management of dealers' long and short positions and so reduce costs of market making and increase liquidity. Hence, the development of repo facilities may reduce the privileges required to induce market making. The World Bank (1995a, 8) notes that, in practice, the introduction and use of repos has been hampered in several countries by regulatory restrictions and taxes.

In the case study countries, the development of the securities market in Ghana led to the emergence of discount houses. In March 1995, the Reserve Bank of India published guidelines and procedures for enlisting primary dealers in government debt. The new system started officially on 1 February 1996. To further promote the secondary market, a system of satellite (sub) dealers to distribute securities at the retail level is now under consideration. In Jamaica, primary dealers consisting of commercial banks, merchant banks and dealers were created in April 1994. They are intended to provide underwriting support for all new issues of government debt and to provide liquidity for two-way transactions. Because commercial banks also act as primary dealers in Sri Lanka, a conflict of interest exists particularly since the market structure there is highly oligopolistic; two state-owned commercial banks hold 60 percent of total bank assets.

The 23 primary dealers in Malaysia, who act as underwriters and market makers, have been attributed with injecting considerable liquidity into the secondary market. Their main privileges consist of exclusive rights to implement open-market operations and to tap the Bank Negara Malaysia's rediscount facility. Indeed, attractive rediscount rates have been offered to promote trading (Cole, Scott and Wellons 1995, 35). Primary dealers are obliged to provide two-way quotes for benchmark issues of government debt at all times (Lin and Chung 1995, 233).

In contrast, one of the early 1984 reforms in New Zealand consisted of scrapping official short-term money market dealers. The level playing-field philosophy ensured that "no serious consideration was given to introducing preferred primary dealers. Our general approach was to encourage as wide, and competitively neutral, access to the market as possible." Australia also abandoned its system of primary dealers in 1992 when the market appeared mature enough to operate efficiently without them.

In Zimbabwe, stockbrokers and discount houses have failed to play any market-making role. Nor are the discount houses crucial any more as market makers. As the sophistication of the commercial banks' treasury operations have increased, the role of the discount houses has become peripheral. Without their privilege of sole right to the Reserve Bank's discount window, they would disappear unless they expanded activities into other areas.

7.4   Market Structure

Minimising debt-service costs under the constraints of a level playing field necessitates competitive markets. If a bank cartel manages to dissuade or prevent others from participating at auctions of government debt, prices will obviously be lower than they otherwise would be. On the one hand, competition dictates allowing and encouraging all agents to participate. On the other hand, efficiency and fairness dictate that players be subject to appropriate regulatory restraints, e.g., to identify and deal with insolvent institutions. Encouraging competition and enforcing regulations often appear to conflict.

In the case study countries, competition was promoted in Ghana by ensuring that all players had full access to the debt instruments. New banks and financial institutions were licensed to increase competition. The financial system was completely deregulated during this period.

In Jamaica, high liquid asset ratio requirements have limited competition because price has still been determined by the demand of captive buyers.

Initially, the only authorised participants at auctions of government debt in Mexico were brokerage houses. Recently, however, authorised participants have been expanded to include commercial banks, stockbrokers, mutual funds and insurance companies. There is now a substantial number of participants in the secondary market that contributes to efficient pricing. Nevertheless, the Banco de México has devoted considerable resources, with apparent success, to devising clear and transparent procedures to prevent collusion at the *Cetes* auctions.

Until recently, collusion was prevalent in Zimbabwe due to the small number of financial institutions. Furthermore, only commercial and merchant banks were allowed to deal with discount houses. With the doubling of discount houses from two to four, an increase in brokers and finance houses, as well as the participation of insurance companies, pension funds and unit trusts, competition has improved. One indicator here is the decline in discount house spreads from 3 to 4 percent a few years ago to 0.1 to 0.25 percent in 1995.

7.5   Primary Markets

Carlo Cottarelli (1996, 2) identifies four broad methods of selling government debt in primary markets:

- Announcing a price and soliciting public subscription over a fixed time period (usually a few days).

- Announcing a price and offering sales on tap over an unlimited period during which the announced price is changed with varying frequency.

- Private placement in which sales are negotiated with a consortium of specialised dealers or investors.

- Auctions.

In the vast majority of countries that have taken steps to develop voluntary domestic markets for government debt, auctions have been adopted as the sales mechanism in the primary market on the grounds that they minimise the cost of government borrowing.

From the central bank's viewpoint, auctions offer the advantage of separating debt and monetary management. This separation necessitates that prices rather than quantities adjust to clear the debt market. As Cottarelli (1996, 5) points out, auctions clearly satisfy this requirement as well as providing advantages on most other criteria. However, they do so only when the switch has been made from minimum price tenders (setting a reserve price) to a market-clearing auction (fixing the quantity).

There is an extensive market microstructure literature that shows how "the pricing of assets cannot be determined independently from the institutional structure of the market (particularly the organization and mechanics of trading)" (Dattels 1996, 2). Hence, adopting auctions as the main method of selling government debt affects the cost of government borrowing. So too do choices with respect to:

- Auction participation.

- Bid screening and dealing with risks of noncompliance.

- Central bank participation.

- Competitive bids.

- Price determination and the allocation mechanism for competitive bids.

- Noncompetitive bids and post-auction sales.

- Announcing the quantity offered and setting reserve prices.

- Scheduling auctions.

- Advertising.

While Peter Dattels' (1996) point is undoubtedly true, the choice of the particular detailed arrangements of the auction system appears to be of second-order importance at the initial stages of developing a voluntary market for government debt, provided the system chosen is internally consistent and covers all eventualities. For example, whether one chooses an English or Dutch auction, a uniform or discriminatory price system, open outcry or sealed bid, etc., seems relatively unimportant. What is important is ensuring that the chosen system works smoothly and efficiently.

None of the case study countries reported that their auction mechanism had caused any specific problems. However, setting a reserve or cutoff price simply in the belief that the authorities know the "appropriate rate" can have and has had a major impact, as witnessed by experience in several case study countries, e.g., Jamaica and Mexico. If any reserve price is to be set, it might best take a relative form such as automatically excluding bids one standard deviation or more below the mean bid at either the current or previous auction or even the average of the two (Cottarelli 1996, 22). When competition is weak or nonexistence, however, the central bank will have to devise more sophisticated strategies to simulate competitive outcomes.

In contrast, as part of the development of markets for government debt in New Zealand, the authorities adopted a "clean" tendering system for government bonds and bills in 1984. In other words, no reserve prices were set and yields were determined by the free interaction of demand and supply as depicted in Figure 6.3. Bernie Fraser explained that the Australian authorities have also found "benefits in always filling a tender rather than rejecting bids on the basis that yields are too high. This avoids the risk of the authorities being seen as opportunistic and contributes to more consistent bidding and better [lower] yields in the long run." At the Symposium, Miguel Mancera reinforced this point by stating that one crucial element in the development of a market for Mexican public debt lay in "the willingness of the government to place the securities at whatever interest rate the market demanded."

7.6   Secondary Markets

While many countries have developed primary markets for government securities through auctions, developing active secondary markets has been much more difficult. Experience in developing countries indicates that secondary market development is not automatic or easy; it takes time and patience. Peter Stebbing (1994) suggests that the adoption of an auction system for selling government securities in 1982 was the single most important factor that boosted secondary market development in Australia. A second key factor is the elimination of captive buyers. A third crucial prerequisite are legal provisions permitting at least some participants to take short positions (Stebbing 1994). Finally, an efficient clearing and settlement system is essential (Sheng 1994, 76).

A number of participants at the Symposium made the point that fewer large issues of benchmark stocks improved liquidity and hence lowered the government's costs in comparison to a larger number of smaller issues. In Australia, for example, there are now 15 benchmark lines on issue through which the Treasury can raise funds. The Australian Treasury adds one or two new benchmark maturities every year to compensate for maturing issues. In this way, a benchmark yield curve has been established.

Present arrangements in Australia are relatively new. In 1987, over 110 government bonds existed and the yield curve was far from smooth. Evidently, the market did not want the large degree of product differentiation that had been provided. In the next two years, therefore, the Reserve Bank of Australia bought unpopular stock in exchange for the more popular and therefore liquid issues. In this way, the number of treasury bond issues outstanding was halved and trading activity in all the remaining issues increased. By 1992, a relatively smooth yield curve for Australian government debt had been achieved (Stebbing 1994).[3]

Another example is provided by the Hong Kong Monetary Authority, which started the Exchange Fund Bills and Notes programme in 1990. While one objective was to facilitate monetary management, another was to establish a benchmark yield curve (Sheng 1994, 76; World Bank 1995a, 23). One of the effects of the Hong Kong benchmark yield curve has been the reduction in the spread between yields on domestic-

---

[3]Over a somewhat longer period, the UK has also rationalised a plethora of government stocks and adopted a benchmark system.

currency and US government bonds.[4] Another has been increased liquidity; the daily turnover of Exchange Fund Bills and Notes approached 50 percent of the outstanding value in 1996. The Hong Kong Monetary Authority has actively promoted the development of a government debt market in various ways, including the provision of an efficient clearing and settlement system, without providing any subsidies.

Among the case study countries, there is still no secondary market trading in Ghana. In 1996, Ghana's retail auction for government and central bank securities is scheduled to be replaced by a wholesale auction. Limited access to a central bank rediscount window is expected to attract primary dealers who will develop a secondary market.

Although it is recognised as a *sine qua non* of a strong primary market, the secondary market in India is virtually nonexistent because of the preponderance of captive buyers in the market for government debt. As all the players are final investors, a secondary market of adequate depth has failed to develop. Plans to develop the secondary market include improving institutional infrastructure and the payment and settlement system. Among various recent measures, the establishment of the Securities Trading Corporation by the Reserve Bank in 1994, approval of six primary dealers under the Guidelines for Primary Dealers issued in 1995, accounting requirements to mark to market and the introduction of an electronic delivery-versus-payments system in July 1995 are expected to promote secondary trading. The National Stock Exchange of India was established in 1993 with an automated screen-based dealing system. Complementing telephone-based transactions, the National Stock Exchange offers its wholesale debt market segment for trading in government securities.

In Jamaica, use of the standard accounting practice of not marking to market is also cited as one of the deterrents to the development of a secondary market. For financial institutions engaging in maturity intermediation, i.e., borrowing short and lending long, using book values rather than market values produces a better balance sheet situation when interest rates rise. Financial institutions are reluctant to sell assets whose market values have fallen because only then would their reduced values have to be incorporated in their balance sheets. Concealing insolvency by using book rather than market values has been widespread in both

---

[4] Since October 1983, the Hong Kong dollar has been fixed against the US dollar under a currency board system.

developing and developed countries, as witnessed, for example, by the US Savings and Loan débâcle in the early 1980s.

In Zimbabwe, lack of interest and skill among stockbrokers as well as the lack of appropriate legislation have been responsible for the nonexistence of secondary markets.

Among the case study countries, only in New Zealand was there a sufficient number of competitive players to develop active secondary markets in government bonds without obstacles. Treasury bills proved more difficult because of the lack of a steady issue volume; they were issued simply for seasonal liquidity needs. This problem disappeared once a steady issue schedule was adopted.

7.7   Spillover to Markets for Private Sector Debt

One anticipated effect of developing voluntary domestic markets for government debt is the encouragement of markets for private sector debt. Indeed, this was one reason why the Hong Kong Monetary Authority has taken active steps to develop a government debt market, despite the fact that the government posts a budget surplus and therefore does not use the funds raised (World Bank 1995b). Where fiscal discipline is not so strong, however, the danger arises that developing government debt markets in the absence of a funding need could produce a moral hazard: governments might be tempted to increase budget expenditures to absorb the newly raised funds.

In the case study countries, developing markets for government debt does appear to have encouraged markets for private sector debt in Ghana, at least to a limited degree. More generally, it has increased the public's financial awareness, e.g., banking habit and investment culture.

The deregulation of corporate debenture rates is expected to stimulate the private sector bond market in India. Already, several innovative corporate bonds have been issued, with government security yields used as reference rates. Establishing a reference rate for pricing in the markets for commercial paper, certificates of deposits, interbank claims and other repo markets is also one of the benefits accruing from the development of the government debt market in Jamaica. There has also been increased trading in new financial instruments. However, the Bank of Jamaica suggests that an active interbank market is a prerequisite for developing markets for government debt.

In Malaysia, the infrastructure and procedures established for the government debt market have acted as models for markets in private sector debt. The development process for the government debt market has also provided market participants with the skills needed to trade in other debt instruments.

Specialised Mexican financial institutions such as brokerage houses that started operations only in government securities have expanded activities using the same techniques and facilities to develop markets for private debt. "Thus, economies of scale in the development of a government paper market have facilitated the introduction and evolution of a sound and solid private sector debt market." At the Symposium, Miguel Mancera linked the use of treasury bill yields as reference rates to the adoption of a system of book-entry transfer: "Even though this particular step may seem trivial, it can be safely stated that it was absolutely essential for the fast development of a significant market."

Liberalised markets in New Zealand led to rapid financial innovation with big Euro and Yankee kiwi bonds in the early years followed by futures and options on domestic bonds, domestic interest rate swaps, fixed-rate mortgages and some strips.

The yield on Sri Lankan treasury bills is now used as a reference rate by the Sri Lankan financial system. New market instruments such as treasury bill-backed securities have also emerged.

7.8 Conclusion

Experience in the case study countries indicates that developing a voluntary domestic market for government debt involves major changes in both outlook and activities on the parts of ministries of finance, central banks and the financial institutions. Although no questionnaire response doubted the advantages that could accrue from the successful development of a market for government debt, they all indicated many of the practical difficulties encountered during the development process.

Other developing countries may benefit from these and other lessons of experience. To some extent, however, delving into the details of these experiences involves an understanding of chaos theory. As this theory indicates, it is not that markets are necessarily chaotic, but rather that their development paths are highly dependent on initial conditions. Most obviously, New Zealand's experience differs from the Ghanaian and Zimbabwean experiences; their starting points were entirely different.

Nevertheless, interest in this topic has produced a wealth of detailed research over the past few years. As James Duesenberry (1995, vi) stresses: "The devil is in the details." Both to avoid repetition and to keep the length of this book within reasonable bounds, the final chapter focuses on the specific roles that a central bank may play in this process rather than on the myriad of details that must be considered by those involved in the process of developing markets for government debt.[5]

---

[5] Among other relevant references in the bibliography, those involved in this development process might consult Pierre-Richard Agénor and Peter Montiel (1996), William E. Alexander, Tomás J. T. Baliño and Charles Enoch (1995), Leonardo Bartolini and Carlo Cottarelli (1994), Günter F. Bröker (1993), Gerard Caprio, Izak Atiyas and James Hanson (1994), Christophe Chamley and Patrick Honohan (1993), David Cole, Hal Scott and Philip Wellons (1995), Carlo Cottarelli (1993), Peter Dattels (1996), Morris Goldstein and David Folkerts-Landau (1994), Simon Gray (1996), Randall Kroszner (1996), Lin See-Yan and Chung Tin Fah (1995), David Lynch (1995), Robin McConnachie (1996), Ronald McKinnon (1993), Venkataraman Sundararajan, Hans J. Blommestein and Peter Dattels (1996), Venkataraman Sundararajan, Peter Dattels, Ian McCarthy, Marta Castello-Branco and Hans Blommestein (1996), David Wilton (1995 & 1996) and World Bank (1995a, 1995b & 1995c).

Chapter 8

Roles for the Central Bank

8.1 Introduction

ONE VIEW OF THE APPROPRIATE CONDUCT of central banking holds that the central bank should confine its activities as narrowly as possible to the primary objective—price stability—of monetary policy. In this view, government debt management, auctioneering, registry, payment and settlement systems, electronic delivery-versus-payment mechanisms, and prudential supervision and regulation of financial institutions are outside the proper scope of central banking and should therefore be conducted by other public or private sector institutions.

Since monetary policy must be coordinated with fiscal and exchange rate policy, however, the central bank cannot, in practice, stand aloof from policies in these areas. Dialogue is essential and the central bank's influence on appropriate and coordinated macroeconomic policies will usually depend, at least in part, on the expertise that it can proffer. Central bank independence may well be more a matter of possessing the necessary expertise to argue its case than of any formal legal arrangements (Fry, Goodhart and Almeida 1996, 108–110).

Indeed, a major justification for central bank involvement in creating voluntary domestic markets for government debt may lie in the lack of skills elsewhere. In some countries, the central bank is the only source of financial and market skills needed to make any progress. Even where its own skills are inadequate, the central bank may serve as a focal point for external technical assistance that would be unavailable, except at extremely high cost, to any other institutions.

At the Symposium, there was considerable support for the view that the central bank could play an important role in this process, certainly as a catalyst, but more often as a promoter or facilitator. While modest expenditure in the form of pump-priming might be useful in some circumstances, experience suggests that coordination and expertise are typically far more important and effective than any subsidies. Indeed, the Hong Kong Monetary Authority and the Reserve Bank of New Zealand stress the fact that their successful developmental roles have not involved any direct or indirect costs to taxpayers.

There is also general agreement that implementing monetary policy to achieve price stability can be pursued most efficiently through the use of indirect market-based techniques of monetary control. If this is impossible because of the lack of appropriate markets, then the central bank may perforce be obliged to play a role in creating these markets. This together with the belief that debt markets promote efficient financial intermediation are the rationales behind the considerable efforts by the Hong Kong Monetary Authority to develop voluntary domestic markets for government debt in Hong Kong.

The process of developing voluntary domestic markets for government debt requires not only conducive macroeconomic conditions and appropriate market structures, but also financial infrastructure. As Ian Plenderleith stated at the Symposium, this infrastructure is being developed and improved continuously even in the most sophisticated financial markets of the world. But the appropriate financial infrastructure is highly country specific. It depends on the legal system, the ways fiscal and monetary policy are implemented, the structure of the financial system, as well as accounting conventions, geographical characteristics, the state of telecommunications, etc.

This chapter focuses on some activities that central banks can and have performed in the pursuit of the market development objective in its earlier stages. While there are a myriad of detailed issues relating to the development of financial markets, here I concentrate on those that appear not only particularly important in the early stages of this process but also to offer comparative advantage for central bank involvement. Hence, for example, such issues as tax treatment and contract enforcement, despite their obvious importance, are not discussed. Nonetheless, some central bankers may well feel that they do have a comparative advantage in proffering advice on tax matters, particularly when government deficits are undermining monetary policy or specific taxes on financial transactions are seriously impeding market development.

At the Symposium, Ian Plenderleith pointed out that, although the Bank of England had been involved in government debt financing for over 300 years, practice was still developing. Recent measures included, for example, the introduction of a specific and published auction programme, the increased transparency of monetary policy, the introduction of repos in 1996 and the planned introduction of stripping in 1997. Over time, the Bank of England has developed four guiding principles for the UK's debt management policy:

1. The marketing exercise: since the government has a product to sell, market intelligence is crucial. The Bank of England maintains a dialogue with both financial intermediaries and final investors.

2. Keep it simple: experience indicated that, since the markets' understanding of new products could be patchy, it was important to keep products clear and comprehensible. Index-linked securities offered several benefits to both issuer and investor, but they are inherently complex and the UK market has taken some time to digest them. The conference on index-linked securities organised by the Bank of England in 1995 constituted part of the Bank's efforts to educate the market (Bank of England 1996b).

3. A variety of instruments and selling techniques could broaden appeal.

4. The central bank's involvement in the secondary market should be developmental. For example, with the introduction of index-linked government securities in the UK, the Bank of England acted initially as a market maker to promote this market. Obviously, however, care was taken not to substitute for the market.

Lars Kalderen (1996) suggests that, in countries that are just starting to develop voluntary domestic markets for government debt, considerable central bank involvement in government debt management "is likely to be the best solution." In any event, it is essential that the planning process addresses and resolves the issue of who does what in each aspect of government debt management.

8.2   Information Provider

While all central banks produce annual reports and many also publish quarterly bulletins presumably to provide information, these are hardly the most appropriate and effective vehicles for the dissemination of relevant market information. An ideal system both for obtaining and disseminating such information must be continuous and on-line (Dattels 1996, Kalderen 1996).

Information is an essential ingredient in the development of voluntary markets for government debt. Given that it is a public good, i.e., its use by someone else does not remove it from one's own use, information provision will be suboptimal in perfectly competitive markets. Yet transparency is crucial for efficient market development. Hence, there is an economic case for allocating some public funds to improving information systems. Among the case study countries, lack of adequate information was mentioned specifically as an impediment to development of the market in Ghana.

To the extent that the central bank collects much information from financial institutions as part of its supervisory role, the central bank may well have a comparative advantage in operating various types of information systems for financial markets. For example, the general adoption of Reuters screens may be facilitated by central bank initiative in negotiating with Reuters and dealing with any local legal impediments. In some countries, central banks have provided trading systems for government securities in conjunction with clearing and settlement facilities. For example, the National Bank of Poland has developed a special network for its primary dealers in the money markets. In other countries, central banks have been instrumental in developing trading systems rather than in providing the networks themselves. Transparency and efficiency improvements have been noted.

8.3 Issue Manager

In some circumstances, a case can be made for assigning the task of managing the issue of government debt to the central bank as the fiscal agent of the government. Most importantly, the central bank is best placed to conduct the necessary market research prior to each issue. Communication with market participants is vital to prevent disorderly market conditions. Part of this communication process involves a pre-announced calendar of issues. Another part involves market intelligence to forecast demand.

In some countries, e.g., Germany, Italy, Spain, Denmark and the UK among OECD countries, the central bank manages the issue of government debt, while in others this task is done by the ministry of finance or by a specialised semi-independent government debt management agency, as in Hungary, Ireland, New Zealand and Sweden. While it may be largely a matter of historical accident as to who does what in countries where voluntary markets for government debt have existed for many years, this question must be addressed explicitly at the start of any programme to develop voluntary markets for government debt. If a specialised agency has greater flexibility over salaries, it may be able to recruit highly qualified personnel more easily than either a central bank or ministry of finance.

At the same time that the advantages and disadvantages of appointing the central bank as the issue manager of government debt are analysed, the advantages and disadvantages, if any, of separating management of treasury bill issues from issues of longer-term government debt might be considered. While the separation of monetary policy (treasury bill issue) and debt management (longer-term debt issue) raises a matter of principle, the decision may well depend primarily on the institutional setting in each country. Whatever decision on the location of the issue manager is reached, it is imperative to recognise that the management of the government's debt has important macroeconomic effects that necessitate coordination with all other aspects of macroeconomic policy.

8.4   Market Maker

Another important matter to be considered at the outset of the market development programme is the potential role of the central bank as a market maker. In this capacity, the central bank would stand ready to buy and sell government debt from and to market participants.

In the OECD countries, primary dealers rather than the central bank are generally obliged to act as market makers. Central banks facilitate this primary dealer role by providing privileged repo, rediscount or overdraft facilities. If a viable system of primary dealers already exists, the central bank might only undermine it by intervening as a market maker as well.

In many developing countries, however, no system of primary dealers or its equivalent exists. Several developing country central banks have established secondary market windows during the initial stages of market development. The Central Bank of Malta still acts as a market maker, since no one else does. However, it maintains a relatively high bid-ask spread to encourage the development of private sector market makers. The fact that the Bank of England acted as a market maker for index-linked bonds when they were first introduced suggests that there is a case for the central bank acting as market maker in the early stages of the market development process, provided it is careful not to undermine the market.

If there is a case, market making activities must be arranged carefully to ensure that the central bank neither uses portfolio adjustments to prevent market price adjustments nor becomes a residual buyer again. Chapters 6 and 7 already make the point that markets cannot develop if the central bank effectively offers a rediscount facility without limit at a fixed interest rate approximately equal to the treasury bill yield. Some modes of market making could produce exactly this effect. For example, the National Bank of Hungary initially undermined the primary dealership system it had established by continuing to act as a market maker for government securities using on-line computers in all its 19 branches and charging low commissions. Other modes of market making, however, can inject competition where it is weak or nonexistent.

8.5   Auction Participation

While a "clean" auction may be accepted as an ultimate goal, the absence of sufficient market participants to ensure competitive bidding in the early stages of the market development process may justify some participation by the central bank in the auctions of government debt. Such participation could be designed to counteract collusive behaviour on the part of other bidders, to prevent wild swings in yields and to ensure that the government's financing needs were satisfied. To foster the objective of developing voluntary markets for government debt, this third possible objective of central bank participation in the auctions should be strongly rejected.

Venkataraman Sundararajan, Peter Dattels, Ian McCarthy, Marta Castello-Branco and Hans Blommestein (1996, 30) recommend that where the central bank does participate in auctions of government debt as a buyer it should be a noncompetitive residual buyer taking up debt at the weighted average auction price. Preferably, the maximum quantity of the central bank bid should be preannounced together with the total offer, so providing the market with the net minimum quantity on offer for competitive bids. In any event, central bank participation should not lead back down the path to inflationary deficit finance.

The point was made at the Symposium that central banks may wish to issue their own bills for monetary policy purposes. Indeed, several central banks have issued their own paper in order to mop up excess liquidity, sometimes produced by central bank financing of government deficits. Particularly in small countries, however, liquidity and hence a smooth yield curve might be impeded by simultaneous circulation of treasury and central bank bills. Furthermore, frequent switches between treasury and central bank bills could be unnecessarily confusing and disruptive to the market development process, perhaps particularly deterring nonbank participation at the auctions. Marc Quintyn (1996) also argues in favour of using government securities rather than central bank paper "because they are better able to serve as catalysts in financial market development." Quintyn notes that markets for central bank securities tend to remain very thin and fail to integrate with the rest of the money market, so impeding the transmission of monetary policy; he cites Indonesia and Korea as two examples.[1]

In order to divorce monetary policy from fiscal policy but still prevent any overfunding of the government's borrowing requirements from becoming a direct fiscal burden, the central bank could deposit any funds from treasury bill auctions that exceeded the government's financing needs (as indicated to the central bank each month by the ministry of finance) in a special account bearing interest at exactly the treasury bill auction yield. Conversely, should monetary policy dictate underfunding of the government's borrowing requirements from time to time, this special account could be depleted to make up the shortfall. Any overdraft in this account would be charged exactly the same interest rate as a positive balance. In this way, the central bank could conduct auctions of treasury bills solely from the perspective of their monetary policy implications. The ministry of finance should not be concerned by any direct consequences of any week-to-week or month-to-month over- or underfunding.

---

[1] Quintyn (1996) also finds that in practice issuing central bank bills increases the risk of central bank losses with the concomitant erosion of the prestige and autonomy of the central bank. Among the case study countries, Jamaica provides a relevant example of this problem.

8.6 Clearing and Settlement Systems

As lender of last resort, the central bank has an obvious interest in ensuring that clearing and settlement systems for government debt are well designed to minimise credit, liquidity and operational risks. If a commercial bank pays for government debt that is not duly transferred, the central bank might have to intervene to prevent a systemic crisis. At the heart of a country's payment system, the central bank is ideally placed to develop a delivery-versus-payment system, "a prerequisite for the success of transactions involving a chain of separate deals" (Kalderen 1996).

Sundararajan, Dattels, McCarthy, Castello-Branco and Blommestein (1996, 36) identify four key elements in the clearing and settlement process:

1. Trade comparison and clearing arrangements.

2. A depository that handles securities and maintains a book-entry transfer system.

3. A money transfer system.

4. A custodial/safekeeping arrangement where members of the depository can safely keep securities on behalf of clients.

David Sheppard (1996) provides a general discussion of the role of the central bank in the development and provision of payment systems.

Among the case study countries, a Committee on Electronic Funds Transfer (EFT) and Other Payments submitted its proposals to the Reserve Bank of India in January 1996. It recommended the introduction of a national EFT system for interbank and intrabank credit transfers which will require an amendment to the Reserve Bank of India Act of 1934.

In 1994 the Banco de México initiated a reform of the national payment system. The three major elements of this reform are: (a) limits and penalties on commercial banks' daylight and overnight overdrafts with the central bank; (b) reform of the clearing and settlement system including the introduction of a large-value transfer system; and (c) introduction of an electronic delivery-versus-payment scheme for transactions in bank securities. This delivery-versus-payment system will soon be expanded to include secondary market transactions in government debt as well as other stock market transactions.

In primary markets, auction participants in some countries must deposit cash before the auction, while in others this is not required. Clearly, full cash deposits ensure that bids are honoured, but such a requirement is costly and can deter some agents from participating at all. The problem of nonpayment, however, is far more serious in the secondary markets. In the primary market, the worst that can happen is that the sale is not consummated with the resulting minor pricing distortion. In the secondary market, nonpayment could produce major systemic problems.

Among the OECD countries, an electronic assured payment system is provided by the Bank of England to ensure simultaneous transfer of title and payment for government debt at the end of each day.[2] Similarly, in New Zealand the government securities registry system is operated by the Reserve Bank. Among the case study countries, the absence of a central registry for securities delays transactions in Jamaica. Because treasury bills are bearer instruments in Jamaica, this creates an additional risk. The absence of a central depository system in Zimbabwe has impeded market development there too; Zimbabwean debt securities are also issued in bearer form. The introduction of a registry for a book-entry system run by a reputable organisation would apparently be welcomed by most Zimbabwean market participants.

Given the cost reductions achieved by computerised registry systems and the obvious advantage to the government of systems that discourage tax avoidance, it is difficult to find any strong justification for bearer instruments. In the absence of bearer instruments, all clearing systems must feature a central depository or registry in which ownership is recorded and through which ownership transfers are effected.

David Wilton (1995) demonstrates that the cost of poor clearing and settlement systems can be measured in China because the quality of depositories varies between trading centres. Identical bonds fetch higher prices in Shanghai than elsewhere because Shanghai has the best depository and so the least delivery risk.

The Banco de México operates as a centralised depository for government securities and performs all the necessary custodial and book-entry operations. The advantage of this book-entry system is that it "significantly reduces operating and transaction costs as there is no need for the physical transfer of titles among market participants." Most

---

[2]This system will be replaced by a true delivery-versus-payment system as soon as the Central Gilts Office system has adapted to encompass a real-time gross settlement system.

participants in the market for government debt can access the Bank's electronic communications system (*Siac-Banxico*), which is equivalent to the US Fedwire. In this way, participants can conduct direct purchases and sales or repo agreements. Repayment on maturity is also effected through this electronic system. The delivery-versus-payment system already used for bank securities will be adopted for government debt in the near future.

At the Symposium, Donald Brash stated that the market for government debt has developed rapidly in New Zealand with the active encouragement of the Reserve Bank in such areas as the provision of an electronic delivery-versus-payment system, but without any tax or other incentives, without the Reserve Bank acting as market maker and without any system of privileged primary dealers.

8.7 Regulation and Supervision

The rationale for regulation and supervision of government debt markets is essentially the same as the rationale for bank supervision and regulation. This is the primary justification for placing this function in the central bank, which typically supervises commercial banks. Furthermore, market confidence may be enhanced by central bank rather than government supervision of government debt markets. If supervision is conducted by the central bank, this function needs to be separated by some form of Chinese wall from any issue management function that the central bank may perform. Among OECD countries, government debt markets are supervised by the central bank in Italy, Spain, Netherlands and the UK.

8.8 Secondary Market Development

Even if the central bank does not act as market maker, it can certainly play a role as market developer. In particular, it can offer its expertise to the government on steps needed for this development. As Sundararajan, Dattels, McCarthy, Castello-Branco and Blommestein (1996, 32–33) point out, active and efficient secondary markets in government securities are generally associated with the following features:

- No price or tax distortions or other inefficient portfolio regulations that produce market segmentation and captive buyers.

- An efficient primary market in which the authorities are prepared to sell government debt at true market-clearing prices.

- A sufficient volume of government debt and widespread holdings among diverse agents.

- Active liquidity management by the central bank, on the one hand to ensure adequate interest-rate flexibility and, on the other hand, to avoid excessive interest-rate volatility or instability.

- Strong interbank and money markets supported by an efficient clearing and settlement system.

- A well-defined microstructure for secondary market trading.

- A transparent and equitable regulatory and supervisory framework.

Measures taken by the Reserve Bank of India include an attempt to broaden the investor base and the introduction of a repo market. The Hong Kong Monetary Authority stimulated secondary market development by permitting market makers to take short positions, although these positions must be closed out at the end of each day. Indeed, some intra-day limits on the taking of short positions might be appropriate in most countries to reduce systemic risk.

8.9 Conclusion

The appropriate roles of a central bank in the process of developing voluntary markets for government debt are country-specific and, as Miguel Mancera suggests, may change over time:

> At different stages in the process of developing a voluntary market for government securities, the activities of a central bank may not be confined to those described as "belonging to the proper role" of central banking. Yet, over the years some of these activities may be transferred to other public and private sector institutions, as is happening in Mexico in the case of the book-entry transfer system for government securities. The speed and scope of actual divestiture depends on many factors, including those of a historical nature. At times, the availability of trained personnel at the central bank is the deciding factor in whether or not the institution embarks on a particular activity to support the development of a market for government securities.

In all countries, central banks are uniquely placed to promote the development of voluntary domestic markets for government debt at some stage in the process. Given this role as well as roles in prudential supervision and monetary policy implementation, I would not hesitate to answer Kurt Schuller's (1996) question "Should developing countries have central banks?" in the affirmative. Once governments are persuaded that cheap finance from their central banks or through financial repression and inflation-unemployment tradeoffs are mere illusions, central banks can then pursue unimpeded their primary monetary policy objective of price stability. Emancipating the banking system in the process of developing markets for government debt should enable every country's financial system to perform its two basic functions—administering the country's payments mechanism and intermediating between savers and investors—effectively and efficiently. As the earlier parts of this book argue, the end results should be lower inflation, higher saving ratios and higher growth.

Appendix 1

Central Bank Case Study Questionnaire

*[Please indicate any answers that you wish
to be kept confidential or unattributed.]*

1. What were the main perceived incentives for or benefits from developing voluntary domestic markets for government debt (e.g., implementing monetary policy through indirect instruments, financing government deficits in a less inflationary way, etc.)?

2. How were the main political actors (e.g., minister of finance) persuaded of the benefits of abandoning system of captive buyers (including the central bank) of government securities in favour of developing a market in which government securities would be bought voluntarily and hence would have to compete with markets for other financial claims?

3. Were any prerequisites for developing voluntary domestic markets for government debt identified before the process started? If so, please elaborate.

4. What sequencing was followed, whether deliberate or not, in the development of markets for government debt?

5. Were there any features of the banking system (or the financial sector in general) changed as prerequisites for or as consequences of the development of domestic markets for government debt? If so, please elaborate.

6. Please outline problems encountered in the process of developing domestic markets for government debt under the following four headings:

    • macroeconomic policy issues (e.g., government deficit, inflation, coordination between monetary, fiscal and exchange rate policies, legal system and ability to enforce contracts, etc.).

- operational issues (e.g., treasury management capabilities in ministry of finance and banks, information systems, absence of profit motive or incentives in state banks, need for primary dealers, the learning process, etc.).
- market structure issues (e.g., lack of competition, excessive regulation, etc.).
- financial infrastructure (e.g., payments system, recording and transferring title to securities, other legal issues, etc.).

7. Did the development of domestic markets for government debt affect the government's attitude towards its deficit or the deficit itself? If so, please elaborate.

8. Did the development of domestic markets for government debt affect the private sector in any way, e.g., crowd out private sector borrowers or facilitate the development of markets for private sector debt? If so, please elaborate.

9. Has the development of domestic markets for government debt affected the role of the central bank, e.g., has it affected implementation of monetary policy, the independence of the central bank, etc.? If so, please elaborate.

10. In hindsight, what pitfalls in the process of developing domestic markets for government debt can be identified?

11. In hindsight, what benefits from the process of developing domestic markets for government debt can be identified, particularly those that were not foreseen at the outset?

Appendix 2

Government Deficits as Percent of GDP

Country	1979–93	1979–83	1984–88	1989–93
Australia	1.2	1.6	1.9	0.2
Austria	4.6	4.2	5.1	4.4
Belgium	8.8	10.4	9.8	6.3
Canada	4.0	4.3	4.2	3.1
Denmark	1.6	4.9	−1.2	1.1
Finland	3.1	2.1	0.6	6.6
France	2.5	2.1	2.5	2.9
Germany	1.7	2.0	1.3	1.9
Iceland	2.8	1.9	3.3	3.3
Ireland	8.2	14.1	9.0	1.5
Italy	11.9	11.6	12.7	11.0
Japan	4.1	6.8	4.3	0.6
Luxembourg	−1.9	0.5	−5.9	0.9
Netherlands	4.6	6.2	4.4	3.1
New Zealand	3.3	7.3	2.7	−0.9
Norway	0.3	0.5	−1.8	2.5
Spain	5.1	5.2	5.7	4.2
Sweden	5.4	8.4	4.2	3.5
Switzerland	0.3	0.5	−0.3	0.7
United Kingdom	2.7	4.6	1.5	2.1
United States	3.9	3.4	4.3	4.1
Bahrain	1.7	−2.4	2.3	5.3
Cyprus	5.5	7.1	4.8	4.5
Egypt	6.0	9.1	8.6	2.8
Greece	10.7	6.3	11.3	14.5
Hungary	1.2	1.8	1.1	0.5
Iran	5.5	8.0	6.5	2.0
Israel	10.3	19.4	6.7	4.9
Jordan	5.3	7.6	7.6	0.7
Kuwait	11.5	−20.5	9.2	34.0
Malta	2.3	−0.6	2.8	4.5
Oman	7.6	1.7	12.7	8.4
Poland	1.2	n.a.	1.2	n.a.
Portugal	9.0	10.4	11.2	4.6
Romania	−3.4	−2.6	−5.3	−1.6
Syria	2.0	5.1	3.2	−0.6
Turkey	4.3	n.a.	3.1	4.6
United Arab Republic	−0.3	−1.4	0.5	0.0

Government Deficits as Percent of GDP (Continued)

Country	1979–93	1979–83	1984–88	1989–93
Botswana	−9.9	−1.6	−17.6	−10.5
Burundi	−0.1	1.3	−0.5	−1.5
Cameroon	1.5	0.2	n.a.	4.5
Chad	5.4	n.a.	3.5	7.2
Ethiopia	5.9	5.3	5.3	8.1
Gabon	−0.5	−1.6	−0.1	1.2
Gambia	3.3	7.8	n.a.	−1.1
Ghana	2.2	5.1	0.6	1.0
Guinea-Bissau	13.0	n.a.	12.3	13.2
Kenya	4.9	6.1	5.2	3.4
Lesotho	9.7	n.a.	19.5	3.2
Madagascar	4.1	n.a.	3.5	4.2
Malawi	7.0	9.0	7.6	2.2
Mauritius	4.4	10.8	1.8	0.5
Morocco	6.5	10.4	5.7	2.7
Namibia	0.8	n.a.	−0.7	1.6
Nigeria	5.2	−1.3	6.7	10.2
Rwanda	3.8	1.7	n.a.	4.9
Seychelles	7.7	n.a.	10.6	5.3
Sierra Leone	8.0	11.7	7.9	4.4
South Africa	4.4	3.3	4.7	5.6
Swaziland	0.2	2.3	0.7	−6.2
Tanzania	6.9	10.1	6.2	4.5
Tunisia	4.7	4.8	5.1	4.1
Uganda	2.8	3.0	2.0	3.5
Zaire	8.8	n.a.	8.0	9.0
Zambia	13.0	13.4	13.9	11.1
Zimbabwe	8.7	8.8	8.9	7.8

Government Deficits as Percent of GDP (Concluded)

Country	1979–93	1979–83	1984–88	1989–93
Bhutan	3.6	0.3	2.5	9.3
China	0.8	1.2	0.5	0.8
Fiji	3.6	4.8	3.3	2.6
India	7.1	6.0	8.4	7.0
Indonesia	1.3	2.2	1.4	0.2
Korea	0.9	2.3	0.1	0.4
Malaysia	8.6	14.3	7.7	3.6
Myanmar	1.4	−1.3	1.7	3.8
Nepal	5.9	4.4	6.6	7.0
Pakistan	7.1	6.5	7.5	7.4
Papua New Guinea	3.2	4.1	1.9	3.5
Philippines	2.5	2.5	2.8	2.1
Singapore	−5.3	−2.1	−2.4	−11.5
Solomon Islands	6.8	6.0	7.6	n.a.
Sri Lanka	10.9	13.5	9.6	8.6
Thailand	1.3	4.4	2.9	−3.4
Tonga	2.1	0.5	2.5	2.4
Argentina	2.7	4.7	3.1	0.4
Bahamas	2.5	2.9	1.2	3.3
Barbados	3.5	3.4	4.0	1.0
Belize	1.6	n.a.	−0.8	3.1
Bolivia	10.4	14.4	15.6	1.3
Brazil	7.0	2.5	11.3	7.4
Chile	−0.8	−1.8	1.2	−1.7
Colombia	1.5	2.9	2.0	−0.4
Costa Rica	2.3	4.0	1.9	1.2
Dominican Republic	1.1	3.3	0.9	−0.8
Ecuador	0.5	2.8	0.7	−1.9
El Salvador	2.5	4.4	0.9	2.2
Guatemala	2.2	4.1	1.6	0.8
Guyana	33.3	38.0	43.0	15.2
Haiti	4.0	4.5	3.2	4.1
Honduras	4.1	4.7	6.4	1.1
Mexico	6.0	6.5	10.4	1.2
Netherlands Antilles	3.7	4.7	2.3	n.a.
Nicaragua	18.0	10.9	20.1	24.1
Panama	3.3	8.9	4.3	−3.1
Paraguay	−0.3	0.1	0.4	−1.4
Peru	3.4	3.5	4.2	2.6
St Kitts and Nevis	3.5	n.a.	7.1	0.0
St Lucia	0.5	1.2	0.1	−0.6
St Vincent and Grenadine	0.6	0.7	−0.1	2.1
Trinidad and Tobago	4.5	2.8	6.3	3.9
Uruguay	1.8	2.9	2.3	0.3
Venezuela	0.6	1.1	0.6	0.3

Appendix 3

Government Domestic Debt as Percent of GDP

Country	1979–93	1979–83	1984–88	1989–93
Australia	16.0	15.3	17.4	12.9
Austria	30.0	18.8	31.7	39.6
Belgium	79.2	52.2	82.4	103.0
Canada	30.5	24.7	35.3	34.9
Denmark	n.a.	n.a.	n.a.	n.a.
Finland	5.6	4.0	6.5	6.7
France	n.a.	n.a.	n.a.	n.a.
Germany	14.8	13.9	15.1	15.5
Iceland	9.8	6.9	8.3	14.1
Ireland	n.a.	n.a.	n.a.	n.a.
Italy	72.0	53.7	77.6	93.1
Japan	49.0	40.3	54.8	56.2
Luxembourg	5.8	6.5	6.5	3.6
Netherlands	47.6	n.a.	47.3	47.6
New Zealand	32.9	31.6	35.0	28.4
Norway	22.0	23.1	24.6	17.3
Spain	28.1	15.9	35.2	33.3
Sweden	31.5	25.5	37.9	31.2
Switzerland	15.3	15.8	15.7	14.4
United Kingdom	n.a.	n.a.	n.a.	n.a.
United States	37.5	27.5	38.6	46.6
Bahrain	7.0	1.7	5.1	13.6
Cyprus	21.0	14.7	19.8	28.6
Egypt	n.a.	n.a.	n.a.	n.a.
Greece	n.a.	n.a.	n.a.	n.a.
Hungary	n.a.	n.a.	n.a.	n.a.
Iran	n.a.	n.a.	n.a.	n.a.
Israel	107.2	104.8	114.1	102.6
Jordan	23.8	14.1	21.5	35.9
Kuwait	61.3	n.a.	15.6	74.9
Malta	10.6	5.6	6.7	17.4
Oman	3.1	0.4	n.a.	5.8
Poland	n.a.	n.a.	n.a.	n.a.
Portugal	n.a.	n.a.	n.a.	n.a.
Romania	n.a.	n.a.	n.a.	n.a.
Syria	n.a.	n.a.	n.a.	n.a.
Turkey	13.2	n.a.	n.a.	13.2
United Arab Republic	n.a.	n.a.	n.a.	n.a.

Government Domestic Debt as Percent of GDP (Continued)

Country	1979–93	1979–83	1984–88	1989–93
Botswana	0.6	1.0	0.0	n.a.
Burundi	n.a.	n.a.	n.a.	n.a.
Cameroon	9.9	n.a.	n.a.	9.9
Chad	7.5	n.a.	n.a.	7.5
Ethiopia	21.7	15.3	24.9	29.8
Gabon	n.a.	n.a.	n.a.	n.a.
Gambia	14.1	14.1	n.a.	n.a.
Ghana	n.a.	n.a.	n.a.	n.a.
Guinea-Bissau	n.a.	n.a.	n.a.	n.a.
Kenya	n.a.	n.a.	n.a.	n.a.
Lesotho	22.5	n.a.	31.4	19.6
Madagascar	n.a.	n.a.	n.a.	n.a.
Malawi	n.a.	n.a.	n.a.	n.a.
Mauritius	28.4	31.8	30.6	22.9
Morocco	18.8	13.6	16.6	26.4
Namibia	n.a.	n.a.	n.a.	n.a.
Nigeria	27.4	21.2	34.3	26.8
Rwanda	7.5	0.8	n.a.	12.0
Seychelles	n.a.	n.a.	n.a.	n.a.
Sierra Leone	20.8	32.3	22.8	7.3
South Africa	31.3	30.2	29.0	35.7
Swaziland	3.3	3.6	4.1	1.6
Tanzania	n.a.	n.a.	n.a.	n.a.
Tunisia	10.4	8.4	10.6	13.4
Uganda	n.a.	n.a.	n.a.	n.a.
Zaire	6.2	10.1	n.a.	3.0
Zambia	n.a.	n.a.	n.a.	n.a.
Zimbabwe	33.8	32.5	33.8	37.1

Government Domestic Debt as Percent of GDP (Concluded)

Country	1979–93	1979–83	1984–88	1989–93
Bhutan	1.7	1.2	2.1	1.5
China	n.a.	n.a.	n.a.	n.a.
Fiji	19.8	16.2	22.8	24.5
India	38.7	31.5	39.7	45.0
Indonesia	1.1	0.6	0.9	1.8
Korea	5.2	4.8	6.0	4.9
Malaysia	n.a.	n.a.	n.a.	n.a.
Myanmar	n.a.	n.a.	n.a.	n.a.
Nepal	13.8	n.a.	13.7	13.8
Pakistan	27.7	21.9	31.1	39.7
Papua New Guinea	10.0	7.7	8.5	13.7
Philippines	18.5	8.1	18.4	29.0
Singapore	71.7	57.6	80.4	77.3
Solomon Islands	n.a.	n.a.	n.a.	n.a.
Sri Lanka	38.0	37.8	36.9	39.2
Thailand	16.5	16.6	21.8	11.0
Tonga	n.a.	n.a.	n.a.	n.a.
Argentina	n.a.	n.a.	n.a.	n.a.
Bahamas	18.0	16.3	15.4	22.2
Barbados	n.a.	n.a.	n.a.	n.a.
Belize	9.5	n.a.	n.a.	9.5
Bolivia	n.a.	n.a.	n.a.	n.a.
Brazil	n.a.	n.a.	n.a.	n.a.
Chile	n.a.	n.a.	n.a.	n.a.
Colombia	n.a.	n.a.	n.a.	n.a.
Costa Rica	n.a.	n.a.	n.a.	n.a.
Dominican Republic	n.a.	n.a.	n.a.	n.a.
Ecuador	n.a.	n.a.	n.a.	n.a.
El Salvador	n.a.	n.a.	n.a.	n.a.
Guatemala	n.a.	n.a.	n.a.	n.a.
Guyana	131.9	127.4	220.6	47.6
Haiti	n.a.	n.a.	n.a.	n.a.
Honduras	n.a.	n.a.	n.a.	n.a.
Mexico	n.a.	n.a.	n.a.	n.a.
Netherlands Antilles	13.4	12.4	15.6	n.a.
Nicaragua	n.a.	n.a.	n.a.	n.a.
Panama	18.8	15.1	21.6	19.6
Paraguay	n.a.	n.a.	n.a.	n.a.
Peru	n.a.	n.a.	n.a.	n.a.
St Kitts and Nevis	n.a.	n.a.	n.a.	n.a.
St Lucia	n.a.	n.a.	n.a.	n.a.
St Vincent and Grenadine	13.4	n.a.	16.2	10.6
Trinidad and Tobago	n.a.	n.a.	n.a.	n.a.
Uruguay	7.1	5.7	10.1	5.5
Venezuela	n.a.	n.a.	n.a.	n.a.

Appendix 4

Government Foreign Debt as Percent of GDP

Country	1979–93	1979–83	1984–88	1989–93
Australia	3.7	3.3	4.2	2.6
Austria	8.2	8.0	8.7	7.8
Belgium	14.6	7.7	19.1	16.9
Canada	4.8	2.8	6.0	9.1
Denmark	n.a.	n.a.	n.a.	n.a.
Finland	7.3	5.9	7.2	9.0
France	n.a.	n.a.	n.a.	n.a.
Germany	6.2	2.9	6.3	9.4
Iceland	15.2	11.2	16.1	18.1
Ireland	n.a.	n.a.	n.a.	n.a.
Italy	0.0	0.0	0.0	0.0
Japan	0.3	0.2	0.3	0.3
Luxembourg	0.5	0.2	0.9	0.6
Netherlands	12.4	n.a.	10.2	12.9
New Zealand	24.5	18.8	28.7	32.1
Norway	4.7	8.4	1.8	3.8
Spain	2.4	1.2	1.9	4.0
Sweden	9.4	6.4	12.4	9.4
Switzerland	0.0	0.0	0.0	0.0
United Kingdom	n.a.	n.a.	n.a.	n.a.
United States	0.0	0.0	0.0	0.0
Bahrain	5.0	6.1	5.6	3.5
Cyprus	21.2	14.3	26.3	22.9
Egypt	n.a.	n.a.	n.a.	n.a.
Greece	n.a.	n.a.	n.a.	n.a.
Hungary	n.a.	n.a.	n.a.	n.a.
Iran	n.a.	n.a.	n.a.	n.a.
Israel	53.0	67.0	58.2	33.9
Jordan	66.5	23.0	44.2	132.3
Kuwait	26.8	n.a.	n.a.	28.4
Malta	6.4	7.6	7.4	4.8
Oman	16.2	9.7	n.a.	22.8
Poland	n.a.	n.a.	n.a.	n.a.
Portugal	n.a.	n.a.	n.a.	n.a.
Romania	n.a.	n.a.	n.a.	n.a.
Syria	n.a.	n.a.	n.a.	n.a.
Turkey	13.4	n.a.	n.a.	13.4
United Arab Republic	n.a.	n.a.	n.a.	n.a.

Government Foreign Debt as Percent of GDP (Continued)

Country	1979–93	1979–83	1984–88	1989–93
Botswana	17.6	15.8	19.9	n.a.
Burundi	n.a.	n.a.	n.a.	n.a.
Cameroon	43.0	n.a.	n.a.	43.0
Chad	36.6	n.a.	n.a.	36.6
Ethiopia	18.2	12.8	20.2	27.0
Gabon	n.a.	n.a.	n.a.	n.a.
Gambia	21.4	21.4	n.a.	n.a.
Ghana	n.a.	n.a.	n.a.	n.a.
Guinea-Bissau	n.a.	n.a.	n.a.	n.a.
Kenya	n.a.	n.a.	n.a.	n.a.
Lesotho	56.5	n.a.	58.3	55.9
Madagascar	n.a.	n.a.	n.a.	n.a.
Malawi	n.a.	n.a.	n.a.	n.a.
Mauritius	18.5	18.4	23.4	13.8
Morocco	50.0	33.2	59.6	66.2
Namibia	n.a.	n.a.	n.a.	n.a.
Nigeria	45.5	5.2	43.5	87.9
Rwanda	27.6	11.1	n.a.	38.6
Seychelles	n.a.	n.a.	n.a.	n.a.
Sierra Leone	42.6	27.3	37.2	63.1
South Africa	1.7	1.8	2.2	0.8
Swaziland	34.0·	28.0	44.6	26.2
Tanzania	n.a.	n.a.	n.a.	n.a.
Tunisia	32.8	25.8	36.8	37.9
Uganda	n.a.	n.a.	n.a.	n.a.
Zaire	36.9	15.3	n.a.	54.2
Zambia	n.a.	n.a.	n.a.	n.a.
Zimbabwe	18.3	12.2	22.6	22.8

Government Foreign Debt as Percent of GDP (Concluded)

Country	1979–93	1979–83	1984–88	1989–93
Bhutan	24.8	0.9	4.1	42.0
China	n.a.	n.a.	n.a.	n.a.
Fiji	10.1	10.0	11.5	8.2
India	6.5	7.4	6.5	5.7
Indonesia	32.1	20.0	37.2	39.1
Korea	6.1	8.3	7.3	2.7
Malaysia	n.a.	n.a.	n.a.	n.a.
Myanmar	n.a.	n.a.	n.a.	n.a.
Nepal	29.4	n.a.	23.1	31.6
Pakistan	29.0	28.8	29.0	29.8
Papua New Guinea	28.2	20.2	35.9	28.6
Philippines	16.0	9.5	17.9	20.5
Singapore	1.5	3.3	1.1	0.1
Solomon Islands	n.a.	n.a.	n.a.	n.a.
Sri Lanka	41.6	30.8	41.5	52.6
Thailand	5.6	4.3	7.9	4.5
Tonga	n.a.	n.a.	n.a.	n.a.
Argentina	n.a.	n.a.	n.a.	n.a.
Bahamas	3.9	3.1	4.6	4.0
Barbados	n.a.	n.a.	n.a.	n.a.
Belize	18.1	n.a.	n.a.	18.1
Bolivia	n.a.	n.a.	n.a.	n.a.
Brazil	n.a.	n.a.	n.a.	n.a.
Chile	n.a.	n.a.	n.a.	n.a.
Colombia	n.a.	n.a.	n.a.	n.a.
Costa Rica	n.a.	n.a.	n.a.	n.a.
Dominican Republic	n.a.	n.a.	n.a.	n.a.
Ecuador	n.a.	n.a.	n.a.	n.a.
El Salvador	n.a.	n.a.	n.a.	n.a.
Guatemala	n.a.	n.a.	n.a.	n.a.
Guyana	172.5	114.8	177.8	224.7
Haiti	n.a.	n.a.	n.a.	n.a.
Honduras	n.a.	n.a.	n.a.	n.a.
Mexico	n.a.	n.a.	n.a.	n.a.
Netherlands Antilles	24.1	25.1	22.1	n.a.
Nicaragua	n.a.	n.a.	n.a.	n.a.
Panama	45.2	43.0	47.1	45.6
Paraguay	n.a.	n.a.	n.a.	n.a.
Peru	n.a.	n.a.	n.a.	n.a.
St Kitts and Nevis	n.a.	n.a.	n.a.	n.a.
St Lucia	n.a.	n.a.	n.a.	n.a.
St Vincent and Grenadine	23.9	n.a.	20.9	26.9
Trinidad and Tobago	n.a.	n.a.	n.a.	n.a.
Uruguay	13.6	7.7	16.3	16.9
Venezuela	n.a.	n.a.	n.a.	n.a.

Appendix 5

Government Debt as Percent of GDP

Country	1979–93	1979–83	1984–88	1989–93
Australia	19.7	18.7	21.7	15.5
Austria	38.2	26.8	40.4	47.4
Belgium	93.7	59.9	101.5	119.8
Canada	35.3	27.5	41.3	44.0
Denmark	n.a.	n.a.	n.a.	n.a.
Finland	12.9	9.8	13.7	15.7
France	n.a.	n.a.	n.a.	n.a.
Germany	21.0	16.8	21.4	24.9
Iceland	24.9	18.2	24.4	32.2
Ireland	n.a.	n.a.	n.a.	n.a.
Italy	72.0	53.7	77.6	93.1
Japan	49.3	40.5	55.1	56.4
Luxembourg	6.3	6.7	7.4	4.1
Netherlands	60.0	n.a.	57.5	60.5
New Zealand	57.4	50.5	63.8	60.4
Norway	26.7	31.5	26.4	21.1
Spain	30.5	17.1	37.1	37.3
Sweden	40.9	31.9	50.3	40.6
Switzerland	15.3	15.8	15.7	14.4
United Kingdom	n.a.	n.a.	n.a.	n.a.
United States	37.5	27.5	38.6	46.6
Bahrain	12.0	7.8	10.7	17.1
Cyprus	42.2	29.0	46.2	51.5
Egypt	n.a.	n.a.	n.a.	n.a.
Greece	n.a.	n.a.	n.a.	n.a.
Hungary	n.a.	n.a.	n.a.	n.a.
Iran	n.a.	n.a.	n.a.	n.a.
Israel	160.2	171.8	172.4	136.5
Jordan	90.3	37.0	65.7	168.2
Kuwait	61.7	n.a.	13.0	86.3
Malta	17.0	13.2	14.1	22.3
Oman	19.3	10.0	n.a.	28.7
Poland	n.a.	n.a.	n.a.	n.a.
Portugal	n.a.	n.a.	n.a.	n.a.
Romania	n.a.	n.a.	n.a.	n.a.
Syria	n.a.	n.a.	n.a.	n.a.
Turkey	26.6	n.a.	n.a.	26.6
United Arab Republic	n.a.	n.a.	n.a.	n.a.

Government Debt as Percent of GDP (Continued)

Country	1979–93	1979–83	1984–88	1989–93
Botswana	18.2	16.8	19.9	n.a.
Burundi	n.a.	n.a.	n.a.	n.a.
Cameroon	52.9	n.a.	n.a.	52.9
Chad	44.2	n.a.	n.a.	44.2
Ethiopia	40.0	28.1	45.1	56.8
Gabon	n.a.	n.a.	n.a.	n.a.
Gambia	35.5	35.5	n.a.	n.a.
Ghana	n.a.	n.a.	n.a.	n.a.
Guinea-Bissau	n.a.	n.a.	n.a.	n.a.
Kenya	n.a.	n.a.	n.a.	n.a.
Lesotho	79.1	n.a.	89.7	75.5
Madagascar	n.a.	n.a.	n.a.	n.a.
Malawi	n.a.	n.a.	n.a.	n.a.
Mauritius	47.0	50.2	54.0	36.7
Morocco	68.8	46.9	76.2	92.5
Namibia	n.a.	n.a.	n.a.	n.a.
Nigeria	73.0	26.4	77.8	114.8
Rwanda	35.1	11.9	n.a.	50.5
Seychelles	n.a.	n.a.	n.a.	n.a.
Sierra Leone	63.4	59.6	60.0	70.4
South Africa	33.0	31.9	31.2	36.5
Swaziland	37.3	31.6	48.8	27.8
Tanzania	n.a.	n.a.	n.a.	n.a.
Tunisia	43.2	34.2	47.4	51.3
Uganda	n.a.	n.a.	n.a.	n.a.
Zaire	43.1	25.4	n.a.	57.2
Zambia	n.a.	n.a.	n.a.	n.a.
Zimbabwe	52.1	44.7	56.4	59.9

Government Debt as Percent of GDP (Concluded)

Country	1979–93	1979–83	1984–88	1989–93
Bhutan	26.5	2.1	6.2	43.5
China	n.a.	n.a.	n.a.	n.a.
Fiji	29.9	26.2	34.3	32.7
India	45.2	38.9	46.1	50.7
Indonesia	33.2	20.6	38.1	40.9
Korea	11.3	13.1	13.3	7.6
Malaysia	n.a.	n.a.	n.a.	n.a.
Myanmar	n.a.	n.a.	n.a.	n.a.
Nepal	43.2	n.a.	36.8	45.3
Pakistan	56.7	50.7	60.1	69.5
Papua New Guinea	38.2	27.8	44.5	42.3
Philippines	34.4	17.6	36.3	49.5
Singapore	73.2	60.9	81.5	77.4
Solomon Islands	n.a.	n.a.	n.a.	n.a.
Sri Lanka	79.6	68.6	78.4	91.8
Thailand	22.0	20.9	29.7	15.5
Tonga	n.a.	n.a.	n.a.	n.a.
Argentina	n.a.	n.a.	n.a.	n.a.
Bahamas	21.9	19.4	20.0	26.3
Barbados	n.a.	n.a.	n.a.	n.a.
Belize	27.6	n.a.	n.a.	27.6
Bolivia	n.a.	n.a.	n.a.	n.a.
Brazil	n.a.	n.a.	n.a.	n.a.
Chile	n.a.	n.a.	n.a.	n.a.
Colombia	n.a.	n.a.	n.a.	n.a.
Costa Rica	n.a.	n.a.	n.a.	n.a.
Dominican Republic	n.a.	n.a.	n.a.	n.a.
Ecuador	n.a.	n.a.	n.a.	n.a.
El Salvador	n.a.	n.a.	n.a.	n.a.
Guatemala	n.a.	n.a.	n.a.	n.a.
Guyana	304.3	242.2	398.4	272.3
Haiti	n.a.	n.a.	n.a.	n.a.
Honduras	n.a.	n.a.	n.a.	n.a.
Mexico	n.a.	n.a.	n.a.	n.a.
Netherlands Antilles	37.6	37.5	37.6	n.a.
Nicaragua	n.a.	n.a.	n.a.	n.a.
Panama	64.0	58.1	68.7	65.2
Paraguay	n.a.	n.a.	n.a.	n.a.
Peru	n.a.	n.a.	n.a.	n.a.
St Kitts and Nevis	n.a.	n.a.	n.a.	n.a.
St Lucia	n.a.	n.a.	n.a.	n.a.
St Vincent and Grenadine	37.3	n.a.	37.1	37.5
Trinidad and Tobago	n.a.	n.a.	n.a.	n.a.
Uruguay	20.7	13.4	26.4	22.4
Venezuela	n.a.	n.a.	n.a.	n.a.

Appendix 6

*Government and Government-Guaranteed Foreign Debt
as Percent of GDP*

Country	*1979–93*	*1979–83*	*1984–88*	*1989–93*
Bahrain	n.a.	n.a.	n.a.	n.a.
Cyprus	n.a.	n.a.	n.a.	n.a.
Egypt	64.4	65.1	57.6	70.7
Greece	n.a.	n.a.	n.a.	n.a.
Hungary	42.0	29.6	45.3	52.5
Iran	1.3	2.9	1.1	0.5
Israel	n.a.	n.a.	n.a.	n.a.
Jordan	83.4	38.6	64.9	146.7
Kuwait	61.7	n.a.	13.0	86.3
Malta	6.4	7.4	7.3	4.8
Oman	19.2	9.4	24.4	23.9
Poland	45.8	n.a.	45.8	n.a.
Portugal	34.9	31.0	45.5	26.4
Romania	9.5	16.7	10.6	2.6
Syria	44.2	19.3	44.2	59.1
Turkey	27.9	n.a.	34.2	25.4
United Arab Republic	n.a.	n.a.	n.a.	n.a.

Government and Government-Guaranteed Foreign Debt
as Percent of GDP (Continued)

Country	1979–93	1979–83	1984–88	1989–93
Botswana	19.7	17.2	25.4	15.6
Burundi	45.3	14.2	42.5	79.3
Cameroon	32.7	27.4	n.a.	37.9
Chad	28.3	n.a.	25.3	31.4
Ethiopia	31.2	17.2	29.5	50.7
Gabon	35.5	29.5	20.0	55.6
Gambia	70.2	37.9	n.a.	102.4
Ghana	25.8	5.9	26.9	44.5
Guinea-Bissau	212.1	n.a.	185.6	231.9
Kenya	44.7	30.8	43.3	60.1
Lesotho	56.0	n.a.	57.2	55.2
Madagascar	130.4	n.a.	144.5	127.6
Malawi	62.7	50.3	70.3	74.6
Mauritius	27.2	25.5	30.1	26.1
Morocco	73.0	54.0	89.0	76.6
Namibia	n.a.	n.a.	n.a.	n.a.
Nigeria	48.1	7.3	48.3	88.8
Rwanda	28.1	11.6	n.a.	36.3
Seychelles	39.8	n.a.	43.6	36.9
Sierra Leone	51.6	28.0	49.1	77.7
South Africa	n.a.	n.a.	n.a.	n.a.
Swaziland	38.1	33.9	47.4	29.8
Tanzania	99.2	42.2	96.5	158.8
Tunisia	47.4	38.7	53.1	51.0
Uganda	32.0	7.7	22.1	66.3
Zaire	70.1	32.6	81.0	97.8
Zambia	114.9	55.3	160.9	132.0
Zimbabwe	26.9	14.1	36.0	36.2

Government and Government-Guaranteed Foreign Debt as Percent of GDP (Concluded)

Country	1979–93	1979–83	1984–88	1989–93
Bhutan	16.5	0.6	7.0	30.4
China	6.2	1.6	4.8	11.5
Fiji	20.6	16.4	26.4	19.0
India	16.3	10.4	14.2	24.4
Indonesia	32.4	20.4	37.8	38.9
Korea	17.6	23.4	22.1	7.4
Malaysia	31.9	20.7	47.0	28.1
Myanmar	25.6	24.9	36.9	14.8
Nepal	22.3	9.0	23.8	41.9
Pakistan	35.9	33.9	35.4	38.4
Papua New Guinea	34.1	21.1	44.1	36.9
Philippines	40.9	20.9	50.6	51.3
Singapore	n.a.	n.a.	n.a.	n.a.
Solomon Islands	26.4	12.5	40.4	n.a.
Sri Lanka	46.4	32.2	48.8	58.1
Thailand	16.1	12.4	22.1	13.7
Tonga	36.7	n.a.	39.1	35.2
Argentina	20.6	9.4	31.1	21.3
Bahamas	n.a.	n.a.	n.a.	n.a.
Barbados	22.8	15.5	28.8	29.6
Belize	31.3	19.9	37.3	32.3
Bolivia	57.1	48.3	59.1	63.9
Brazil	21.9	18.2	27.7	19.2
Chile	39.0	20.8	65.2	31.0
Colombia	24.9	13.1	28.9	32.6
Costa Rica	65.8	59.4	83.0	54.9
Dominican Republic	34.3	17.6	40.8	44.5
Ecuador	59.7	28.1	67.8	83.2
El Salvador	27.1	18.4	30.2	32.6
Guatemala	18.7	8.8	23.8	23.4
Guyana	212.8	117.0	175.1	346.4
Haiti	24.3	20.8	28.3	25.6
Honduras	56.1	39.5	56.8	71.9
Mexico	32.9	22.9	48.1	27.5
Netherlands Antilles	n.a.	n.a.	n.a.	n.a.
Nicaragua	145.6	74.2	47.2	315.5
Panama	69.0	64.1	71.4	71.5
Paraguay	25.2	13.8	33.1	28.7
Peru	32.7	30.7	40.6	26.7
St Kitts and Nevis	19.8	n.a.	17.2	21.8
St Lucia	16.4	n.a.	14.4	19.3
St Vincent and Grenadine	22.3	19.3	22.7	27.2
Trinidad and Tobago	20.9	10.6	27.0	41.7
Uruguay	36.0	20.2	46.6	41.2
Venezuela	33.9	17.7	38.8	45.1

Appendix 7

Continuously Compounded Rates of Economic Growth

Country	1979–93	1979–83	1984–88	1989–93
Australia	2.9	2.2	4.5	1.9
Austria	2.2	2.1	2.1	2.5
Belgium	1.8	1.4	2.2	1.8
Canada	2.5	1.7	4.6	0.1
Denmark	1.8	1.5	2.7	1.1
Finland	2.0	3.9	3.5	−1.3
France	1.9	1.8	2.5	1.5
Germany	2.0	0.4	2.4	2.8
Iceland	2.5	3.2	4.3	0.1
Ireland	3.6	2.3	3.9	4.5
Italy	2.5	2.3	3.0	2.1
Japan	3.9	3.7	4.3	3.6
Luxembourg	3.2	1.3	4.4	4.2
Netherlands	1.9	0.5	2.7	2.5
New Zealand	2.2	3.3	2.0	0.9
Norway	2.8	3.0	3.3	2.0
Spain	2.2	1.0	3.5	2.0
Sweden	1.4	1.7	2.8	−0.3
Switzerland	1.7	1.6	2.6	1.0
United Kingdom	1.8	0.9	4.0	0.5
United States	2.2	1.1	3.8	1.7
Bahrain	2.5	−0.3	2.5	5.4
Cyprus	5.8	5.9	6.3	5.2
Egypt	5.7	6.2	7.5	3.7
Greece	1.6	1.2	2.3	1.2
Hungary	1.7	2.1	2.8	−1.4
Iran	0.4	−0.5	−4.6	6.5
Israel	5.0	6.6	3.8	4.6
Jordan	4.0	7.6	2.6	1.8
Kuwait	0.4	−3.0	−2.6	0.3
Malta	4.3	2.9	3.9	6.1
Oman	7.8	10.4	6.6	6.4
Poland	4.1	n.a.	4.1	n.a.
Portugal	2.9	2.8	2.8	3.0
Romania	−2.0	3.3	1.6	−10.5
Syria	5.0	8.0	3.1	4.3
Turkey	3.8	n.a.	2.3	4.1
United Arab Republic	9.5	16.2	1.6	8.5

Continuously Compounded Rates of Economic Growth (Continued)

Country	1979–93	1979–83	1984–88	1989–93
Botswana	9.6	10.8	9.6	8.1
Burundi	4.1	4.5	4.5	3.0
Cameroon	5.8	8.9	n.a.	−2.1
Chad	3.4	n.a.	2.6	4.1
Ethiopia	2.0	5.0	1.3	−1.7
Gabon	3.2	2.1	2.4	5.7
Gambia	4.4	6.9	n.a.	2.0
Ghana	2.2	−2.4	4.6	4.4
Guinea-Bissau	4.0	n.a.	6.7	3.3
Kenya	3.4	3.2	4.9	1.9
Lesotho	6.9	n.a.	8.6	5.9
Madagascar	1.2	n.a.	3.3	0.8
Malawi	2.5	0.3	3.1	4.3
Mauritius	4.5	0.9	7.4	5.3
Morocco	3.4	2.7	5.1	2.2
Namibia	3.5	n.a.	4.8	2.8
Nigeria	2.2	−1.4	3.2	5.0
Rwanda	2.8	9.9	n.a.	−0.7
Seychelles	5.7	n.a.	4.8	6.4
Sierra Leone	−0.8	3.3	−1.2	−4.4
South Africa	1.7	2.6	2.0	0.1
Swaziland	9.1	3.6	12.3	14.6
Tanzania	2.9	0.6	3.7	4.3
Tunisia	4.5	5.3	3.2	5.2
Uganda	4.3	6.7	3.6	4.1
Zaire	−5.5	n.a.	0.6	−7.0
Zambia	0.7	0.2	2.1	−1.1
Zimbabwe	5.1	6.0	4.2	5.2

Continuously Compounded Rates of Economic Growth (Concluded)

Country	1979–93	1979–83	1984–88	1989–93
Bhutan	5.4	6.4	5.3	4.6
China	9.0	7.4	11.0	8.2
Fiji	2.8	–0.7	3.3	6.6
India	4.4	3.7	5.6	4.1
Indonesia	5.9	5.9	5.1	6.7
Korea	7.5	6.0	9.6	6.9
Malaysia	6.5	6.9	4.3	8.4
Myanmar	3.3	7.8	–1.9	4.1
Nepal	4.1	1.7	5.7	5.4
Pakistan	5.9	6.5	6.2	4.8
Papua New Guinea	3.2	1.0	2.7	5.9
Philippines	1.9	3.9	–0.2	2.2
Singapore	7.3	8.4	5.5	7.9
Solomon Islands	7.1	8.9	5.2	n.a.
Sri Lanka	2.7	0.9	3.6	4.3
Thailand	7.3	5.2	7.4	9.2
Tonga	2.7	5.7	1.8	2.2
Argentina	1.5	0.6	0.5	3.3
Bahamas	3.8	6.0	5.0	0.5
Barbados	2.6	0.8	4.0	4.9
Belize	6.2	n.a.	3.9	7.6
Bolivia	0.9	–1.1	0.3	3.4
Brazil	2.2	1.8	4.7	–0.5
Chile	4.6	1.0	5.5	7.2
Colombia	3.6	2.8	4.2	3.7
Costa Rica	3.0	–0.3	4.4	5.0
Dominican Republic	3.1	4.5	2.9	2.1
Ecuador	2.7	2.4	3.0	2.7
El Salvador	0.5	–4.9	1.8	4.5
Guatemala	1.9	0.5	1.5	3.8
Guyana	–1.8	–6.4	0.3	1.3
Haiti	0.9	1.8	0.4	–1.2
Honduras	3.0	1.4	3.9	3.8
Mexico	2.6	3.9	1.1	2.9
Netherlands Antilles	–1.0	–0.4	–2.0	n.a.
Nicaragua	–2.8	–3.5	–4.2	–0.4
Panama	3.2	5.6	–1.4	5.3
Paraguay	4.0	5.2	3.5	3.4
Peru	0.6	0.5	3.2	–2.0
St Kitts and Nevis	5.6	n.a.	7.0	4.2
St Lucia	4.5	2.2	7.5	4.2
St Vincent and Grenadine	5.6	5.2	6.4	4.7
Trinidad and Tobago	–1.0	2.4	–4.5	–0.8
Uruguay	2.0	–0.4	3.3	3.1
Venezuela	1.6	–1.2	3.3	2.8

Appendix 8

Real Interest Rates

Country	1979–93	1979–83	1984–88	1989–93
Australia	5.1	1.0	6.7	9.0
Austria	1.4	1.0	1.5	1.8
Belgium	4.5	2.4	4.7	5.4
Canada	4.8	3.6	5.2	6.1
Denmark	5.0	3.3	5.2	6.5
Finland	2.8	−0.7	3.6	4.0
France	3.1	0.1	5.3	5.5
Germany	4.6	3.9	4.5	5.4
Iceland	−5.0	−11.8	−3.1	−0.1
Ireland	1.7	−2.2	3.6	3.9
Italy	1.9	−1.2	4.2	3.2
Japan	1.9	1.3	2.7	1.9
Luxembourg	2.6	0.1	4.3	3.1
Netherlands	3.6	2.9	4.4	3.5
New Zealand	3.7	−0.8	3.6	7.2
Norway	3.4	−1.3	4.7	7.7
Spain	2.8	−0.9	3.7	5.6
Sweden	4.0	2.5	5.5	3.9
Switzerland	1.8	0.3	2.4	2.3
United Kingdom	3.3	1.1	4.8	4.0
United States	3.9	4.1	4.9	2.8
Bahrain	7.6	n.a.	7.6	n.a.
Cyprus	1.3	−1.7	3.3	2.1
Egypt	−2.9	−0.9	−4.2	−3.5
Greece	0.4	−4.3	0.2	5.3
Hungary	−2.3	n.a.	n.a.	−2.3
Iran	n.a.	n.a.	n.a.	n.a.
Israel	5.3	4.6	9.2	1.5
Jordan	−1.8	n.a.	n.a.	−1.8
Kuwait	3.7	2.0	5.8	4.5
Malta	2.8	−1.4	5.4	3.6
Oman	10.0	n.a.	13.9	6.1
Poland	n.a.	n.a.	n.a.	n.a.
Portugal	2.9	−0.3	4.4	5.1
Romania	n.a.	n.a.	n.a.	n.a.
Syria	−13.5	−8.1	−30.8	−6.3
Turkey	2.4	n.a.	−2.6	4.4
United Arab Republic	n.a.	n.a.	n.a.	n.a.

Real Interest Rates (Continued)

Country	1979–93	1979–83	1984–88	1989–93
Botswana	−1.3	−1.7	0.2	−2.8
Burundi	−2.0	−5.3	1.3	n.a.
Cameroon	3.7	−1.4	n.a.	10.1
Chad	9.3	n.a.	9.0	9.7
Ethiopia	−0.6	n.a.	3.6	−4.9
Gabon	1.0	−1.8	3.0	4.3
Gambia	5.3	2.8	n.a.	7.7
Ghana	−23.1	−38.5	−7.6	n.a.
Guinea-Bissau	−15.5	n.a.	−23.9	−13.4
Kenya	0.4	−2.2	2.9	0.8
Lesotho	0.2	n.a.	−1.3	1.1
Madagascar	−12.9	n.a.	−12.9	n.a.
Malawi	−0.3	1.8	−4.0	3.8
Mauritius	1.6	−4.8	6.2	3.6
Morocco	0.0	−2.9	1.3	2.6
Namibia	2.2	n.a.	n.a.	2.2
Nigeria	−8.4	−6.5	−9.4	−9.4
Rwanda	0.2	−3.5	n.a.	2.0
Seychelles	9.1	n.a.	n.a.	9.1
Sierra Leone	−25.3	−14.9	−44.2	−16.8
South Africa	0.1	−2.3	0.2	3.0
Swaziland	−2.1	−4.2	−2.3	1.8
Tanzania	−14.1	−15.5	−15.1	−2.3
Tunisia	−2.7	−5.4	0.2	−4.0
Uganda	−38.6	−19.2	−67.1	−4.1
Zaire	−152.9	n.a.	−28.8	−177.7
Zambia	−23.8	−4.8	−19.4	−62.6
Zimbabwe	−1.2	−1.2	0.0	−4.1

Real Interest Rates (Concluded)

Country	1979–93	1979–83	1984–88	1989–93
Bhutan	–0.1	–7.9	2.2	–0.6
China	–0.6	2.3	–1.8	–6.2
Fiji	0.9	–1.1	3.2	0.7
India	2.4	0.7	3.4	3.2
Indonesia	5.5	–4.5	10.3	12.0
Korea	2.1	–2.5	6.0	2.7
Malaysia	4.2	2.6	6.4	3.4
Myanmar	–5.9	0.0	–8.0	–15.1
Nepal	–0.8	–2.5	0.3	2.2
Pakistan	0.0	0.0	1.4	–1.6
Papua New Guinea	4.0	1.8	5.2	4.5
Philippines	1.9	0.3	0.8	4.5
Singapore	3.5	3.8	4.7	1.9
Solomon Islands	–1.3	–2.9	–0.3	n.a.
Sri Lanka	1.9	0.3	3.5	2.0
Thailand	7.3	3.8	10.5	7.7
Tonga	–1.1	–2.2	–2.2	1.7
Argentina	57.8	11.1	18.0	144.4
Bahamas	1.9	0.7	2.7	2.1
Barbados	1.7	–0.3	3.1	0.7
Belize	7.8	n.a.	5.0	8.4
Bolivia	–44.8	–31.6	–116.9	13.9
Brazil	45.1	14.1	27.3	98.4
Chile	9.7	15.8	5.3	8.0
Colombia	6.6	4.7	7.8	7.2
Costa Rica	–4.8	–22.0	2.8	4.7
Dominican Republic	n.a.	n.a.	n.a.	n.a.
Ecuador	–10.5	–26.4	–9.7	–8.1
El Salvador	–2.7	0.3	–5.9	0.0
Guatemala	–0.7	3.0	–3.7	–1.5
Guyana	1.1	–5.0	–8.1	20.1
Haiti	n.a.	n.a.	n.a.	n.a.
Honduras	3.1	4.3	7.9	–2.2
Mexico	–4.8	–8.8	–10.9	5.3
Netherlands Antilles	4.5	2.9	6.1	n.a.
Nicaragua	–131.7	n.a.	240.8	–224.8
Panama	8.1	n.a.	8.4	7.8
Paraguay	2.0	n.a.	n.a.	2.0
Peru	–42.7	–25.1	–72.5	–30.5
St Kitts and Nevis	5.9	n.a.	7.0	4.8
St Lucia	2.8	–0.3	5.8	2.8
St Vincent and Grenadine	2.1	–3.2	6.1	3.0
Trinidad and Tobago	–2.6	–4.6	–1.1	–2.1
Uruguay	8.4	10.1	8.1	6.9
Venezuela	–5.0	0.4	–7.7	–7.8

Appendix 9

Continuously Compounded CPI Inflation Rates

Country	1979–93	1979–83	1984–88	1989–93
Australia	6.8	9.6	6.8	4.1
Austria	3.7	5.0	2.7	3.3
Belgium	4.2	6.8	3.0	2.9
Canada	6.3	9.2	4.1	5.0
Denmark	5.6	9.6	4.5	2.6
Finland	6.1	9.3	4.9	4.2
France	6.1	11.1	4.3	2.9
Germany	3.0	4.9	1.2	3.3
Iceland	25.8	45.4	22.4	9.6
Ireland	7.4	14.7	4.5	3.0
Italy	10.1	15.6	6.9	6.1
Japan	2.6	4.1	1.1	2.5
Luxembourg	4.4	7.1	2.2	3.3
Netherlands	2.9	5.1	1.1	2.5
New Zealand	9.2	13.0	10.7	2.7
Norway	6.7	9.3	6.7	3.5
Spain	8.9	13.5	7.5	5.8
Sweden	7.2	9.6	5.7	6.4
Switzerland	3.6	4.4	2.1	4.3
United Kingdom	6.9	10.6	4.6	5.5
United States	5.3	8.5	3.4	4.0
Bahrain	1.8	5.6	−1.2	1.1
Cyprus	5.7	8.6	3.6	4.8
Egypt	15.9	14.9	16.6	15.4
Greece	17.3	19.8	16.6	15.5
Hungary	10.2	5.8	8.6	20.5
Iran	17.0	17.1	16.7	17.1
Israel	55.3	77.6	73.6	14.7
Jordan	7.4	8.7	2.6	10.9
Kuwait	5.0	7.4	1.2	4.9
Malta	3.1	7.6	0.5	2.0
Oman	2.4	10.8	−5.3	1.6
Poland	22.0	n.a.	22.0	n.a.
Portugal	15.3	19.5	14.5	10.9
Romania	22.3	7.6	1.4	59.5
Syria	18.4	13.0	35.7	11.2
Turkey	51.0	n.a.	55.2	50.1
United Arab Republic	3.5	6.9	2.9	1.2

Continuously Compounded CPI Inflation Rates (Continued)

Country	1979–93	1979–83	1984–88	1989–93
Botswana	10.7	11.9	8.6	12.0
Burundi	8.5	11.7	6.0	7.7
Cameroon	7.5	10.6	n.a.	–0.3
Chad	–1.0	n.a.	–1.9	0.0
Ethiopia	7.1	6.1	3.9	14.4
Gabon	8.5	10.6	6.4	6.4
Gambia	8.2	7.2	n.a.	9.2
Ghana	32.7	52.3	25.2	20.5
Guinea-Bissau	46.6	n.a.	47.2	46.5
Kenya	14.3	12.2	8.9	21.7
Lesotho	12.6	n.a.	11.0	13.7
Madagascar	12.5	n.a.	23.8	10.2
Malawi	14.9	11.1	18.6	11.5
Mauritius	9.9	15.7	4.9	9.2
Morocco	7.2	9.0	6.5	5.8
Namibia	12.2	n.a.	12.2	12.2
Nigeria	20.7	13.6	20.1	28.5
Rwanda	9.0	10.8	n.a.	8.0
Seychelles	1.9	n.a.	1.4	2.4
Sierra Leone	46.1	25.7	59.8	52.6
South Africa	13.2	12.9	14.0	12.6
Swaziland	13.2	14.4	13.6	9.2
Tanzania	24.9	22.2	28.2	24.2
Tunisia	8.3	10.6	7.3	6.8
Uganda	54.6	30.8	88.9	29.9
Zaire	175.4	n.a.	60.3	204.2
Zambia	35.4	12.6	34.3	75.2
Zimbabwe	12.7	13.0	11.8	14.1

Continuously Compounded CPI Inflation Rates (Concluded)

Country	1979–93	1979–83	1984–88	1989–93
Bhutan	9.0	13.0	6.9	9.0
China	7.2	3.3	9.0	8.6
Fiji	6.6	8.0	5.6	6.9
India	8.8	9.6	7.8	9.0
Indonesia	9.3	12.7	7.4	7.8
Korea	8.2	14.3	3.5	6.7
Malaysia	3.6	5.7	1.5	3.6
Myanmar	12.7	3.4	11.4	23.1
Nepal	9.9	10.1	9.4	10.3
Pakistan	7.7	8.5	5.6	9.2
Papua New Guinea	6.0	7.5	4.9	5.4
Philippines	13.1	12.9	14.9	11.6
Singapore	2.8	5.0	0.7	2.7
Solomon Islands	11.2	10.7	11.6	n.a.
Sri Lanka	12.3	14.7	9.0	14.0
Thailand	5.6	9.6	2.3	4.8
Tonga	9.2	9.8	9.9	7.8
Argentina	131.9	96.6	139.9	159.3
Bahamas	5.9	8.1	4.7	5.0
Barbados	7.1	10.9	3.5	6.0
Belize	2.7	n.a.	4.2	1.8
Bolivia	84.5	59.5	180.2	13.8
Brazil	141.9	66.3	128.4	253.4
Chile	19.3	22.1	18.9	17.0
Colombia	21.9	22.0	19.9	23.9
Costa Rica	20.5	29.9	14.2	17.4
Dominican Republic	19.8	8.7	23.3	27.4
Ecuador	30.2	18.4	28.9	43.3
El Salvador	16.3	13.4	19.8	15.8
Guatemala	13.7	7.3	14.8	18.9
Guyana	14.1	16.5	20.6	3.1
Haiti	8.3	11.2	1.8	19.3
Honduras	10.1	10.7	3.8	15.6
Mexico	39.0	36.2	63.7	17.2
Netherlands Antilles	4.6	6.7	1.3	n.a.
Nicaragua	168.7	28.0	209.4	293.7
Panama	2.8	6.8	0.8	0.9
Paraguay	19.6	15.5	21.7	21.7
Peru	121.2	55.7	98.9	209.2
St Kitts and Nevis	2.5	n.a.	0.9	4.0
St Lucia	6.1	9.4	2.9	4.3
St Vincent and Grenadine	5.3	10.0	1.9	4.4
Trinidad and Tobago	11.3	13.7	9.0	10.8
Uruguay	49.3	37.4	50.5	60.0
Venezuela	21.9	12.3	16.7	36.9

Appendix 10

Change in Reserve Money as Percent of GDP

Country	1979–93	1979–83	1984–88	1989–93
Australia	0.4	0.5	0.5	0.2
Austria	0.4	0.6	0.2	0.6
Belgium	0.1	0.2	0.1	0.0
Canada	0.2	0.3	0.2	0.2
Denmark	0.5	0.3	0.7	0.6
Finland	0.7	0.8	1.1	0.3
France	0.3	0.6	0.5	−0.2
Germany	0.5	0.2	0.6	0.7
Iceland	1.7	3.7	1.5	0.0
Ireland	0.6	1.0	0.6	0.2
Italy	1.6	1.9	1.6	1.2
Japan	0.6	0.5	0.8	0.4
Luxembourg	n.a.	n.a.	n.a.	n.a.
Netherlands	0.5	0.5	0.5	0.6
New Zealand	0.1	0.2	0.2	0.0
Norway	0.3	0.4	0.3	0.2
Spain	1.8	4.1	1.3	0.1
Sweden	0.8	0.6	0.7	1.2
Switzerland	−0.1	−0.3	−0.2	0.1
United Kingdom	0.2	0.2	0.3	0.2
United States	0.4	0.3	0.4	0.4
Bahrain	0.4	0.8	0.1	0.4
Cyprus	3.0	4.9	2.7	1.5
Egypt	5.3	8.8	3.8	4.0
Greece	2.8	3.8	2.9	1.8
Hungary	0.7	−4.1	−0.3	5.7
Iran	5.0	6.4	7.7	2.8
Israel	1.7	1.9	2.5	0.7
Jordan	5.6	5.7	2.7	8.3
Kuwait	0.2	1.5	−1.5	−0.5
Malta	2.1	4.1	2.5	0.1
Oman	0.6	1.2	0.2	0.3
Poland	2.9	n.a.	2.9	n.a.
Portugal	3.9	4.9	1.7	5.4
Romania	3.1	2.3	0.0	6.8
Syria	4.9	4.5	2.3	7.3
Turkey	3.0	n.a.	3.6	2.8
United Arab Republic	0.6	0.4	1.8	0.3

Change in Reserve Money as Percent of GDP (Continued)

Country	1979–93	1979–83	1984–88	1989–93
Botswana	1.7	1.8	1.9	1.2
Burundi	0.5	0.7	0.4	0.3
Cameroon	0.3	1.1	n.a.	−0.5
Chad	0.2	n.a.	0.0	0.4
Ethiopia	2.0	1.3	2.0	3.0
Gabon	0.5	0.4	0.2	0.8
Gambia	2.0	2.6	n.a.	1.4
Ghana	2.3	2.8	2.9	1.2
Guinea-Bissau	6.5	n.a.	n.a.	6.5
Kenya	1.5	0.8	1.2	2.7
Lesotho	2.1	n.a.	5.3	0.0
Madagascar	1.1	n.a.	0.2	1.2
Malawi	1.6	0.8	3.5	−1.3
Mauritius	1.8	0.6	1.8	3.1
Morocco	1.7	1.5	1.6	2.1
Namibia	n.a.	n.a.	n.a.	n.a.
Nigeria	1.6	1.5	1.2	2.5
Rwanda	0.6	1.1	n.a.	0.4
Seychelles	1.6	n.a.	0.7	2.3
Sierra Leone	4.1	3.0	6.1	3.3
South Africa	−0.4	n.a.	n.a.	−0.4
Swaziland	1.5	1.4	2.1	0.5
Tanzania	n.a.	n.a.	n.a.	n.a.
Tunisia	1.1	1.6	0.7	1.1
Uganda	2.5	1.9	4.0	0.9
Zaire	7.3	1.7	4.5	12.3
Zambia	3.0	1.1	4.0	4.7
Zimbabwe	1.1	1.1	1.0	1.5

Change in Reserve Money as Percent of GDP (Concluded)

Country	1979–93	1979–83	1984–88	1989–93
Bhutan	3.4	n.a.	2.0	4.8
China	6.5	n.a.	4.8	7.5
Fiji	0.7	0.4	1.5	0.1
India	2.0	1.7	2.2	2.2
Indonesia	0.9	1.3	0.7	0.9
Korea	0.9	0.6	1.0	1.3
Malaysia	1.6	1.4	0.8	2.5
Myanmar	3.8	2.2	1.4	13.8
Nepal	1.8	1.4	1.8	2.6
Pakistan	2.3	2.3	2.1	2.6
Papua New Guinea	–0.1	–0.7	0.0	0.3
Philippines	1.4	1.1	1.3	1.9
Singapore	1.6	2.0	1.2	1.6
Solomon Islands	0.0	–0.7	0.8	n.a.
Sri Lanka	1.6	1.8	1.5	1.6
Thailand	1.0	0.9	0.9	1.2
Tonga	3.7	8.7	3.4	2.6
Argentina	6.4	8.5	5.7	5.2
Bahamas	0.5	0.6	0.6	0.2
Barbados	0.9	1.4	0.7	–0.3
Belize	0.8	0.0	1.3	0.9
Bolivia	4.2	5.4	5.6	1.7
Brazil	4.8	2.3	4.3	8.4
Chile	9.1	6.9	14.5	5.9
Colombia	2.1	2.3	1.6	2.4
Costa Rica	4.3	5.0	4.0	4.0
Dominican Republic	2.0	0.8	2.7	2.6
Ecuador	2.1	1.5	2.4	2.7
El Salvador	2.2	2.5	1.6	2.4
Guatemala	1.2	0.3	1.6	1.6
Guyana	10.2	6.6	19.3	4.6
Haiti	2.1	1.3	2.7	3.2
Honduras	0.9	0.6	0.6	1.6
Mexico	3.4	6.2	3.1	0.7
Netherlands Antilles	1.3	0.3	3.3	n.a.
Nicaragua	13.9	5.6	25.9	10.1
Panama	n.a.	n.a.	n.a.	n.a.
Paraguay	2.4	2.0	2.5	2.6
Peru	6.3	5.2	7.9	5.6
St Kitts and Nevis	1.7	n.a.	1.5	1.9
St Lucia	1.7	1.0	2.6	1.8
St Vincent and Grenadine	1.4	–0.5	3.1	1.1
Trinidad and Tobago	0.7	2.4	–1.0	1.2
Uruguay	6.5	3.4	7.9	8.2
Venezuela	1.7	1.8	0.7	2.7

Appendix 11

Reserve Money as Percent of Broad Money (M2)

Country	1979–93	1979–83	1984–88	1989–93
Australia	12.2	14.3	13.2	9.0
Austria	12.6	14.8	12.3	10.5
Belgium	18.7	23.1	18.1	14.0
Canada	10.1	11.2	9.9	8.6
Denmark	8.5	8.3	8.6	8.6
Finland	11.0	8.8	11.5	12.8
France	8.8	9.0	9.3	8.1
Germany	17.1	18.2	16.5	16.7
Iceland	26.1	36.3	27.2	14.7
Ireland	23.7	27.2	25.1	19.0
Italy	23.1	21.8	23.6	24.7
Japan	9.9	10.7	9.7	9.4
Luxembourg	n.a.	n.a.	n.a.	n.a.
Netherlands	10.0	9.5	10.0	10.5
New Zealand	9.3	14.2	9.3	3.4
Norway	11.0	13.9	10.4	8.2
Spain	22.8	18.6	29.4	20.3
Sweden	13.8	13.4	12.6	15.5
Switzerland	14.8	20.1	14.5	9.9
United Kingdom	9.3	15.4	8.2	4.4
United States	8.9	9.5	8.4	8.9
Bahrain	15.4	17.5	14.5	14.1
Cyprus	37.7	39.1	42.1	31.8
Egypt	43.6	52.2	47.6	32.6
Greece	30.2	33.2	30.6	26.7
Hungary	62.0	81.1	62.2	52.0
Iran	53.0	51.3	61.6	51.0
Israel	8.9	13.8	7.0	5.9
Jordan	40.6	46.0	36.4	39.5
Kuwait	11.6	16.5	12.6	9.4
Malta	54.1	65.3	60.0	39.4
Oman	32.8	44.2	29.3	25.0
Poland	51.6	n.a.	51.6	n.a.
Portugal	25.5	26.2	20.5	30.8
Romania	54.5	69.0	46.5	50.8
Syria	71.6	65.9	84.8	65.9
Turkey	29.6	n.a.	31.6	28.9
United Arab Republic	19.6	23.4	19.2	17.4

Reserve Money as Percent of Broad Money (M2) (Continued)

Country	1979–93	1979–83	1984–88	1989–93
Botswana	30.2	29.8	30.3	30.4
Burundi	47.7	50.8	47.9	39.2
Cameroon	27.7	28.3	n.a.	27.0
Chad	69.8	n.a.	67.8	71.9
Ethiopia	58.4	60.3	56.2	58.9
Gabon	26.0	28.3	23.5	23.8
Gambia	51.6	62.9	n.a.	40.4
Ghana	62.0	72.1	66.3	47.5
Guinea-Bissau	83.7	n.a.	n.a.	83.7
Kenya	28.3	26.3	27.6	31.1
Lesotho	40.5	n.a.	42.6	39.1
Madagascar	44.7	n.a.	48.6	43.9
Malawi	41.3	27.7	51.0	51.0
Mauritius	26.0	30.5	21.9	25.6
Morocco	33.1	34.7	31.5	33.1
Namibia	n.a.	n.a.	n.a.	n.a.
Nigeria	39.1	41.3	34.8	42.4
Rwanda	42.5	56.6	n.a.	35.4
Seychelles	26.8	n.a.	26.8	26.9
Sierra Leone	62.3	56.7	65.1	65.1
South Africa	8.9	n.a.	n.a.	8.9
Swaziland	39.2	38.1	45.8	30.0
Tanzania	n.a.	n.a.	n.a.	n.a.
Tunisia	22.6	24.5	22.7	20.3
Uganda	56.3	54.1	61.7	51.5
Zaire	75.3	61.7	82.5	84.8
Zambia	35.2	31.3	35.0	42.2
Zimbabwe	24.1	22.5	24.9	24.4

Reserve Money as Percent of Broad Money (M2) (Concluded)

Country	1979–93	1979–83	1984–88	1989–93
Bhutan	66.6	n.a.	41.2	91.9
China	42.2	n.a.	42.9	41.8
Fiji	20.5	22.0	21.0	18.5
India	33.1	33.7	32.7	32.8
Indonesia	29.9	42.2	28.9	15.7
Korea	20.6	24.9	16.9	20.1
Malaysia	21.6	23.5	19.5	21.9
Myanmar	79.4	82.5	61.9	115.4
Nepal	41.5	43.3	40.8	39.7
Pakistan	40.5	38.7	38.6	44.3
Papua New Guinea	18.1	24.7	15.7	13.8
Philippines	29.2	28.7	27.8	31.1
Singapore	22.9	26.8	23.4	18.6
Solomon Islands	41.8	49.6	33.9	n.a.
Sri Lanka	34.2	32.2	34.2	36.3
Thailand	16.1	21.5	14.7	12.2
Tonga	110.3	115.0	114.4	102.1
Argentina	46.8	47.1	46.9	46.4
Bahamas	16.1	16.4	16.7	15.2
Barbados	22.9	23.3	22.9	21.2
Belize	26.7	24.8	28.9	26.1
Bolivia	51.4	61.3	58.2	34.7
Brazil	33.7	44.5	32.8	21.5
Chile	93.3	45.4	143.4	91.3
Colombia	54.5	58.6	49.0	53.3
Costa Rica	42.0	34.9	42.1	49.0
Dominican Republic	49.6	51.0	46.9	51.0
Ecuador	45.0	48.6	40.3	46.2
El Salvador	34.4	25.9	39.6	37.9
Guatemala	38.3	40.3	38.0	36.7
Guyana	52.2	43.1	64.5	49.0
Haiti	53.3	51.5	53.5	61.8
Honduras	29.3	32.8	26.0	29.2
Mexico	41.8	58.2	46.0	21.2
Netherlands Antilles	21.1	22.1	19.0	n.a.
Nicaragua	52.4	44.6	54.9	57.8
Panama	n.a.	n.a.	n.a.	n.a.
Paraguay	55.8	55.0	60.4	51.9
Peru	52.4	51.1	59.7	46.5
St Kitts and Nevis	19.4	n.a.	19.2	19.5
St Lucia	20.9	18.1	23.7	22.7
St Vincent and Grenadine	26.0	22.2	29.0	26.0
Trinidad and Tobago	27.5	31.2	25.2	19.9
Uruguay	30.8	21.0	35.3	36.1
Venezuela	29.4	30.6	28.4	29.3

Appendix 12

Bank Reserves as Percent of Bank Deposits

Country	1979–93	1979–83	1984–88	1989–93
Australia	4.1	5.5	4.5	2.3
Austria	5.2	6.3	5.1	4.1
Belgium	1.1	1.4	1.1	0.8
Canada	3.5	4.8	3.1	2.3
Denmark	2.2	0.8	2.7	3.1
Finland	7.0	3.3	7.9	9.9
France	2.4	2.0	3.2	2.0
Germany	8.4	9.7	8.0	7.5
Iceland	22.7	31.4	24.0	12.6
Ireland	8.3	10.3	8.5	6.0
Italy	15.7	13.9	16.4	17.4
Japan	2.2	2.5	2.1	1.9
Luxembourg	n.a.	n.a.	n.a.	n.a.
Netherlands	0.6	0.5	0.7	0.7
New Zealand	1.9	1.9	1.2	2.9
Norway	1.5	2.1	1.5	0.8
Spain	15.6	9.4	21.6	15.8
Sweden	3.1	2.8	2.4	3.9
Switzerland	6.1	9.6	6.2	2.4
United Kingdom	2.4	4.0	2.0	1.2
United States	2.2	2.8	2.1	1.8
Bahrain	8.6	7.8	5.8	12.0
Cyprus	24.3	22.3	26.7	23.8
Egypt	25.9	24.7	31.2	21.6
Greece	23.3	17.0	26.9	25.9
Hungary	34.7	48.7	32.1	34.1
Iran	36.5	27.7	46.5	39.5
Israel	62.7	128.6	38.6	21.1
Jordan	20.3	16.7	11.6	32.6
Kuwait	5.4	10.5	6.3	3.2
Malta	22.2	28.4	28.4	11.0
Oman	15.0	23.7	12.4	8.7
Poland	38.1	n.a.	38.1	n.a.
Portugal	15.1	13.4	10.7	22.9
Romania	18.9	37.2	9.5	13.8
Syria	30.9	14.9	59.4	21.5
Turkey	21.9	n.a.	26.3	20.1
United Arab Republic	12.9	15.1	13.7	11.2

Bank Reserves as Percent of Bank Deposits (Continued)

Country	1979–93	1979–83	1984–88	1989–93
Botswana	22.1	20.8	23.4	22.1
Burundi	4.7	2.9	7.1	3.1
Cameroon	4.9	4.3	n.a.	5.5
Chad	15.6	n.a.	11.6	19.5
Ethiopia	28.9	27.8	30.8	28.0
Gabon	5.4	6.5	4.6	4.1
Gambia	25.0	35.2	n.a.	14.9
Ghana	43.0	44.8	45.5	38.8
Guinea-Bissau	70.6	n.a.	n.a.	70.6
Kenya	10.1	8.5	9.9	12.0
Lesotho	32.7	n.a.	34.9	31.2
Madagascar	21.7	n.a.	24.2	21.2
Malawi	25.8	11.1	37.3	33.6
Mauritius	12.4	11.9	9.4	16.0
Morocco	4.6	2.5	3.2	8.9
Namibia	n.a.	n.a.	n.a.	n.a.
Nigeria	11.0	13.9	7.5	12.1
Rwanda	12.1	18.3	n.a.	9.0
Seychelles	11.6	n.a.	8.3	14.2
Sierra Leone	56.0	69.6	62.6	36.0
South Africa	3.0	n.a.	n.a.	3.0
Swaziland	33.3	31.2	40.8	24.1
Tanzania	n.a.	n.a.	n.a.	n.a.
Tunisia	2.8	3.5	2.4	2.4
Uganda	28.0	26.0	34.5	17.8
Zaire	49.2	35.0	59.3	58.5
Zambia	25.0	19.7	23.7	36.0
Zimbabwe	10.3	9.5	10.7	10.6

Bank Reserves as Percent of Bank Deposits (Concluded)

Country	1979–93	1979–83	1984–88	1989–93
Bhutan	56.3	n.a.	27.3	85.3
China	20.4	n.a.	20.1	20.6
Fiji	9.7	8.1	10.4	10.7
India	13.8	12.3	13.9	15.2
Indonesia	16.4	22.3	14.5	11.4
Korea	9.6	12.0	5.7	11.1
Malaysia	7.0	7.1	5.9	8.2
Myanmar	60.4	71.4	11.9	154.4
Nepal	10.6	11.3	9.4	11.4
Pakistan	12.2	10.0	11.1	15.6
Papua New Guinea	6.6	13.1	4.2	2.5
Philippines	13.4	11.8	12.5	16.1
Singapore	8.6	9.1	8.8	7.8
Solomon Islands	27.8	37.8	17.8	n.a.
Sri Lanka	14.8	13.2	16.3	15.0
Thailand	3.9	4.7	3.6	3.4
Tonga	112.2	117.8	116.8	102.5
Argentina	30.2	34.5	33.5	22.6
Bahamas	7.9	8.2	7.8	7.9
Barbados	9.9	10.1	9.7	9.6
Belize	12.9	9.0	13.5	14.1
Bolivia	34.1	35.0	46.9	20.3
Brazil	17.2	17.9	20.4	12.1
Chile	11.2	18.2	8.0	7.3
Colombia	38.2	43.2	33.9	34.0
Costa Rica	33.5	23.4	33.6	43.4
Dominican Republic	33.2	35.2	32.2	32.2
Ecuador	22.4	23.7	21.0	22.6
El Salvador	25.2	25.8	22.5	27.2
Guatemala	22.3	20.1	22.4	24.5
Guyana	39.9	27.6	55.5	36.8
Haiti	25.0	20.8	27.3	37.0
Honduras	10.1	11.8	7.8	10.8
Mexico	30.4	49.1	35.5	6.4
Netherlands Antilles	7.5	8.2	6.0	n.a.
Nicaragua	29.7	17.5	29.2	42.5
Panama	n.a.	n.a.	n.a.	n.a.
Paraguay	40.3	41.1	45.8	34.2
Peru	34.1	32.7	43.2	26.3
St Kitts and Nevis	13.8	n.a.	14.2	13.4
St Lucia	9.8	4.8	14.3	13.3
St Vincent and Grenadine	15.5	10.7	17.6	19.8
Trinidad and Tobago	19.2	23.0	17.0	11.8
Uruguay	30.4	14.0	38.3	38.9
Venezuela	17.2	16.1	12.8	22.6

Appendix 13
Growth Rates in Eight Case Study Countries

Year	Ghana	India	Jamai- ca	Malay- sia	Mexico	New Zealand	Sri Lanka	Zim- babwe
1979	-3.2	-4.9	-1.8	8.9	8.8	2.5	5.9	3.7
1980	0.0	6.3	-5.9	7.2	8.0	1.1	5.5	10.0
1981	-1.8	6.3	2.5	6.7	7.6	4.7	5.4	11.8
1982	-7.5	3.7	1.2	5.8	-0.6	2.3	-17.1	2.6
1983	0.7	7.2	2.3	6.1	-4.3	5.7	4.8	1.6
1984	2.6	3.6	-0.9	7.5	3.5	5.1	5.0	-1.9
1985	5.0	5.3	-4.7	-1.0	2.5	-0.2	4.9	6.2
1986	5.1	4.8	1.7	1.0	-3.7	3.2	4.2	0.9
1987	4.7	4.7	7.4	5.3	1.8	0.6	1.5	7.6
1988	5.5	9.5	2.8	8.6	1.3	1.5	2.7	8.4
1989	5.0	6.4	6.6	8.8	3.2	-1.3	2.3	10.9
1990	3.3	5.5	5.3	9.3	4.4	-0.8	6.0	-4.1
1991	5.2	0.5	0.5	8.3	3.6	-1.3	4.7	3.6
1992	3.8	4.5	1.9	7.5	2.7	0.0	n.a.	-7.0
1993	4.9	3.4	0.7	8.0	0.7	5.8	n.a.	4.1
1994	n.a.	n.a.	n.a.	8.4	3.4	3.3	n.a.	5.2
1995	n.a.	n.a.	n.a.	n.a.	n.a.	n.a.	n.a.	-3.2

Appendix 14
Inflation Rates in Eight Case Study Countries

Year	Ghana	India	Jamai- ca	Malay- sia	Mexico	New Zealand	Sri Lanka	Zim- babwe
1979	43.5	6.1	25.5	3.6	16.7	12.8	10.2	16.7
1980	40.6	10.8	24.1	6.5	23.4	15.8	23.2	5.3
1981	77.2	12.3	12.0	9.3	24.6	14.3	16.5	12.4
1982	20.1	7.6	6.3	5.7	46.3	15.0	10.3	10.1
1983	80.1	11.2	11.0	3.6	70.2	7.1	13.1	20.8
1984	33.4	8.0	24.5	3.8	50.4	6.0	15.4	18.4
1985	9.8	5.4	22.9	0.3	45.6	14.3	1.5	8.2
1986	22.0	8.4	14.1	0.7	62.2	12.4	7.7	13.4
1987	33.5	8.4	6.4	0.3	84.1	14.6	7.4	11.8
1988	27.3	9.0	7.9	2.5	76.2	6.2	13.1	7.2
1989	22.5	6.0	13.4	2.8	18.2	5.6	10.9	12.1
1990	31.7	8.6	19.9	2.6	23.6	5.9	19.5	16.0
1991	16.6	13.0	41.3	4.3	20.4	2.6	11.5	21.0
1992	9.6	11.1	57.3	4.7	14.4	1.0	10.8	35.1
1993	22.3	6.2	19.9	3.5	9.3	1.3	11.1	24.4
1994	22.2	9.7	30.1	3.7	6.7	1.7	8.1	20.1
1995	n.a.	n.a.	n.a.	5.2	30.0	3.7	7.4	20.4

Appendix 15

Government Deficits as Percent of GDP
in Eight Case Study Countries

Year	Ghana	India	Jamai-ca	Malay-sia	Mexico	New Zealand	Sri Lanka	Zim-babwe
1979	6.4	5.5	12.6	7.9	3.0	5.7	12.0	10.4
1980	4.2	6.5	15.5	13.3	3.0	6.7	18.3	10.9
1981	6.5	5.5	13.6	19.1	6.5	7.5	12.4	5.9
1982	5.6	6.0	15.2	17.9	12.0	7.6	14.0	10.5
1983	2.7	6.4	19.9	13.1	8.2	9.2	10.6	6.2
1984	1.8	7.6	5.8	8.9	7.2	8.2	6.8	10.1
1985	2.2	8.5	8.6	7.4	7.6	4.5	9.7	7.0
1986	−0.1	9.3	n.a.	10.5	13.1	3.6	10.1	7.7
1987	−0.5	8.4	n.a.	7.7	14.2	−1.0	8.7	10.9
1988	−0.4	8.1	−0.3	4.3	9.6	−2.0	12.7	8.8
1989	−0.7	7.9	−1.5	5.1	5.0	n.a.	8.6	8.0
1990	−0.2	8.1	−0.2	4.8	2.8	−4.0	7.8	6.8
1991	−1.5	5.8	−0.3	4.4	0.2	−1.9	9.5	7.1
1992	4.8	5.7	1.5	4.2	−1.5	2.2	5.4	6.1
1993	2.5	7.4	0.8	−0.2	−0.4	−0.1	6.4	7.3
1994	n.a.	n.a.	n.a.	−2.4	0.8	−0.8	8.5	4.5
1995	n.a.	n.a.	n.a.	n.a.	n.a.	n.a.	n.a.	11.1

Appendix 16

Government Domestic Debt as Percent of GDP
in Eight Case Study Countries

Year	Ghana	India	Jamai-ca	Malay-sia	Mexico	New Zealand	Sri Lanka	Zim-babwe
1979	n.a.	29.3	n.a.	n.a.	n.a.	32.2	34.2	35.8
1980	n.a.	30.0	n.a.	n.a.	n.a.	30.7	35.9	36.3
1981	n.a.	30.6	45.5	n.a.	n.a.	28.9	38.0	32.7
1982	n.a.	33.5	48.7	n.a.	n.a.	31.3	40.7	30.1
1983	n.a.	34.2	63.2	n.a.	n.a.	35.0	40.2	27.5
1984	n.a.	35.2	64.4	n.a.	n.a.	37.2	34.0	32.3
1985	n.a.	37.4	56.5	n.a.	n.a.	36.2	35.4	32.4
1986	n.a.	40.8	n.a.	n.a.	n.a.	34.4	37.1	32.4
1987	n.a.	42.6	n.a.	n.a.	n.a.	34.0	38.1	36.7
1988	n.a.	42.3	n.a.	n.a.	n.a.	31.1	40.0	35.2
1989	n.a.	44.0	n.a.	n.a.	n.a.	29.2	42.7	35.5
1990	n.a.	44.8	n.a.	n.a.	n.a.	29.3	39.0	36.1
1991	n.a.	45.0	22.8	n.a.	n.a.	28.8	38.3	32.1
1992	n.a.	44.7	19.2	n.a.	n.a.	29.2	37.8	28.2
1993	n.a.	46.6	22.5	n.a.	n.a.	28.9	38.1	23.4
1994	n.a.	n.a.	n.a.	n.a.	n.a.	25.8	39.9	7.2
1995	n.a.	n.a.	n.a.	n.a.	n.a.	n.a.	n.a.	3.1

Appendix 17

Government Foreign Debt as Percent of GDP in Eight Case Study Countries

Year	Ghana	India	Jamai-ca	Malay-sia	Mexico	New Zealand	Sri Lanka	Zim-babwe
1979	n.a.	8.5	n.a.	n.a.	n.a.	16.4	29.0	10.3
1980	n.a.	7.6	n.a.	n.a.	n.a.	16.8	28.2	11.5
1981	n.a.	7.1	36.7	n.a.	n.a.	17.3	30.4	11.3
1982	n.a.	7.0	41.1	n.a.	n.a.	20.8	32.9	13.4
1983	n.a.	6.7	49.9	n.a.	n.a.	22.8	33.4	14.4
1984	n.a.	6.6	67.1	n.a.	n.a.	25.5	32.7	18.6
1985	n.a.	6.5	83.5	n.a.	n.a.	29.5	37.4	21.4
1986	n.a.	6.6	102.7	n.a.	n.a.	32.5	42.8	23.4
1987	n.a.	6.5	125.1	n.a.	n.a.	31.0	45.6	26.4
1988	n.a.	6.2	113.2	n.a.	n.a.	26.9	48.7	23.3
1989	n.a.	5.9	102.6	n.a.	n.a.	26.0	55.7	21.8
1990	n.a.	5.6	96.9	n.a.	n.a.	28.1	51.7	23.2
1991	n.a.	5.5	119.5	n.a.	n.a.	31.6	52.3	27.6
1992	n.a.	5.6	113.6	n.a.	n.a.	31.3	52.9	36.4
1993	n.a.	5.6	103.2	n.a.	n.a.	30.2	50.4	38.8
1994	n.a.	n.a.	n.a.	n.a.	n.a.	28.6	49.2	35.9
1995	n.a.	n.a.	n.a.	n.a.	n.a.	n.a.	49.2	35.7

Appendix 18

Government Debt as Percent of GDP in Eight Case Study Countries

Year	Ghana	India	Jamai-ca	Malay-sia	Mexico	New Zealand	Sri Lanka	Zim-babwe
1979	n.a.	37.8	n.a.	n.a.	n.a.	48.6	63.2	46.1
1980	n.a.	37.6	n.a.	n.a.	n.a.	47.6	64.1	47.8
1981	n.a.	37.7	82.2	n.a.	n.a.	46.2	68.4	44.0
1982	n.a.	40.5	89.8	n.a.	n.a.	52.1	73.6	43.5
1983	n.a.	40.8	113.1	n.a.	n.a.	57.8	73.6	42.0
1984	n.a.	41.8	131.4	n.a.	n.a.	62.6	66.7	50.9
1985	n.a.	43.9	140.1	n.a.	n.a.	65.7	72.8	53.8
1986	n.a.	47.3	n.a.	n.a.	n.a.	66.9	79.9	55.8
1987	n.a.	49.1	n.a.	n.a.	n.a.	65.0	83.7	63.2
1988	n.a.	48.5	n.a.	n.a.	n.a.	58.1	88.8	58.5
1989	n.a.	49.9	n.a.	n.a.	n.a.	55.1	98.5	57.3
1990	n.a.	50.4	n.a.	n.a.	n.a.	57.4	90.7	59.3
1991	n.a.	50.5	142.3	n.a.	n.a.	60.4	90.7	59.7
1992	n.a.	50.4	132.8	n.a.	n.a.	60.5	90.7	64.7
1993	n.a.	52.2	125.7	n.a.	n.a.	59.1	88.6	62.2
1994	n.a.	n.a.	n.a.	n.a.	n.a.	54.4	89.0	43.1
1995	n.a.	n.a.	n.a.	n.a.	n.a.	n.a.	n.a.	38.9

Appendix 19

*Government and Government-Guaranteed Foreign Debt
as Percent of GDP in Eight Case Study Countries*

Year	Ghana	India	Jamai-ca	Malay-sia	Mexico	New Zealand	Sri Lanka	Zim-babwe
1979	8.8	11.4	45.8	13.3	20.2	n.a.	29.3	11.2
1980	6.8	10.1	48.5	14.5	16.2	n.a.	28.0	11.4
1981	4.4	9.7	52.4	18.5	15.4	n.a.	30.8	11.3
1982	3.7	10.3	57.7	24.9	24.3	n.a.	35.4	15.4
1983	5.9	10.5	78.7	32.2	38.7	n.a.	37.7	21.0
1984	16.9	11.6	109.3	36.8	38.6	n.a.	37.2	29.4
1985	19.6	12.7	133.5	43.2	40.4	n.a.	42.7	35.2
1986	21.6	14.5	126.7	53.9	55.2	n.a.	48.8	38.2
1987	33.4	15.8	116.1	54.6	59.1	n.a.	56.5	41.2
1988	42.7	16.2	106.0	46.3	47.0	n.a.	59.1	36.1
1989	42.4	19.2	95.6	35.9	37.5	n.a.	60.8	34.2
1990	40.1	21.6	90.9	29.5	30.8	n.a.	57.3	34.8
1991	40.5	24.8	115.2	27.9	26.9	n.a.	58.7	40.9
1992	45.8	27.6	112.7	24.8	22.6	n.a.	58.6	50.6
1993	53.7	28.9	102.1	22.3	19.9	n.a.	55.2	49.2

Appendix 20

*Change in Reserve Money as Percent of GDP
in Eight Case Study Countries*

Year	Ghana	India	Jamai-ca	Malay-sia	Mexico	New Zealand	Sri Lanka	Zim-babwe
1979	2.4	2.3	1.4	1.6	4.3	0.4	1.9	0.9
1980	3.1	1.7	3.1	1.9	4.7	−0.5	1.6	1.8
1981	4.4	1.2	−0.4	1.2	5.3	0.4	1.4	1.8
1982	1.5	2.0	−0.9	1.9	10.5	0.2	1.9	1.2
1983	2.4	1.4	4.4	0.5	6.5	0.4	2.1	0.3
1984	2.7	1.9	7.3	0.4	5.6	0.2	1.3	0.7
1985	2.3	2.7	4.4	0.9	1.8	0.3	2.3	1.3
1986	3.5	2.1	2.6	0.6	3.5	−0.3	0.3	1.0
1987	2.6	2.4	2.7	0.7	3.1	0.4	1.0	0.5
1988	3.4	2.1	5.2	1.4	1.6	0.3	2.4	1.5
1989	1.7	2.5	3.6	2.8	0.4	−0.1	0.6	1.3
1990	0.2	1.8	2.4	2.9	1.2	0.0	1.8	1.6
1991	0.0	2.5	3.4	2.0	1.0	0.0	2.5	1.8
1992	3.8	1.2	8.3	3.1	0.6	0.0	0.8	0.8
1993	0.3	2.9	6.0	1.8	0.4	0.1	2.3	2.8
1994	n.a.	n.a.	n.a.	5.5	0.8	0.2	1.9	1.5
1995	n.a.	n.a.	n.a.	n.a.	n.a.	n.a.	n.a.	0.6

Appendix 21

Net Domestic Credit to Government as Percent of
Aggregate Domestic Credit in Eight Case Study Countries

Year	Ghana	India	Jamai-ca	Malay-sia	Mexico	New Zealand	Sri Lanka	Zim-babwe
1979	68.1	39.4	58.3	1.5	46.5	36.5	35.2	n.a.
1980	67.4	41.1	59.1	−1.3	45.3	33.0	40.6	n.a.
1981	68.7	42.8	57.6	5.8	44.5	28.9	45.3	45.3
1982	63.8	42.9	57.4	10.9	52.4	26.0	45.9	42.3
1983	72.6	42.6	56.1	11.2	59.7	24.1	44.1	43.9
1984	81.7	42.4	56.1	9.7	55.3	12.9	38.3	33.6
1985	69.3	43.4	52.2	6.3	54.7	13.9	36.8	28.1
1986	63.0	44.8	52.3	4.0	60.2	21.7	39.4	26.2
1987	70.3	45.9	45.5	6.5	58.3	17.6	40.6	30.1
1988	76.1	46.6	24.5	7.1	54.9	16.2	42.0	29.5
1989	60.5	46.2	4.6	6.1	49.3	12.9	43.2	24.0
1990	46.2	46.8	−15.5	5.2	39.5	8.2	42.2	24.1
1991	57.9	48.9	−49.8	3.0	30.9	7.9	39.5	19.6
1992	68.5	48.6	−53.1	2.8	18.0	8.8	35.1	17.2
1993	70.6	48.0	−29.4	4.2	4.5	7.0	29.5	23.4
1994	67.8	48.4	−29.5	2.5	−6.0	5.5	25.6	25.7
1995	n.a.	n.a.	n.a.	n.a.	n.a.	n.a.	n.a.	23.4

Appendix 22

Reserve Money as Percent of Broad Money (M2)
in Eight Case Study Countries

Year	Ghana	India	Jamai-ca	Malay-sia	Mexico	New Zealand	Sri Lanka	Zim-babwe
1979	73.2	34.6	25.0	26.2	54.2	17.1	36.3	n.a.
1980	73.1	34.9	27.6	24.5	54.7	14.9	32.3	n.a.
1981	73.2	33.8	26.0	22.9	54.7	13.3	30.9	21.7
1982	71.5	32.9	18.9	22.2	60.8	12.8	30.4	22.7
1983	69.6	32.5	18.4	21.7	66.5	12.7	30.9	23.2
1984	69.3	31.7	27.5	20.4	61.9	12.3	31.7	24.2
1985	65.8	32.5	35.4	19.8	53.2	10.7	33.8	24.6
1986	65.8	33.1	35.5	19.3	43.7	8.3	35.6	26.3
1987	65.8	33.2	35.3	18.8	33.5	6.9	34.6	25.4
1988	64.8	33.2	37.0	19.4	37.7	8.2	35.4	23.8
1989	59.6	33.3	40.5	20.6	36.3	7.7	36.6	24.0
1990	50.3	33.5	42.3	22.5	21.7	4.7	36.2	24.9
1991	42.8	33.4	38.1	23.4	17.5	3.2	36.9	29.9
1992	42.3	32.2	36.2	22.5	15.6	2.9	36.4	33.9
1993	42.8	31.6	38.7	20.6	14.8	2.8	35.4	32.1
1994	43.2	32.9	39.0	21.3	14.5	2.8	35.7	28.9
1995	n.a.	n.a.	n.a.	n.a.	n.a.	n.a.	n.a.	25.1

Appendix 23
Bank Reserves as Percent of Bank Deposits in Eight Case Study Countries

Year	Ghana	India	Jamai-ca	Malay-sia	Mexico	New Zealand	Sri Lanka	Zim-babwe
1979	47.6	11.5	15.8	7.3	44.5	2.6	14.6	n.a.
1980	44.9	12.6	20.0	7.0	45.4	1.9	12.8	n.a.
1981	44.4	12.2	21.4	6.9	45.8	1.6	12.6	8.7
1982	44.8	12.5	9.1	7.0	51.5	1.6	12.5	9.5
1983	42.2	12.6	7.1	7.1	58.5	1.6	13.3	10.2
1984	51.4	11.5	19.4	7.0	55.8	1.3	15.2	10.8
1985	53.0	12.9	27.4	6.6	45.6	1.1	17.9	10.9
1986	49.9	14.2	33.5	5.6	33.8	1.0	19.8	11.4
1987	43.6	14.7	37.0	5.1	22.4	1.1	15.8	10.6
1988	29.9	16.1	36.2	5.1	20.0	1.6	12.6	10.1
1989	28.0	16.0	39.6	6.1	16.0	1.6	13.4	10.5
1990	26.0	15.3	39.8	8.3	6.1	2.7	13.5	10.8
1991	38.8	15.2	34.0	9.8	4.1	3.4	15.5	14.8
1992	46.9	14.7	33.2	9.2	3.2	2.9	16.7	20.1
1993	54.2	14.7	34.7	7.6	2.5	2.7	15.8	17.8
1994	72.6	16.2	32.6	8.8	2.3	2.6	16.2	15.6
1995	n.a.	n.a.	n.a.	n.a.	n.a.	n.a.	n.a.	14.8

Appendix 24
Real Interest Rates in Eight Case Study Countries

Year	Ghana	India	Jamai-ca	Malay-sia	Mexico	New Zealand	Sri Lanka	Zim-babwe
1979	−29.7	3.0	−15.4	3.2	−3.0	n.a.	1.5	−9.4
1980	−26.8	−0.6	−12.6	0.8	−4.6	n.a.	−7.9	2.3
1981	−63.5	−1.8	0.2	−0.5	0.9	−2.8	0.4	−0.8
1982	−6.3	3.2	6.1	3.5	−11.3	−3.5	6.0	6.6
1983	−66.4	−0.3	3.2	5.8	−25.9	3.9	1.4	−4.9
1984	−17.0	2.9	−8.7	6.1	−10.1	4.8	−0.4	−4.0
1985	7.0	5.8	−2.9	9.5	0.0	0.2	12.7	4.2
1986	−5.0	2.8	6.3	7.8	−1.9	3.5	3.6	−2.5
1987	−14.3	3.1	11.8	5.6	−16.8	1.7	2.7	−1.2
1988	−8.6	2.5	10.2	2.9	−25.7	7.9	−1.0	3.5
1989	n.a.	5.5	4.9	3.1	15.6	6.8	2.8	−1.9
1990	n.a.	2.9	4.0	3.9	5.7	6.9	−4.7	−0.3
1991	n.a.	−0.2	−16.7	3.2	−2.5	8.0	3.4	4.8
1992	n.a.	2.6	−24.5	n.a.	1.4	7.3	3.6	2.8
1993	n.a.	5.1	9.9	n.a.	6.3	6.5	4.9	13.7
1994	n.a.	2.0	5.3	n.a.	6.7	5.8	5.1	10.3
1995	n.a.	n.a.	n.a.	1.3	5.1	6.0	n.a.	10.0

Appendix 25

Central Bank Governors' Symposium Participants

Heads of Delegation

Mr Eddie George Governor Bank of England	Mr Bernard Bonin Senior Deputy Governor Bank of Canada
Mr Martin Etchegoyhen Director Central Bank of Argentina	Mr Afxentis Afxentiou Governor Central Bank of Cyprus
Mr Bernie Fraser Governor Reserve Bank of Australia	Mr K. Dwight Venner Governor Eastern Caribbean Central Bank
Mr James H. Smith Governor Central Bank of The Bahamas	Mr Momodou C. Bajo Governor Central Bank of The Gambia
Mr Khorshed Alam Governor Bangladesh Bank	Dr Godfried Agama Governor Bank of Ghana
Mr Calvin Springer Governor Central Bank of Barbados	Mr Joseph Yam Chief Executive Hong Kong Monetary Authority
Mr Keith Arnold Governor Central Bank of Belize	Dr Chakravarthi Rangarajan Governor Reserve Bank of India
Mr H. C. L. Quill Hermans Governor Bank of Botswana	Mr Derick M. Latibeaudiere Governor Bank of Jamaica

Mr Micah Cheserem
Governor
Central Bank of Kenya

HE Sheikh Salem Abdul Aziz
    Al-Sabah
Governor
Central Bank of Kuwait

Mr Felix Borotho
Deputy Governor
Central Bank of Lesotho

Prof Matthew A. P. Chikaonda
Governor
Reserve Bank of Malawi

Mr Ahmad Mohd Don
Governor
Bank Negara Malaysia

Mr Francis J. Vassallo
Governor
Central Bank of Malta

Mr Mitrajeet D. Maraye
Governor
Bank of Mauritius

Mr Miguel Mancera
Governor
Banco de México

Dr Jaafar Bin Ahmad
Governor
Bank of Namibia

Dr Donald Brash
Governor
Reserve Bank of New Zealand

Dr Paul A. Ogwuma
Governor
Central Bank of Nigeria

HE Sheikh Hamad Al-Sayari
Governor
Saudi Arabian Monetary Agency

Mr Rick N. Houenipwela
Governor
Central Bank of Solomon Islands

Dr Chris L. Stals
Governor
South African Reserve Bank

Mr Amarananda S. Jayawardena
Governor
Central Bank of Sri Lanka

Mr James Nxumalo
Governor
Central Bank of Swaziland

Dr Idris M. Rashidi
Governor
Bank of Tanzania

Mr T. Ainsworth Harewood
Governor
Central Bank of Trinidad
    & Tobago

Mr Charles Kikonyogo
Governor
Bank of Uganda

HE Sultan Bin Nasser
    Al-Suwaidi
Governor
Central Bank of the United
    Arab Emirates

Mr Sampson Ngwele
Governor
Reserve Bank of Vanuatu

Dr Situmbeko Musokotwane
Deputy Governor
Bank of Zambia

Dr Leonard L. Tsumba
Governor
Reserve Bank of Zimbabwe

Others: Bank of England

Mr Bill Allen
Deputy Director
Monetary Analysis

Mr Creon Butler
Head
Monetary Instruments
    & Markets Division

Ms Rebecca Emerson
Analyst
Monetary Instruments
    & Markets Division

Mr John Footman
The Secretary of the Bank

Mr Simon Gray
Adviser
Centre for Central Banking
    Studies

Mr Peter Hayward
Senior Adviser
Developing World Division
Supervision & Surveillance

Mr Tony Latter
Director, Technical Assistance
Centre for Central Banking
    Studies

Mr Colin Miles
Senior Adviser
Developing World Division
Supervision & Surveillance

Mr Lionel Price
Director
Centre for Central Banking
   Studies

Mr Ian Plenderleith
Executive Director

Mr David Reid
Head
Developing World Division
Supervision & Surveillance

Mr Tim Smith
Senior Adviser
Developing World Division
Supervision & Surveillance

Mr John Townend
Deputy Director
Market Operations

Mr Michael Stephenson
Senior Economist
Developing World Division
Supervision & Surveillance

Ms Christine Walsh
Senior Manager
Financial Stability
Supervision & Surveillance

Others: Overseas

Mr Oduetse Motshidisi
Acting Director
Administrative Services
Bank of Botswana

Mr Herbert Carr
Senior Administrative Officer
Central Bank of The Gambia

Mr Alex Bernasko
Bank of Ghana

Mr James Lau, Jr
Executive Director
External Department
Hong Kong Monetary Authority

Mr Sandip Ghose
Governor's Executive Assistant
Reserve Bank of India

Mr Brian Wynter
Deputy Governor
Bank of Jamaica

Mr Mark Lesiit
Governor's Personal Assistant
Central Bank of Kenya

Mr Nabil H. Al-Saqabi
Manager, Governor's Office
Central Bank of Kuwait

Mrs Mabatho M. Mokhothu
Foreign Exchange Control
Central Bank of Lesotho

Mr Fusi Morokole
Banking Supervision
Central Bank of Lesotho

Mr Elias J. Kambalame
General Manager
Reserve Bank of Malawi

Dr Zeti Akhtar Aziz
Assistant Governor
Bank Negara Malaysia

Mr Godfrey Huber
Manager, Financial Controller
Central Bank of Malta

Mr Ramesh Basant Roi
Director of Research
Bank of Mauritius

Dr O. Joseph Nnanna
Governor's Special Assistant
Central Bank of Nigeria

Mr Mahey R. Rasheed
Director, Foreign Operations
Central Bank of Nigeria

Mr Tirmidhi M. Yakubu
Manager
Foreign Operations Department
Central Bank of Nigeria

Mr Hendrik Van Gass
Governor's Assistant
South African Reserve Bank

Dr Joseph Masawe
Manager
Economic Research and Policy
Bank of Tanzania

Dr Joshua Mugyenyi
Executive Director
Administration
Bank of Uganda

Mr Amrit V. Jogia
General Adviser
Reserve Bank of Vanuatu

Mr Max Chisaka
Director of Computer Services
Bank of Zambia

Mr Matthew Chisunka
Assistant Bank Secretary
Bank of Zambia

Bibliography

Agénor, Pierre-Richard and Peter Montiel (1996), *Development Macroeconomics* (Princeton, NJ: Princeton University Press).

Alexander, William E., Tomás J. T. Baliño and Charles Enoch (1995), *The Adoption of Indirect Instruments of Monetary Policy* (Washington, DC: International Monetary Fund, Occasional Paper 126, June).

Aristophanes (1964), *The Frogs and Other Plays* translated by David Barrett (Harmondsworth: Penguin).

Asian Development Bank (1984), *Domestic Resource Mobilization through Financial Development* (Manila: Asian Development Bank, Economics Office, February).

——— (1985), *Improving Domestic Resource Mobilization through Financial Development* (Manila: Asian Development Bank, Economics Office, September).

Banco de Portugal (1963), *Report of the Board of Directors for the Year 1962* (Lisbon: Banco de Portugal).

Bank of England (1996a), "The Gilt Repo Market," *Bank of England Quarterly Bulletin,* 36(2), May, 142–145.

——— (1996b), *The UK Index-Linked Gilt-Edged Market: Future Development* (London: Bank of England, Papers from the Conference on Indexed Bonds).

Barro, Robert J. (1974), "Are Government Bonds Net Wealth?" *Journal of Political Economy,* 82(6), November/December, 1095–1117.

——— (1989), "The Ricardian Approach to Budget Deficits," *Journal of Economic Perspectives,* 3(2), Spring, 37–54.

——— (1991), "Economic Growth in a Cross Section of Countries," *Quarterly Journal of Economics,* 106(2), May, 407–443.

——— (1995), "Inflation and Economic Growth," *Bank of England Quarterly Bulletin,* 35(2), May, 166–176.

Barth, James R., George R. Iden and Frank S. Russek (1986), "The Economic Consequences of Federal Deficits: An Examination of the Net Wealth and Instability Issues," *Southern Economic Journal,* 53(1), July, 27–50.

Bartolini, Leonardo and Carlo Cottarelli (1994), "Treasury Bill Auctions: Issues and Uses" (Washington, DC: International Monetary Fund, WP/94/135, November).

Blanchard, Olivier and Stanley Fischer (1989), *Lectures on Macroeconomics* (Cambridge, Mass.: MIT Press).

Blejer, Mario I. and Mohsin S. Khan (1984), "Government Policy and Private Investment in Developing Countries," *International Monetary Fund Staff Papers*, 31(2), June, 379–403.

Board of Governors of the Federal Reserve System (1947), *Annual Report, 1947* (Washington, DC: Federal Reserve System).

Bröker, Günter F. (1993), "Strategies for the Development of a Viable and Efficient National Bond Market" in *Emerging Bond Markets in the Dynamic Asian Economies* (Paris: Organisation for Economic Co-operation and Development), 8–41.

Bruno, Michael (1985), "The Reforms and Macroeconomic Adjustments: Introduction," *World Development,* 13(8), August, 867–869.

Buchanan, James M. (1976), "Barro on the Ricardian Equivalence Theorem," *Journal of Political Economy,* 84(2), April, 337–342.

Buffie, Edward F. (1984), "Financial Repression, the New Structuralists, and Stabilization Policy in Semi-Industrialized Economies," *Journal of Development Economics,* 14(3), April, 305–322.

Burgon, John William (1839), *The Life and Times of Sir Thomas Gresham, Knt., Founder of the Royal Exchange* (London: Effingham Wilson).

Calvo, Guillermo A. and Fabrizio Coricelli (1992), "Stagflationary Effects of Stabilization Programs in Reforming Socialist Countries: Enterprise-Side vs. Household-Side Factors," *World Bank Economic Review,* 6(1), January, 71–90.

Capie, Forrest, Charles A. E. Goodhart, Stanley Fischer and Norbert Schnadt (1994), *The Future of Central Banking: The Tercentenary Symposium of the Bank of England* (Cambridge: Cambridge University Press).

Caprio, Gerard, Jr, Izak Atiyas and James A. Hanson, eds (1994), *Financial Reform: Theory and Experience* (Cambridge: Cambridge University Press).

Chamley, Christophe and Patrick Honohan (1993),"Financial Repression and Banking Intermediation," *Savings and Development,* 17(3), 301–308.

Cole, David C., Hal S. Scott and Philip A. Wellons (1995), "The Asian Money Markets: An Overview" in *Asian Money Markets* edited by David C. Cole, Hal S. Scott and Philip A. Wellons (New York: Oxford University Press), 3–38.

Cooper, Richard N. and Jeffrey D. Sachs (1985), "Borrowing Abroad: The Debtor's Perspective" in *International Debt and the Developing Countries* edited by Gordon W. Smith and John T. Cuddington (Washington, DC: World Bank, March), 21–60.

Cottarelli, Carlo (1993), *Limiting Central Bank Central to the Government: Theory and Practice* (Washington, DC: International Monetary Fund, Occasional Paper 110, December).

———— (1996), "Treasury Bill Auctions: Issues in Design" in *Coordination of Monetary and Public Debt Management: Design and Management of Operational Arrangements* edited by Venkataraman Sundararajan, Hans Blommestein and Peter Dattels (Washington, DC: International Monetary Fund).

Cuddington, John T. (1986), "Capital Flight: Issues, Estimates, and Explanations," *Princeton Studies in International Finance,* (58), December.

Darity, William and Bobbie L. Horn (1986), "Some Repressed Difficulties with the Case for Financial Reform in LDCs" (Chapel Hill, NC: Department of Economics, University of North Carolina. Southern Economic Association Meeting in New Orleans, 23–25 November).

Dattels, Peter (1996), "The Microstructure of Government Securities Markets" in *Coordination of Monetary and Public Debt Management: Design and Management of Operational Arrangements* edited by Venkataraman Sundararajan, Hans Blommestein and Peter Dattels (Washington, DC: International Monetary Fund).

De Gregorio, José (1994), "Inflation, Growth and Central Banks: Theory and Evidence" (Washington, DC: International Monetary Fund, May).

De Gregorio, José and Pablo E. Guidotti (1995), "Financial Development and Economic Growth," *World Development,* 23(3), March, 433–448.

Diaz-Alejandro, Carlos (1985), "Good-Bye Financial Repression, Hello Financial Crash," *Journal of Development Economics,* 19(1–2), September–October, 1–24.

Dollar, David (1992), "Outward-Oriented Developing Economies Really Do Grow More Rapidly: Evidence from 95 LDCs, 1976–1985," *Economic Development and Cultural Change,* 40(3), April, 523–544.

Dooley, Michael P. (1986), "Country-Specific Risk Premiums, Capital Flight and Net Investment Income Payments in Selected Developing Countries" (Washington, DC: International Monetary Fund, DM/86/17, March).

———— (1988), "Capital Flight: A Response to Differences in Financial Risks," *International Monetary Fund Staff Papers,* 35(3), September, 422–436.

Dornbusch, Rudiger (1996), "Debt and Monetary Policy: The Policy Issues" (Cambridge, Mass.: Massachusetts Institute of Technology, Department of Economics, March).

Dornbusch, Rudiger and Mario Henrique Simonsen (1983), *Inflation, Debt, and Indexation* (Cambridge, Mass.: MIT Press).

Duesenberry, James S. (1995), "Foreword" in *Asian Money Markets* edited by David C. Cole, Hal S. Scott and Philip A. Wellons (New York: Oxford University Press), v–vi.

Easterly, William R. (1993), "How Much Do Distortions Affect Growth?" *Journal of Monetary Economics,* 32(2), November, 187–212.

European Commission (1994), *1994 Broad Economic Policy Guidelines* (Brussels: European Commission, no. 58).

Farhadian, Ziba and Robert M. Dunn, Jr (1986), "Fiscal Policy and Financial Deepening in a Monetarist Model of the Balance of Payments," *Kyklos,* 39(1), 66–83.

Feder, Gershon (1982), "On Exports and Economic Growth," *Journal of Development Economics,* 12(1), February–April, 59–73.

Fischer, Stanley (1994), "Modern Central Banking" in *The Future of Central Banking: The Tercentenary Symposium of the Bank of England* by Forrest Capie, Charles Goodhart, Stanley Fischer and Norbert Schnadt (Cambridge: Cambridge University Press), 262–308.

Friedman, Milton and Anna J. Schwartz (1963), *A Monetary History of the United States, 1867–1960* (Princeton, NJ: Princeton University Press for the National Bureau of Economic Research).

Fry, Maxwell J. (1972), *Finance and Development Planning in Turkey* (Leiden: Brill).

―――― (1973), "Manipulating Demand for Money" in *Essays in Modern Economics* edited by Michael Parkin (London: Longman), 371–385.

―――― (1978), "Money and Capital or Financial Deepening in Economic Development?" *Journal of Money, Credit and Banking,* 10(4), November, 464–475.

―――― (1979), "The Cost of Financial Repression in Turkey," *Savings and Development,* 3(2), 127–135.

―――― (1980), "Saving, Investment, Growth and the Cost of Financial Repression," *World Development,* 8(4), April, 317–327.

―――― (1981), "Interest Rates in Asia: An Examination of Interest Rate Policies in Burma, India, Indonesia, Korea, Malaysia, Nepal, Pakistan, the Philippines, Singapore, Sri Lanka, Taiwan and Thailand" (Washington, DC: International Monetary Fund, Asian Department, June).

―――― (1989), "Foreign Debt Instability: An Analysis of National Saving and Domestic Investment Responses to Foreign Debt Accumulation in 28 Developing Countries," *Journal of International Money and Finance,* 8(3), September, 315–344.

―――― (1990), "Sri Lanka's Financial Liberalization and Trade Reforms: *Plus Ça Change?*" *International Economic Journal,* 4(1), Spring, 71–90.

―――― (1991), "Domestic Resource Mobilization in Developing Asia: Four Policy Issues," *Asian Development Review,* 9(1), 15–39.

—— (1993), "Foreign Debt Accumulation: Financial and Fiscal Effects and Monetary Policy Reactions in Developing Countries," *Journal of International Money and Finance,* 12(4), August, 347–367.

—— (1995), *Money, Interest, and Banking in Economic Development,* 2nd edn (Baltimore, Md: Johns Hopkins University Press).

—— (1996), "Saving, Growth, and Financial Distortions in the Pacific Basin and Other Developing Areas" (Birmingham: University of Birmingham, International Finance Group, May 1996).

—— (1997), "In Favour of Financial Liberalisation," *Economic Journal,* 107(442), May.

Fry, Maxwell J., Charles A. E. Goodhart and Alvaro Almeida (1996), *Central Banking in Developing Countries: Objectives, Activities and Independence* (London: Routledge).

Fry, Maxwell J. and Raburn M. Williams (1984), *American Money and Banking* (New York: John Wiley).

Gelb, Alan H. (1989), "Financial Policies, Growth, and Efficiency" (Washington, DC: World Bank, Country Economics Department, PPR Working Paper WPS 202, June).

Gesell, Silvio (1911), *Die natürliche Wirtschaftsordnung durch Freiland und Freigeld* (Berlin: Freiland-Freigeldverlag). [*The Natural Economic Order* translated from the 6th German edn by Philip Pye (Berlin: Neo-Verlag, 1929).]

Ghani, Ejaz (1992), "How Financial Markets Affect Long-Run Growth: A Cross-Country Study" (Washington, DC: World Bank, Country Operations, PR Working Paper WPS 843, January).

Giovannini, Alberto and Martha de Melo (1993), "Government Revenue from Financial Repression," *American Economic Review,* 83(4), September, 953–963.

Gleizer, Daniel L. (1995), "Brazil" in *Financial Systems and Economic Policy in Developing Countries* edited by Stephan Haggard and Chung H. Lee (Ithaca, NY and London: Cornell University Press), 212–256.

Goldstein, Morris and David Folkerts-Landau (1994), "International Capital Markets: Developments, Prospects, and Policy Issues" (Washington, DC: International Monetary Fund, World Economic and Financial Surveys, September).

Gray, Simon (1996), "The Management of Government Debt" (London: Bank of England, Centre for Central Banking Studies, Handbooks in Central Banking 5, May).

Harberger, Arnold C. (1986), "Welfare Consequences of Capital Inflows" in *Economic Liberalization in Developing Countries* edited by Armeane M. Choksi and Demetris Papageorgiou (Oxford: Basil Blackwell), 157–184.

Hermes, Niels and Robert Lensink (1993), "The Financial Sector and Its In-fluence on Economic Growth: Evidence from 14 Latin American Countries, 1963–1989" (Groningen: University of Groningen, Institute of Economic Research, Research Memorandum 531, June).

Hilferding, Rudolf (1910), *Das Finanzkapital. Eine Studie über die jüngste Ent-wicklung des Kapitalismus* (Vienna: Wiener Volksbuchhandlung). [*Finance Capital: A Study of the Latest Phase of Capitalist Development* edited with an introduction by Tom Bottomore from translations by Morris Watnick and Sam Gordon (London: Routledge and Kegan Paul, 1981).]

Hoggarth, Glenn (1996), "Introduction to Monetary Policy" (London: Bank of England, Centre for Central Banking Studies, Handbooks in Central Banking 1, May).

Ize, Alain and Guillermo Ortiz (1987), "Fiscal Rigidities, Public Debt, and Capital Flight," *International Monetary Fund Staff Papers,* 34(2), June, 311–332.

Johnston, John (1984), *Econometric Methods,* 3rd edn (New York: McGraw-Hill).

Kalderen, Lars (1996), "Debt Management Functions and their Location" in *Coordination of Monetary and Public Debt Management: Design and Man-agement of Operational Arrangements* edited by Venkataraman Sundararajan, Hans Blommestein and Peter Dattels (Washington, DC: International Mone-tary Fund).

Keynes, J. Maynard (1936), *The General Theory of Employment Interest and Money* (London: Macmillan).

Khan, Mohsin S. and Nadeem Ul Haque (1985), "Foreign Borrowing and Cap-ital Flight: A Formal Analysis," *International Monetary Fund Staff Papers,* 32(4), December, 606–628.

Khan, Mohsin S. and Delano Villanueva (1991), "Macroeconomic Policies and Long-Term Growth: A Conceptual and Empirical Review" (Washington, DC: International Monetary Fund, WP/91/28, March).

King, Robert G. and Ross Levine (1993a), "Finance and Growth: Schumpeter Might Be Right," *Quarterly Journal of Economics,* 108(3), August, 717–737.

—— (1993b), "Finance, Entrepreneurship, and Growth: Theory and Evi-dence," *Journal of Monetary Economics,* 32(3), December, 513–542.

—— (1993c), "Financial Intermediation and Economic Growth" in *Capital Markets and Financial Intermediation* edited by Colin Mayer and Xavier Vives (Cambridge: Cambridge University Press for the Centre for Economic Policy Research), 156–189.

Kroszner, Randall S. (1996), "Global Government Securities Markets: Eco-nomics and Politics of Market Microstructure Reforms" in *The Debt Burden and Its Consequences for Monetary Policy* edited by Guillermo Calvo and Mervyn King (London: Macmillan).

Krueger, Anne O. (1987), "Debt, Capital Flows, and LDC Growth," *American Economic Review*, 77(2), May, 159–164.

Lanyi, Anthony and Rüşdü Saracoglu (1983), *Interest Rate Policies in Developing Countries* (Washington, DC: International Monetary Fund, Occasional Paper 22, October).

Lee, Yang-Pal (1980), "Inflation Hedges and Economic Growth in a Monetary Economy" (Stanford, Calif.: Stanford University, Ph.D. thesis).

Lin See-Yan and Chung Tin Fah (1995), "Money Markets in Malaysia" in *Asian Money Markets* edited by David C. Cole, Hal S. Scott and Philip A. Wellons (New York: Oxford University Press), 209–272.

Liu, Liang-Yn and Wing Thye Woo (1994), "Saving Behaviour under Imperfect Financial Markets and the Current Account Consequences," *Economic Journal*, 104(424), May, 512–527.

Lundberg, Erik (1964), "The Financial System of Portugal" (Washington, DC: International Monetary Fund and World Bank, October).

Lynch, David (1995), "Links between Asia-Pacific Financial Sector Development and Economic Performance" (Sydney: Macquarie University, Ph.D. thesis, October).

McConnachie, Robin I. (1996), "Primary Dealers in Government Securities Markets" (London: Bank of England, Centre for Central Banking Studies, Handbooks in Central Banking 6, May).

McKinnon, Ronald I. (1973), *Money and Capital in Economic Development* (Washington, DC: Brookings Institution).

—— (1986), "Issues and Perspectives: An Overview of Banking Regulation and Monetary Control" in *Pacific Growth and Financial Interdependence* edited by Augustine H. H. Tan and Basant Kapur (Sydney: Allen and Unwin), 319–336.

—— (1991), "Monetary Stabilization in LDCs" in *Liberalization in the Process of Economic Development* edited by Lawrence B. Krause and Kim Kihwan (Berkeley and Los Angeles: University of California Press), 366–400.

—— (1993), *The Order of Economic Liberalization: Financial Control in the Transition to a Market Economy*, 2nd edn (Baltimore, Md: Johns Hopkins University Press).

McNelis, Paul D. (1988), "Indexation and Stabilization: Theory and Experience," *World Bank Research Observer*, 3(2), July, 157–169.

Mason, Andrew (1987), "National Savings Rates and Population Growth: A New Model and New Evidence" in *Population Growth and Economic Development: Issues and Evidence* edited by D. Gale Johnson and Ronald D. Lee (Madison, Wis.: University of Wisconsin Press), 523–560.

Masson, Paul R., Tamim Bayoumi and Hossein Samiei (1995), "Saving Behavior in Industrial and Developing Countries" in *Staff Studies for the World Economic Outlook* by the Research Department of the International Monetary Fund (Washington, DC: International Monetary Fund, World Economic and Financial Surveys, September), 1–27.

Meek, Paul (1988a), "Government Financing: The Role of the Central Bank" (Sydney: Reserve Bank of Australia, SEANZA Central Banking Seminar, 7 November).

――― (1988b), "Pakistan: Integration of Debt Management and Monetary Policy" (Sydney: Reserve Bank of Australia, SEANZA Central Banking Seminar, 8 November).

――― (1991), "Central Bank Liquidity Management and the Money Market" in *Monetary Policy Instruments for Developing Countries* edited by Gerard Caprio, Jr and Patrick Honohan (Washington, DC: World Bank), 15–29.

Metzler, Lloyd A. (1968), "The Process of International Adjustment under Conditions of Full Employment: A Keynesian View" in *Readings in International Economics* edited by Richard E. Caves and Harry G. Johnson (Homewood, Ill.: Richard D. Irwin for the American Economic Association), 465–486.

Min, Byoung Kyun (1976), "Financial Restriction in Korea, 1965–1974" (Honolulu: University of Hawaii, Ph.D. thesis).

Nichols, Donald A. (1974), "Some Principles of Inflationary Finance," *Journal of Political Economy,* 82(2), March–April, 423–430.

Polak, Jacques J. (1989), *Financial Policies and Development* (Paris: Development Centre of the Organisation for Economic Co-operation and Development).

Quintyn, Marc (1996), "Government Securities versus Central Bank Securities in Developing Market-Based Monetary Operations" in *Coordination of Monetary and Public Debt Management: Design and Management of Operational Arrangements* edited by Venkataraman Sundararajan, Hans Blommestein and Peter Dattels (Washington, DC: International Monetary Fund).

Ricardo, David (1817), *On the Principles of Political Economy, and Taxation* (London: John Murray).

Robinson, David J. and Peter Stella (1988), "Amalgamating Central Bank and Fiscal Deficits" in *Measurement of Fiscal Impact: Methodological Issues* edited by Mario I. Blejer and Ke-Young Chu (Washington, DC: International Monetary Fund, Occasional Paper 59, June), 20–31.

Rojas-Suárez, Liliana and Steven R. Weisbrod (1995), *Financial Fragilities in Latin America: The 1980s and 1990s* (Washington, DC: International Monetary Fund, Occasional Paper 132, October).

Roubini, Nouriel and Xavier Sala-i-Martin (1991), "Financial Development, the Trade Regime, and Economic Growth" (Cambridge, Mass.: National Bureau of Economic Research, NBER Working Paper 3876, October).

—— (1992), "Financial Repression and Economic Growth," *Journal of Development Economics,* 39(1), July, 5–30.

Sachs, Jeffrey D. (1986), "Managing the LDC Debt Crisis," *Brookings Papers on Economic Activity,* (2), 397–431.

——, ed. (1989), *Developing Country Debt and the World Economy* (Chicago: University of Chicago Press for the National Bureau of Economic Research).

——, ed. (1990), *Developing Country Debt and Economic Performance,* Vols 1–3 (Chicago: University of Chicago Press for the National Bureau of Economic Research).

Sargent, Thomas J. and Neil Wallace (1981), "Some Unpleasant Monetarist Arithmetic," *Federal Reserve Bank of Minneapolis Quarterly Review,* Fall, 1–17.

Sayers, Richard S. (1967), *Modern Banking,* 7th edn (Oxford: Oxford University Press).

Schuller, Kurt (1996), *Should Developing Countries Have Central Banks? Currency Quality and Monetary Systems in 155 Countries* (London: Institute of Economic Affairs, Research Monograph 52, June).

Shaw, Edward S. (1973), *Financial Deepening in Economic Development* (New York: Oxford University Press).

—— (1975), "Inflation, Finance and Capital Markets," *Federal Reserve Bank of San Francisco Economic Review,* December, 5–20.

Sheng, Andrew (1994), "Development of the HK Dollar Debt Market" in *The Practice of Central Banking in Hong Kong* by the Hong Kong Monetary Authority (Hong Kong: Hong Kong Monetary Authority, May), 75–81.

Sheppard, David (1996), "Payment Systems" (London: Bank of England, Centre for Central Banking Studies, Handbooks in Central Banking 8, May).

Solow, Robert M. (1956), "A Contribution to the Theory of Economic Growth," *Quarterly Journal of Economics,* 70(1), February, 65–94.

Stebbing, Peter W. (1994), "Developing Secondary Markets" (Suva: Reserve Bank of Fiji, Paper presented at the South Pacific Central Bankers' Seminar on Debt Instruments Market Development in Small Open Developing Economies (SODEs), 24–28 October).

Stiglitz, Joseph E. (1994), "The Role of the State in Financial Markets" in *Proceedings of the World Bank Annual Bank Conference on Development Economics 1993* edited by Michael Bruno and Boris Pleskovic (Washington, DC: World Bank), 19–52.

Stiglitz, Joseph E. and Andrew Weiss (1981), "Credit Rationing in Markets with Imperfect Information," *American Economic Review,* 71(3), June, 393–410.

Sundararajan, Venkataraman and Tomás J. T. Baliño (1991), "Issues in Recent Banking Crises" in *Banking Crises: Cases and Issues* edited by Venkataraman Sundararajan and Tomás J. T. Baliño (Washington, DC: International Monetary Fund), 1–57.

Sundararajan, Venkataraman, Hans J. Blommestein and Peter Dattels, eds (1996), *Coordination of Monetary and Public Debt Management: Design and Management of Operational Arrangements* (Washington, DC: International Monetary Fund).

Sundararajan, Venkataraman, Peter Dattels, Ian S. McCarthy, Marta Castello-Branco and Hans J. Blommestein (1996), "The Coordination of Domestic Public Debt and Monetary Management in Economies in Transition—Issues and Lessons from Experience" in *Coordination of Monetary and Public Debt Management: Design and Management of Operational Arrangements* edited by Venkataraman Sundararajan, Hans Blommestein and Peter Dattels (Washington, DC: International Monetary Fund).

Tanzi, Vito (1977), "Inflation, Lags in Collection, and the Real Value of Tax Revenue," *International Monetary Fund Staff Papers,* 24(1), March, 154–167.

—— (1989), "Lags in Tax Collection and the Case for Inflationary Finance: Theory with Simulations" in *Fiscal Policy, Stabilization, and Growth in Developing Countries* edited by Mario I. Blejer and Ke-Young Chu (Washington, DC: International Monetary Fund), 208–237.

Tanzi, Vito, Mario I. Blejer and Mario O. Teijeiro (1988), "The Effects of Inflation on the Measurement of Fiscal Deficits" in *Measurement of Fiscal Impact: Methodological Issues* edited by Mario I. Blejer and Ke-Young Chu (Washington, DC: International Monetary Fund, Occasional Paper 59, June), 4–19.

Tobin, James (1965), "Money and Economic Growth," *Econometrica,* 33(4), October, 671–684.

—— (1992), "Money" in *The New Palgrave Dictionary of Money and Finance* edited by Peter Newman, Murray Milgate and John Eatwell (London: Macmillan), Vol. 2, 770–778.

Tseng, Wanda and Robert Corker (1991), *Financial Liberalization, Money Demand, and Monetary Policy in Asian Countries* (Washington, DC: International Monetary Fund, Occasional Paper 84, July).

Watson, C. Maxwell, G. Russell Kincaid, Caroline Atkinson, Eliot Kalter and David Folkerts-Landau (1986), "International Capital Markets: Developments and Prospects" (Washington, DC: International Monetary Fund, World Economic and Financial Surveys, December).

Wilson, J. Stuart G. (1993), *Money Markets: The International Perspective* (London: Routledge).

Wilton, David (1995), "Enhancing the Operation of the Government Securities Market" (Washington, DC: World Bank, Presented at a Workshop on Indian Debt Markets, Bombay, 10 November).

———— (1996),"Money Markets in Sub-Sahara Africa" (Washington, DC: World Bank, June).

World Bank (1989), *World Development Report 1989* (New York: Oxford University Press for the World Bank).

———— (1993), *The East Asian Miracle: Economic Growth and Public Policy* (New York: Oxford University Press).

———— (1995a), *The Emerging Asian Bond Market* (Washington, DC: World Bank, June).

———— (1995b), *The Emerging Asian Bond Market: Hong Kong* (Washington, DC: World Bank, June).

———— (1995c), *The Emerging Asian Bond Market: Malaysia* (Washington, DC: World Bank, June).

Index